Building Budget Brits

A Practical Guide for Refurbishing
BSA and Triumph Unit Twins

Mike Brown

A Tech Series Book
Whitehorse Press
Center Conway, New Hampshire

Whitehorse Press books are also available at discounts in bulk quantity for sales and promotional use. For details about special sales or for a catalog of motorcycling books and videos, write to the Publisher:

Whitehorse Press
107 East Conway Road
Center Conway, New Hampshire 03813
Phone: 603-356-6556 or 800-531-1133
Email: Orders@WhitehorsePress.com
Internet: www.WhitehorsePress.com

ISBN 978-1-884313-62-2

5   4   3   2   1

Printed in the United States

CONTENTS

Acknowledgments

Building Budget Brits is the product of many hands and considerable effort. Some individuals whose help was particularly valuable include Mark Appleton of British Cycle Supply, who increased my background knowledge exponentially through his input and the gift of *Modern Motorcycle Mechanics*. Jaye Strait of Britech and Marino Perna of MAP also made themselves readily available for technical questions and contributed images. Dan Kennedy, my publisher and editor, made most of my manuscript pages bleed red ink like I hadn't seen since seventh grade and in so doing improved both content and readability to far surpass what I had ever imagined possible. Also worthy of mention are the many opportunities I've had in *Walneck's Classic Cycle Trader*. I doubt I would have ever accumulated the material needed to put a big project like this together without the privilege of regularly publishing my wrench-turning adventures. Thanks Buzz and Heidi! I'd also like to thank David Bennett, director, BSA Company Limited for allowing the use of BSA copyrighted images and material. Last but certainly not least, I want to thank my wife Mary for all the evenings of proofreading, tolerating oil-stained rugs, and just putting up with a crazy bike freak like me. It's been a great ride.

Mike Brown

Author Mike Brown is shown in front of Mission Espada in San Antonio behind one of his budget creations, a very low-buck BSA A65 now long gone but fondly remembered.

1 *Your Brain: The Most Important Tool*

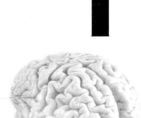

FORWARD INTO THE PAST

This book is a detailed roadmap, a pathway to rebuilding and restoring unit construction Triumph and BSA twins on your own without having to mortgage the house. It all started for me about 20 years ago. I'd been told the BSA A65 I rode then had been repossessed before winding up in a used car lot where I found it half dead. With that thought in mind, as I rode the bike past the motorcycle shop displaying a giant Union Jack, I almost didn't pull over, even though I was being waved at to stop. After nursing the derelict chopper back to life, I wasn't in the mood to fight with a previous owner. Because the motorcycle shop was only a few blocks from the used car lot, I figured if anyone knew the bike's history and held a grudge I'd find the aggrieved person here. Still, the scruffy looking biker at least appeared friendly, so I overcame my resistance and pulled in. Sure enough, the shop's proprietor knew the bike and its sordid history, but he wasn't in a fighting mood. I didn't know it then, but I was starting my first advanced class in Brit bike mechanics.

My instructor-to-be was John Roerich, a talented master builder who soon became a close friend. Much of what is found between these covers owes their origin to this man, a south Texas genius with both wrench and paint gun. Sadly, John died in 2006. Surely there will be Brit bikes in heaven.

Lots of other ideas inside these covers are products of many great pro mechanics I met through John. One in particular, Robert Burge, has been an invaluable resource for this book. Over the years my horizons widened even more through work as a motorcycle journalist for *Old Bike Journal, Walneck's Cycle Trader*, and others, so quite a few tips and tricks flowed from knowledgeable people all over the world. Oh yeah, a couple of these notions are products of my own frustrated thinking deep into the night as I cursed fate, drugged-out chopper builders, English engineers, and wondered why anyone would leave a great motorcycle under a pecan tree for 15 years. Much of the content here is also the product of deep experience. Some, I'm forced to admit, are the result of stupid mistakes. Hunter Thompson coined the term "Gonzo Journalism," which means not simply being an observer but actually living the story. I've lived this for more than 30 years and have the motorcycles and scar tissue to prove it.

My major writing goal was to build a bridge over the many gaps I found in existing literature and repair manuals, and these gaps are frequently deep chasms. I did not, however, intend to make the factory shop manual superfluous. There are certain tools you need to restore any Brit twin, and a factory manual and model-specific parts book are two of them.

SCHOOL BEGINS

In a second life beyond the oil can, I'm a Texas high school teacher who envisioned an extended class for those interested in purchasing, restoring, troubleshooting, and maintaining very popular classic motorcycles: Triumph's unit construction twins and BSA's A50-65 counterparts. Quite a bit of this book, however, is applicable to many Brit bikes of the '60s and '70s.

Whether you seek to build a low-buck get-you-on-the-road daily driver, a full concours restoration, or you just want the dang bike to idle without stalling, learning what John and his many contemporaries were willing to share can make life with a Brit bike much more enjoyable. It is also my prime mission to save you a large chunk of change.

Speaking of change, quite a bit has changed over the past quarter-century, and this most definitely applies to restoring Brit twins. These pages contain contemporary approaches and options, but won't neglect the "old school" either, as a lot of ancient tactics are every bit as good as they once were, but often forgotten in the world of big-budget TV bike shows. You don't have to spend a fortune restoring an old Triumph or BSA, and we've packed this book with lots of economical options. On the other hand, I'll let you know what the consequences are when resorting to cheap alternatives. But mainly I'll show you how to use your own two hands to make a Brit twin the best it can be today.

HOW TO USE THIS BOOK

I've structured this book to help you learn new techniques, but I've also made efforts to keep it readable enough to avoid snores by page twelve. Consequently, I highly suggest a quick cover-to-cover reading first. You don't need to take notes or highlight sections in your first pass through, but I strongly recommend getting the complete picture before diving into a Brit twin project.

REQUIRED TOOLS

As I mentioned, you will need the factory-issued parts book and shop manual for your project bike. Consider them required texts for our class. You will not need any other aftermarket repair manual. The two still widely available are, in my humble opinion, just thin rewrites of the original factory books and contain some highly questionable and outdated information. You also need more than a screwdriver and a pair of pliers, and in subsequent chapters we'll detail just what must be in your conventional toolbox and home shop.

THE COGNITIVE TOOLBOX

Restoring an old Brit Twin can lead a person down countless paths, many of them filled with neat experiences, lasting memories, and new friends. Conversely, taking a major misstep during restoration can produce a financial nightmare, an extremely disappointing project, or worse. Let's take the right road. Although it of-

Sometimes Ebay can produce pretty good deals, as this super clean $463 TR5T rolling chassis demonstrates. What sold us was the excellent condition of the frame, chrome and alloy tank. Another motivator: the owner was within driving distance and had a clear title. The absence of a complete engine was most likely a big factor in others not having an interest, and a $75 T100R engine took care of that problem. A budget builder must do a lot of horse trading, but that's part of the fun.

The almost-final TR5T project is shown above. Pipes were salvaged from an old chopper, just something to get us on the road. Stock pipes will no longer fit, and this is the sort of thing one has to be prepared for when mixing and matching. We won't win best of show, but she's a whole lot of fun, runs great, and looks pretty good for under $1500.

This awful chopper epitomizes a great budget project. It was uglier than a gorilla in makeup, and hadn't been run for 20 years, if the inspection sticker recorded its last gasp on public roads. The early-1972 Bonneville rusted outdoors for years, but the more this $450 wreck was cleaned and inspected, the better it looked. Both tachometer and speedometer worked perfectly, and the odometer registered only 1,800 original miles. What happened? Our theory is that the goofus who "customized" this Triumph was scared to death to ride it. He installed the extended springer by using brass bushings in the neck instead of bearings! He also kept the stock rake, fortunate for our intentions but dumb if you want a long chopper front end like this. It must have handled like a pogo stick from hell.

ten isn't the easiest, the final destination, a really nice motorcycle, is well worth the challenges.

A critical part of a successful restoration begins with brutally honest self-appraisal. Let's look at three T's: time, talent, and treasure, meaning how much time do you have to spend, what are your mechanical talents, and how much gold do you have hidden under the porch?

Talent and treasure can be viewed from dramatically different perspectives. Although I've seen others as good, I've never seen a Triumph restored better than those done by Jaye Strait of Britech. Jaye has all the talent he needs and spares no expense when he applies it. His product is far superior to anything that ever rolled out of what I'll refer to as "Old Triumph." But Jaye markets his bikes today to a special kind of customer, people who want the very best in a classic Triumph, and who are willing—and financially able—to pay for it.

At the opposite end of the time and talent continuum, to use another personal example, would be the 19-year-old miscreant I was when I got my first Triumph. My toolbox consisted of a super-cheap set of SAE sockets, vise grips I found under a garbage can lid, and several abused screwdrivers. I didn't know enough to time an engine, much less fine-tune one, and had about as much patience as Yosemite Sam three minutes into a Bugs Bunny cartoon. My restoration budget was based on minimum wage and whether my girlfriend was willing to hide in the trunk to save two bucks when we went to the drive-in movies. Total class.

Straight up: What sort of mechanical skill do you possess and what is your budget for a final product? My emphasis in this book will be providing information to help common bike freaks like us put together a cool Brit ride at modest expense. For real misers, I offer two examples I acquired and put together for under $1,500. Both are reliable, pleasant to ride, and no embarrassment at the curb or rally, but they sure as heck don't look or run like one of Jaye's. Understand

Here's the same bike 6,000 miles later and now quite presentable. Total cost was under $1,500, including purchase price. This was an exceptionally good deal, but they're out there and within reach if you make the right moves.

the difference? It's very important. If you want a road burner that smokes Harleys off the line, handles in the corners like a good race bike, and never leaves you on the side of the road, you have a certain kind of project in mind. If, however, you're perfectly content with Sunday afternoon jaunts down to the Dairy Queen, this is an entirely different equation.

I don't mean that it's not feasible to produce a super-solid Brit twin relatively inexpensively, because that is indeed possible and it's our primary mission; however it's unlikely to happen quickly, because good projects and parts often take time to find or develop. Budget builders will also spend a whole lot more time sweating and turning wrenches.

Time is money and money can buy time, literally. The Bonneville pictured here before and after restoration first popped into my sights for sale, dead and dirty, for $1,500, a fairly common asking price for many projects we'll cover. But right there, I've blown the bargain basement budget. Instead, I waited almost two years until the guy was sick of watching the bike rust outdoors, and got him to take $450. This was the return for my investment in time, and some might accurately call this patience as well. On the other

extreme, if you get caught in a bidding frenzy on eBay, you'll pay more than you might have ever imagined.

Equally important to budget builders in our time/treasure discussion is refurbishing parts that are commonly cast off. I spend a lot of time fiddling with old Amal carburetors today because I can often make them work well, but if you hired me to restore your bike, I'd pitch many of them too because of the time it takes to fix one and still earn a decent hourly wage.

However, what was once disposable is becoming more and more valuable as time erodes parts availability, so it's important for budget builders to know when to fold 'em and when to hold 'em. Never, for just one example, throw away an original piece of sheet metal no matter how rusty, damaged, or unwanted it may be. If you don't want to use it, you may be pleasantly surprised at what someone else might be willing to pay for it; this goes into the other side of the budget ledger.

ALLIANCES

A smart rebuilder utilizes allies, and a good machinist familiar with Brit bikes is a most important one. Depending on where you live, you

The gold standard for Triumph restorations can be seen in this Bonneville done by Jaye Strait of Britech. The quality is also more than surface deep, unlike some so-called concours restorations, as Jaye builds these bikes he calls Super Twins with many upgraded parts to make the motorcycle as functional as it is beautiful. Quite frankly, it's far superior to anything produced by the original Triumph factory. Consequently, Super Twins aren't cheap, but you most *certainly do get what you pay for. Although Jaye is a widely acknowledged professional bike builder, it would be a mistake to think he's an elitist. From rat bikes to low buck riders to custom choppers, Jaye loves them all and would always include categories for judging budget rides at his Triumph Day shows. Although he has a warm welcome for any Brit bike enthusiast, it is fair to say he's more than a bit partial to Triumphs! (Photos courtesy of Jaye Strait.)*

might have to locate and rely on long distance machine shop service. Do not be afraid to do so, because, for one of many possible examples, it is extremely unwise to let anyone other than a shop very familiar with BSA A65s install and/or ream the timing-side bush. A less-than-qualified machinist will either ream the bush improperly or charge you excessively for set-up time. Someone who does this work frequently will already have the correct tools at hand and can do the job perfectly at much lower cost, even with shipping involved.

A good painter who doesn't charge Rembrandt prices is another valuable ally. I was once a strong advocate of complete DIY painting, but several circumstances changed my mind, and this relates to objective and subjective aspects of the restoration process. In my case, I am no longer satisfied with rattle can paint jobs on gas tanks, nor even my best efforts with my own HVLP spray equipment. I also learned that modern paints contain very dangerous chemistry requiring a lot more protection than the simple cartridge mask I used in the days when I

could easily get acrylic lacquer. This fear was reinforced as I watched several professional painters develop severe health problems caused directly by modern paint. And, I guess it's only fair to add that I finally concluded that I was never going to be a great painter. It took a good friend and ally to reveal my folly.

Perhaps most important with respect to allies is never forgetting that your best ones are the good people around you, and their value is directly related to what sort of ally you are when the need arises. Much of what I learned about motorcycles came through friends. The phrase "What goes around comes around" truly apples to cycle restoration. Networking with a good bunch of guys, either formally in a club or informally, cannot be overstressed.

The newest twist to networking, being on-line on the Internet, is enormously important. If you live in East Overshoe, Alaska you are at a disadvantage for local help, but this is easily overcome on-line. A modern bike builder needs to be computer literate because of the wealth of information, opportunity, and cool people out in cyberspace. The British Empire spread across the world and with it English motorcycles and the people who still love them. I didn't even know Tasmania was a real place, and I never suspected I'd know someone who lives there who would help me with a project. Times have changed dramatically, and using a computer as a resource for your restoration is perhaps the biggest difference today.

Of course, much of what we'll contend with during restorations in the new millennium could be classified as timeless, but modern times truly impact our projects and can alter much of what might have been good advice in 1968 when your shop manual was written. A lot of progress, for two of many possible examples, has been made in sealants and electronics. Using today's technology to its best advantage is just smart and needn't compromise your desire to stay true to original form. Nobody can see an electronic ignition hidden under the seat, and playing around with points today is, well, pointless.

My last opening concept might be the most important, but something I had to learn the hard way. I refer to "false economy," the dangerous temptation to save a few dollars early that requires hundreds of dollars and/or hours later. Reusing connecting rod nuts and having the motor throw a rod without warning is a good example, and it can be lethal. Don't build your coffin. Budgetary considerations should never compromise safety; it's false economy of the worst order.

Okay? Take a break and think things out carefully. You don't need to carve it all in stone, but for lots of people it helps to write details down, and don't forget to share plans with those you trust and respect. The most important tool you'll ever use on your Brit twin rests between your two ears. When this tool is applied judiciously, you'll be very pleased with the outcome.

The payoff? Perhaps most important is knowing that the growl you hear while being nearly pulled off the handlebars under hard acceleration is the product of your own two hands. For me, it seldom gets any better. Let's get dirty, shall we?

► MODERN MOTORCYCLE MECHANICS

BY J.B. "BERNIE" NICHOLSON

It's always great to have alternative resources to put into your mental toolbox, especially if the food for thought originates from a well-respected source, in this case J.B. Nicholson's *Modern Motorcycle Mechanics*. While still the product of human hands and consequently imperfect as all earthly products must be, no one on the planet has ever done a better job covering motorcycle repair in such a broad scope, from BSA to Yamaha, of what are now considered classic motorcycles. First published in 1942 and last updated in 1974, MMM as I will henceforth refer to it, survived seven editions and has been called "the motorcyclist's bible" for good reason.

Unlike so many technical publications that simply organize, illustrate, and regurgitate mechanical knowledge, MMM is the product of extensive hands-on experience, refined over decades. Nicholson began selling and servicing motorcycles in Saskatoon, Canada in 1933. Over this time he bought, sold and serviced A.J.S., Ariel, B.S.A., Matchless, Norton, Royal Enfield, Panther, Sunbeam, Triumph, Villiers, and Indian motorcycles. Nicholson continued to operate a mail-order parts business until he retired in 1993 and finally passed on in December of 2001. Every first-person reference I've read or heard about Nicholson always included "gentleman" and many included "genius." Nicholson, unlike so many others, produced and recorded hard data where lesser technical writers said things like "replace if worn" and for this reason alone MMM is worth owning as a reference source, if you're lucky enough to find a copy.

MMM is long out of print and often goes for ridiculous prices on eBay. As of this writing, however, copies were still available at British Cycle Supply. Throughout *Budget Brits* in various strategic places where appropriate, I'll frequently refer to Mr. Nicholson's facts, figures, and economical repair suggestions as he truly epitomized the *Budget Brit* philosophy. As a professional wrench turner through the Great Depression, hard times of WW II as a military mechanic/engineer, and survivor of the Brit parts-scarce 60s and 70s, J.B. Nicholson has my vote as the greatest budget builder who ever lived. He believed in wringing the most utility out of any given part or machine and knew what worked, and just as importantly, what did not. In many cases, Nicholson's data allow for even greater wear/tolerances than factory specifications, useful information when making decisions. In many other cases, he provides hard data where none was previously provided. In both cases, this is very useful information I'll share where most appropriate or useful.

2 Column A or Column B: BSA or Triumph Twin?

If one ever wants to start an enduring, occasionally volatile, argument in Brit bike circles this topic is an ideal choice: Do you invest your time and treasure restoring a BSA or Triumph twin? Brickbats or not, I hold an opinion. With all things being equal, meaning price and relative condition, I favor the Triumph. However, I own two A65s and one of them is my favorite ride under lots of circumstances. Confused? Let's see if I can clear this up a bit. And hang on to that rock for a moment as we look at the options and model years as logically as possible, although logic is only one factor in this complex decision. We like what we like, and ain't nothin' gonna change that feeling in many cases. That point is well understood.

Few A65s are any nicer than this restored Thunderbolt. Sparkling chrome, excellent frame, and late-model engine add up to a fine motorcycle.

BSA 650S

Starting alphabetically, let's first take at look at BSA's A65 series cycles of 1962–1970. I have deliberated omitted the oil-in-frame A65s of 1971–72 as we'll look at these separately.

A direct descendent of the solid A7/A10 series, the A65s share a lot of common engineering, both good and bad. Even today, parts for these bikes are easy to find and reasonably priced. The used parts market is excellent—even better than Triumph—perhaps owing to the unfortunate way many BSAs were rebuilt, as short-running hand grenades. Many "mechanics" grossly misunderstood BSA twins and created a lot of dead motorcycles. These were frequently stripped to become used parts.

A very big reason A65s carry a rotten reputation for reliability and longevity in many motorcycle circles is directly related to the failure to understand critical differences between Triumph and BSA twins down at Dumbo's Cycle, and then rebuilding them with this ignorance. We'll cover this topic in more detail later in the engine section, but the BSA has two distinctly different components in the lower end that one must understand and plan to service properly.

Most infamous in the BSA is the use of a timing-side bush to support the crankshaft, as opposed to a ball or roller bearing. When a motor runs a bush like this, crankshaft end float is critical. A little too much or not enough and big troubles are right around the corner. Additionally, once installed, the bush must be precisely reamed in perfect alignment with the crankshaft. This job is best left to a specialist or an expert machinist. Also, unlike the Triumph, in which oil is fed through the crankshaft tip, BSAs do this via a slot that feeds a hole in the crank surrounded by the previously mentioned bush running about .001 to .002 clearance. If the bush is machined and or installed improperly—and I'd estimate more than half were so afflicted on this side of the pond the first time the lower end needed service—low oil pressure and attendant high-running temperatures quickly become problems. The problems really got critical with the high-performance Spitfire, which really pounded the bush and thrust bearing under severe service and in racing applications.

A second major difference involves the alloy cap used on BSA connecting rods. Unlike the steel rod caps Triumph used, BSA alloy rod caps have a regular tendency to wear out of round. As with the bush problems, lots of shops didn't fully appreciate this and simply slapped in a new set of bearings. Fortunately, machining the rods back into perfect roundness isn't extremely expensive. Every BSA rod must be carefully checked for this problem.

By 1970 BSA had sorted out the A65 and greatly improved many aspects of it, but by the time they did, they'd managed to wreck its reputation badly. A major image wrecker, ironically, really wasn't even BSA's fault, but that of Lucas, whose reputation wasn't too sterling during the period either. I refer to those A65s running the Lucas 4CA ignition points/advance system. It took way too long for BSA to locate and pinpoint the trouble, a transient spark that fired both cylinders at very inappropriate times. This might not sound like much, but the effect could be enormous: causing the pistons to seize in the cylinders at high speed. One has not lived until he's gone down an interstate sideways because the motor locked up at 75 mph. I have. It is very life-affirming.

But I still ride A65s with great pleasure and regularity today because the problem has a very simple cure. Ditch the points plate and advance unit, and either run a later model Lucas 6A, or really use yer noodle, and go with modern electronic ignition. Problem solved.

Regardless of problems, it has been reported that a properly rebuilt A65 lower end routinely gave over 40,000 miles in stock form in British police motorcycles. Many BSA experts say this is very possible today. The police bikes did, by the way, receive careful maintenance. And after

40,000 miles, it's highly advisable to split the cases on both Triumph and BSA engines because it's due for a good cleaning of the sludge trap. If the bush is replaced with that service, the job isn't expensive. The message: built right, the stock A65 lower end can give good service, so consider one without fear if you so choose. Lots can be done, too, to increase longevity. Much more about that later.

BSA ADVANTAGES

On the plus side, and it's a big plus, the 1963–70 A65 frame was one of the best in the business, and it was mated to a fine set of forks and brakes, especially those running the twin leading shoe units. So long as the frame's straight and the swingarm bushings are in good shape, the A65 rides and handles better than the equivalent Triumph. It's also a lot less likely to leak, owing to BSA running the valve pushrods inside of the cylinder barrels as opposed to two frequently problematic external tubes on Triumph. BSA also runs its rocker assembly inside the head, eliminating external rocker boxers that are also famous leakers and distributors of roadside Triumph parts.

In service, a good running A65 can keep up with modern traffic but long high-speed hauls can become a bit of an endurance issue for both you and the machine. The old saying: BSA=Butt Sore Always has roots in truth. Even when carefully balanced—a very good idea—the A65 is a buzzy little beast that will forever keep you guessing what that blur is in the rear view mirror. The BSA also makes its power higher up the rpm scale than the Triumph so one is apt to keep it there and this also creates more buzz.

Lots of times in life negatives can turn positive, and with BSA twins another positive occurs in parts and project acquisition. Fair or not, the A65 reputation has a direct bearing on market demand and pricing. Even with the additional service work involved in the lower end, one can often build a less expensive BSA than its rival Triumph owing to a lot cheaper initial acquisition costs and the abundance of used parts still available, but in a lot less demand than the Triumph.

UNIT CONSTRUCTION TRIUMPHS

What does one say about a living legend? When Edward Turner brought out the Speed Twin in 1938 it electrified the cycle world and then went on for another 50 years of historic success. Lots of people find the Triumph twin one of the best

Born for the highway and the stuff of legends, the Triumph unit 650 is shown here in Trophy form with alterations to suit a bike that really gets ridden. This single-carb masterpiece may be the greatest motorcycle of its time, but saying so can start lots of arguments. Regardless, a project like this will yield years of satisfaction and is highly recommended.

Perhaps the most underrated motorcycle ever built, oil-in-frame BSAs are outstanding opportunities and are still reasonably priced, even those in top condition like this one. Project BSAs are generally priced well below many other makes and models and are ideal candidates for restoration.

engines ever built in terms of aesthetic qualities, ease of service, and the ability to wring out amazing horsepower without greatly sacrificing reliability.

With respect to the unit construction models under consideration, the lower ends of the 650-750 Triumph twins are reliable and tough, owing to a main bearing arrangement that uses a roller on the drive side and a ball unit at the timing end, controlling the crankshaft firmly and providing exceptionally long service if properly maintained.

Top dollar generally goes to the Bonneville, and one has to consider resale value when purchasing. Still, in later years, about the only difference between the Tiger (and other single-carburetor models) and the illustrious Bonneville was the head and the additional carburetor. The difference in performance is very slight. Same goes with the Thunderbolt, BSA's single-carb 650. In fact single-carburetor bikes have better low-end torque, fewer tuning headaches, and generally better idling. Detect a bias here? It's genuine. I find it hard to justify the cost difference with respect to performance, and I frequently convert both Triumph and BSA motors to single-carb application when I have the parts to do so.

BSA AND TRIUMPH OIL-IN-FRAME (OIF) 650 MODELS 1971–72

The OIF (oil-in-frame) design appeared on both BSA and Triumphs in 1971. And here we come to a period still being howled about, which budget builders can use to excellent advantage.

The Umberslade-designed OIF frame was intended as a modern improvement, and might have been a big hit if not for a couple of major goofs which can be or may already be rectified today or might not make any difference to you.

As originally designed, the OIF chassis was intended to hold more oil, not less as it ended up. Initial designs called for the oil filler being at the front of the top spine, right behind the triple tree. Umberslade's fix to an oil foaming issue was to move the filler neck to the back of the spine right behind the gas tank, seriously reducing oil capacity and directly creating higher operating temperatures—never a good thing. Correcting this problem is simple: just install an aftermarket oil filter and cooler and you regain oil capacity and even better filtration.

In addition to this problem, many riders found the OIF frame too tall, and complained that the center and sidestand restricted the amount of lean one could make before scraping. The frame was also made from thinner-wall steel and stress cracking became an issue. And while this is strictly an aesthetic issue, most find the OIFs with their square breather boxes, much less attractive. The BSA, in my opinion, is made even more unattractive with a gas tank better suited to a lawn tractor. Painting the frame gray also irritated the masses.

So these are bad bikes, right? Lots of people think so, but then, lots of people don't think very well. Actually, the 71–72 A65s, aside from atrocious cosmetics, are arguably the best A65s ever built, except maybe for the '70 that has many of the engine improvements and the older, exceptionally good frame and much nicer cosmetics all around.

The 71–72 BSA engines are especially nice power plants with improved, cast iron oil pump, beefier joint faces, thicker cylinder studs, and better clutch actuation. Another major plus: beginning in 1969 BSA finally got around to fitting an oil pressure sensing switch, which can be used by itself or removed to install a full oil pressure gauge.

As for handling, the OIF is a very sharp performer for both BSA and Triumph, especially if the front forks, also new and identical for both makes in 71, get a set of anti-stiction seals and progressive springing. Which brings us back to why 71–72 BSAs and OIF Triumphs, still found at very reasonable prices, make awfully good choices for a budget Brit project.

OIF 650 Triumphs, however, may carry another black mark if equipped with a 5-speed transmission. Like many new innovations, it had its teething problems. The early Triumph 5-speed boxes suffered from imprecise shifting and fragile gears.

Many of these problems, some of them even the result of deliberate sabotage at the factory by disgruntled workers, were and still are often documented in various publications, but what is frequently overlooked is that the vast majority of really troublesome issues were all repaired by previous owners long ago. Many of these bikes never got out of the U.S. warehouses before getting transmission and leak problems fixed because dealers here knew what would happen to their business if they weren't. Triumph, for example, widely distributed a kit to correct the early 5-speed problems and these kits went into lots of OIF bikes.

It's also good to know that the regular four-speed box had no gear problems and was quite robust. For some reason, probably cost, Triumph decided to go with a leaf spring to index the camplate instead of a plunger; these models can produce problems when worn and they never worked as well as the earlier plunger assembly, which Triumph eventually went back to in the 1973 750s. Leaf-spring transmissions are also much harder to index correctly when rebuilding.

Another common concern for this time period is build quality in general, that suffered for both Triumph and BSA as they pushed their workforce harder in a vain attempt to remain profitable. These problems are non-issues today. You, the restorer, will now be the responsible party and you can be a lot more careful and attentive to detail, producing a cycle better than it was when brand new!

Underway, the unit 650 Triumphs and BSAs are great fun to ride with wonderful engines delivering tractable power and loads of guts. Unlike the 650 BSA, Triumph vibration is less obtrusive and the rock solid lower end can handle anything you dish out, and then some.

TRIUMPH OIF 750S

The Triumph 750s of 1973 on, though very nice machines, bring more vibration, but do respond very well to balancing that alleviates it to a great degree. I've often read that many consider the 750s less vibratory than the 650s, and maybe some are. Still, my seat of the pants assessment, and it's a lot of seat time, is that the 750 produces more vibration, and they sure seems to break off a lot more parts due to harmonic vibration.

A real plus for 750 consideration is the intro-

Just about the end of the line for Triumph, this 750 Bonneville and its Tiger cousin are excellent motorcycles. From 1976 on, they feature left-side shifting as required by U.S. law, and are therefore good choices for those who own another modern cycle. Switching back and forth from left- to right-shifting can be dangerous, as I can attest, having accidentally driven a '77 through a closed garage door! OIF Triumphs of the '70s and '80s are often far less expensive than earlier models, but just as much fun.

duction of disk brakes, first only in the front, but later on both wheels. The only drawback for budget builders is that the entire hydraulic system on most projects will need replacement, a fairly expensive issue.

On the positive side for many is that the rear disk brake models featured left-hand shifting to meet U.S. law. If you grew up on Oriental machines, or own other modern cycles, this can be a lot easier, and safer, to ride. You can even find 750s with reliable electric starting, although they aren't very common.

As for build quality, the 750s were generally excellent, and can be made to do many different things well. Also, there's a continued prejudice against OIF models that keeps them reasonably priced, especially project bikes.

500s

The Triumph 500 also used the same sort of bush on the timing-side up to 1968 that BSA did, but then improved to its big brother's roller/ ball arrangement. The final 500s have been named by numerous Triumph designers, me-

chanics, and employees as "the best engine we ever built," and deserve the accolades.

With respect to 1969-and-on Triumph 500s, one is hard pressed to find a better vintage Brit twin for less money in just about any condition. Because of America's "Bigger is Better" mentality, buyers often left the 500 on the showroom floor in favor of the 650. Ironically, a lot of these little guys had no problems keeping up with their bigger brethren, owing to a great power-to-weight ratio, and with a little fine tuning more than a few were able to outrun bigger twins completely. The late Triumph 500s of '69 and beyond were virtually indestructible and could be beaten mercilessly, as I can personally attest.

BSA's 500 is also extremely undervalued, and like its Triumph cousin, can get up and go, but not quite as well since it is nearly as heavy as the A65. The A50 is virtually identical to the A65 in most respects—so similar, in fact, the factory made only one shop manual for the pair. However, the 500 is so under-stressed, it is much easier on the crank bushing, and vibrates less on the

Don't forget the 500s! This custom Triumph is a little monster that's as fast as it is good looking. Both Triumph and BSA 500s are solid bikes and generally much less expensive than their bigger brothers.

road. Project bikes for both Triumph and BSA 500s are well below the price of the larger twins and often in much better condition. They are both ideal projects for the budget minded.

SPECIALS

I've deliberately avoided much discussion about factory specials or rare bikes like the few BSA 750s, not because I don't like them, but because their owners far too frequently put a value on them that's way out of the budget category. Still, if you can find something neat like a Triumph TT Special on the cheap, grab it, but beware of counterfeit specials because many of them are fakes today.

While not fakes if they are presented honestly, our last category—what the Brits call a Bitsa, meaning a bike built from different models and years, often with parts from different makes as well—certainly deserves consideration, and may well be the way to go for a lot of budget builders. Some are worlds better than the original, while others are rolling death traps, so be careful. Old choppers in particular require careful scrutiny for idiotic engineering, poor welding, and badly mismatched parts. For example, I've seen more than a few choppers raked so severely the extended stock front suspension was only sprung by flexing of the fork tubes and required a parking lot to turn around.

Astute readers will note I haven't spent much time at all discussing various models. One reason is that doing so would require a book itself, and there are good ones already in print. Another is that so little separates the various models mechanically. Also, I mostly skipped over stuff like wheels, brakes, and electrics as they are common issues to all of these bikes. (You did know that BSA owned Triumph and that both makes used many identical pieces?) Finally, most budget builders aren't that fixated on minutiae and are primarily interested in throttle twisting and just enjoying their Brit bikes. In the end the most important thing is that wicked grin we all get riding a classic bike we love.

3 *Finding Budget Projects and Parts*

OVERVIEW

Why is it that some project bikes rest in the dark recesses of garages forever while others go on as top show bikes, classy choppers, or neat daily drivers? There are numerous right answers, but finding the right project to pair with the proper owner is often the key to success. Project and parts sources today involve issues and technologies never imagined when your Brit twin was born. For one example, factory publications say that genuine BSA/Triumph manufactured parts are recommended, but the factories are long gone, and the replacement sources range from better than original to pure garbage. Let's study these issues in today's light by first taking a look at common project categories and then analyzing relevant issues.

This junker of a BSA did make the cut, and for $300 couldn't be passed up. The incorrect Triumph tank was a worthless ball of rust, but the '71 engine resting in a '65 frame proved to be a gold mine. The engine was started as outlined in this chapter, ran perfectly, and didn't smoke a bit. It's spent the last two years burning up Texas highways in a friend's chopper.

PROJECT CATEGORIES

The Rat

A running but rusty, greasy Rat, complete with bald weather-cracked tires, busted headlight, and duct tape seat can make an ideal budget Brit candidate. A good Rat's as scruffy as a New York City wino, just as offensive, often of mixed pedigree, and frequently a seriously wounded runner. Consequently, the first order of business is to make sure the owner can start it. If he can't, completely discount the excuses. One could write a complete book titled, "Reasons the bike for sale won't run now but will be easy for a new owner to start later." It either runs or it doesn't, period. However, it is also wise to at least try starting a dead bike after you buy it, since much can be learned in a very short span of time and considerable expense can be saved or other troubles at least identified clearly.

Before the bike is started, it's best to check out the bottom of the case for evidence of repair. A lot of old cases will have welds underneath and other places, especially around the front where it attaches to the frame. Check carefully in and around both the primary and secondary chain cases, extremely common damage areas caused when either the primary or secondary chain lets go. Also check out the fins on both the head and cylinders for shoddy repair or missing pieces.

Let the owner start the bike now and listen to the engine carefully for noises like knocks, clanks, etc. A little smoke in an old Rat is allowable, but big clouds are cause for demotion to Wounded Rat.

Both BSAs and Triumphs make many sounds even when healthy, but some noises signal terminal illness. Becoming familiar with what's good and isn't is an extremely important advantage in analysis, and if you aren't there yet, get a friend who is to help. Even beginners can become much more proficient after listening carefully to a good running model of interest. Once you become familiar with the sounds of a healthy engine, a bad one is much easier to identify, even if you aren't sure of precisely what sound means trouble.

Specific noises are tough to describe in print, but let's try a little anyway. Clattery sounds from the valve train often aren't serious issues, because just about all Rats need a valve adjustment. Even when new, the valve action is noisy on all Brit twins, compared to modern engines. Bad rattles, however, are often serious and may mean a locked or blown engine is imminent due to something like a loose valve guide—not unusual in either BSA and Triumph heads—especially if they've been rebuilt poorly a few times.

Make sure you're allowed to move the Rat's throttle yourself. Rev it up a bit, and then let off quickly to listen carefully for rod knocks, and knock is pretty descriptive, sort of like two pieces of hardwood being knocked together. It will most often sing it's dying song the second you back off the throttle. Speaking of noise, open pipes can mask lots of sounds, and con artists know it.

As the Rat rattles, use the metal tip of a large wood handle screwdriver on the left and right side of the cases to listen for excessive main bearing noises by putting your ear to the handle end as you hold the other against the case near each main bearing. There's a shop tool, sort of like a doctors stethoscope, that works even better, but the screwdriver will do the job. Squeals, grinding noises, and loud rumbles are bad news.

After letting the bike run for a bit, check to see that you can shift it into all gears while listening to the transmission, and you can do this without a working clutch and on a bike you can't ride by securely blocking up the rear wheel. Listen for excessive gear noise, a high whine, and any other bad sound like mysterious rumbles. Healthy BSA and Triumph transmissions are quiet in operation, so be very suspicious if they aren't. However, nearly all go into first gear with a pretty hard clunk, and did so when they were brand new.

Checking the oil pressure on potential purchases or for diagnostic information is easy on '69 and up BSAs and all unit Triumph twins simply by removing the sending unit and attaching a gauge like this.

Even with something like a busted clutch cable, the bike should go into every gear with ease. Rev the bike sharply and let off quickly to see if you can coax it into jumping a gear after each shift, extremely common with worn boxes but tough to check if the bike can't be ridden. If you can safely saddle the Rat, give the transmission the same test under load for gear jumping, a much better test and very reliable indicator of transmission serviceability.

If nothing nasty turns up so far, shut the engine off and remove the oil pressure sensing switch and replace it with a gauge. BSAs before '69 don't allow this luxury. You want this test done with the bike fully warmed up. Specific oil pressure varies considerably with temperature and engine rpm and will be lower for even good A65s. They never made quite as much pressure even new as a Triumph does. Both call for about 20 psi around idle.

At this point, it's worth remembering that many of the best Rat deals can be had when the machine runs poorly because the fix might not be very expensive but beyond the current owner's understanding. A compression test is most useful here. If it's about the same in both cylinders and well over 100 psi, she may have a lot of life left and not need extensive work. If you have a rough runner with good oil pressure and compression, this is a good one to gamble on if

At a cursory glance, this 1971 Triumph frame looked pretty good. Checking the swingarm for play (as shown) soon revealed its ugly nature as the swingarm would not move freely up and down. Closer inspection revealed considerable collision damage. Shown in the second photo is just one

example on the back part of the frame where the passenger peg attaches. This was pushed in and blocked the swingarm. Both mounting points for the rider's pegs were bent considerably too. This bike was apparently crashed at speed and may have other yet-unseen damage as well.

the price is right and you hope to stay out of the engine for a while.

If things are still looking good, continue checking. Go through the bike as thoroughly as you would with a high-dollar purchase before making any offer. This includes seeing that the brakes hold, the forks and shocks aren't frozen—very common by the way—and that other issues like missing sheet metal, are accounted for and part of the final analysis.

One final test to make on every bike, including basket cases, is checking for swingarm play. Hold the bike securely with one hand, or with some help, and push and pull on the rear tire to see if you can get it to move side to side. If it does, the swingarm bushings are shot. If you find play here, the price had better be exceptionally good because you may have a tough repair job on a bike that's covered many miles. Do this check on any project, especially basket cases, where it's even easier to see if the swingarm moves side to side. Also be sure to check the frame for any signs of collision damage, sometimes evidenced by kinks in the frame tubing but can be a lot subtler.

Later frames, oil-in-frame models 1971 onward, have a tendency to crack around the frame neck and at points around the bottom where the centerstand attaches. On a positive

side, these frames are super-stiff—one of the reasons they handle so well—so they generally don't bend in a crash, they break, making accident detection easier.

Now we come to the offer, a make or break point. I always make the owner start first and prompt hesitant ones with the line, "Hey, it's your bike, you know a lot more about it than I do, what's it worth to you?"

At this critical juncture, a lot of variables come into play, and six other guys drooling over the bike is just one of them. This being said, we must remember the prime objective, reasonable cost. Unless the price is so good you simply can't pass it up, remember the old three-step rule. This strategy involves making a much lower counter offer, and if it isn't accepted, walking away. Lots of times on the third step away from the bike and owner you'll get the lowest offer the owner is willing to accept. Psychologically, it's extremely advantageous to be of the mindset that no one deal is so important that it must be made immediately. This takes a lot of self-discipline, but smart buying is an important part of building budget Brits.

Raising the Dead

It's a good idea to try starting a non-runner and promoting it to Rat bike if you can. Make sure you try this after the sale, as the price can dramatically escalate otherwise.

It really doesn't take long to fire up a dead Brit twin if she's capable of reanimation and you have the parts required. I keep a spare set of coils and carburetors in the shop and a Boyer electronic ignition module for this purpose.

You'll need to drain and refill both the engine and transmission oil, if there's any there to begin with, and lubricate the valve train by removing the valve cover or inspection caps and liberally coating the entire assembly. Also pull the sump plate or plug and check to see that the pickup line isn't blocked, which could happen if it got water inside. Look for water when you pull this plug or plate. Also pull and clean the oil tank screen and line. Don't forget to drain and refill the primary case as well.

Remove both the pickup and return oil lines and replace them with new hose, as they are often obstructed or broken. Check to see that there's nothing obstructing the metal lines the hoses attach to.

Remove the old points set and advance unit and replace it with the Boyer unit wired to your known-good coils. Remove the old carburetor(s) and old fuel hose(s) and replace them with the good carbs and new hoses. If the gas tank is the usual rusty crusty mess, you'll have to provide a means of getting gas to the carburetors via remote tank or use a spare tank as I do.

Set the timing for the bike using the correct tool (see final chapter for this information and other particulars like wiring this rig) and use a known good set of plugs. Don't install them just yet because we want to make sure each plug fires as it should. I use a length of wire from a good battery with a simple off/on toggle switch and another wire to the Boyer unit. After making sure there's spark, continue to kick the engine over until oil begins to dribble out of the port for the oil pressure switch that you removed for this check. If you're trying this on an early A65, kick until you're exhausted and just pray you have oil running to the engine. You can at least check for return circulation by pulling the return line to the oil tank or head. Once you see the oil and/or you're divinely inspired, install the plugs and try starting the bike.

There's method to this madness. By going through these steps, you'll soon know if the engine won't run at all or won't run correctly, or have serious problems and a complete teardown at hand. Also, you pick up a lot of good diagnostic information for later use if it runs well with the test parts but won't when you try something like rebuilding the original carburetors.

I've been pleasantly surprised a number of times by how well some of the ugliest bikes imaginable ran and needed nothing internally. You may be as well, so it's worth checking if the engine turns and has adequate compression.

No dice? Sorry, we're off to the next category.

The Dead Dog

This is a non-runner not worth trying to start because it has an obvious problem, like low compression. The key to success here is finding a bike that can be restored at reasonable expense. What's reasonable for you depends on many variables. Also, don't forget that Dead Dogs can actually be much better deals than running Rats if they have all the right parts resident.

Also of major consideration is how you want to use the bike. For example, is it your intention to restore the bike to concours quality and exactness? If so, then you must place a great deal of emphasis on the bike having all of its factory parts resident and restorable. On the other hand, if all you want is a neat custom bike, then having all the original parts isn't a major issue. Whatever your intentions for the bike, all purchasers need to understand that the market value of a bike is much higher if it is factory correct and engine/frame numbers match when they should.

Make sure you can move the transmission lever and rotate the engine. If either or both are frozen, that's very bad news, even if the owner claims otherwise. Locked assemblies can be terrifically difficult to dismantle and then reveal more broken parts than a junkyard, which might be where the Dead Dog really belongs.

The Basket Case

A basket case can either be the deal of the century or a curse that will torment you for years. As with the Dead Dog, specific knowledge of the

"Stuck from sitting," is one of the lamest excuses going. This sort of damage is very common in both BSAs and Triumphs left exposed outdoors for long periods of time. Water seeps in from the fill plugs and intake ports and can lock up an engine and transmission. This BSA box was "stuck from sitting" and is beyond easy repair, although it still may yield serviceable parts.

make and model is critical. Stay far, far, away from these if you lack both tools and background, and even farther if you seek something quick and easy. That being said, a good basket project can be a super deal if you are careful and the price is too good to pass up.

With basket cases, it's very helpful to work from a component checklist. Believe it or not, it's very easy to buy something like this, throw it into a pickup, and then think going down the road, "Did this thing have a gas tank?" or a thousand different (sometimes very expensive) questions that needed earlier answers. Rooting through every box and checking off critical items makes this a lot less likely to happen. Regardless, every basket bike I've ever seen had more than a few missing parts. Knowing what isn't there also greatly aids final negotiations.

One benefit to basket cases is that it's a lot easier to inspect components for wear and damage. With a disassembled engine, for example, bores can be measured, gears inspected, crankshafts measured, etc. It's very important to check on these things as some basket cases are grown in the back of shops from parts nobody wanted—for good reason.

FINDING THE TREASURE

The thrill of the hunt is a major reward for our passion. And just like conventional hunters, there are good ones and bad ones, as well as

good places to hunt and ones filled with dangerous animals and evil swamps. The best place I know is in this little town that had a Triumph/BSA dealership but the owner died without any heirs. Believe this if you will; it's a classic legend I've heard so many times and so many places I love to compare the regional differences. It doesn't exist. You're on a hunt, brother, competing in the same forest with the rest of us Elmer Fudds and there aren't any definitive maps. However, there are good hunters and bad ones and it is imperative that budget builders be the former.

Like any good hunter, you have to be in the right place at the right time. Sometimes this is pure luck, but this can be greatly increased by the time spent actively hunting. My father was an excellent deer hunter. He'd stay out in blinding snowstorms and torrential rain if he thought the conditions were right for a successful hunt. To put this in a cycle context, it's amazing the sort of deals one can make at a swap meet when both parties are up to their necks in mud. The summer soldiers stay home while the hard core hunters come back with the prize.

Like hunting or fishing, there are ideal times to be in position. At swap meets, being early locates some excellent deals, but waiting until closing time when the tired owner contemplates loading heavy bikes and parts bins is also a good time to make an offer he can't refuse.

Crashing through mechanical brush is also wise. I once spent a full Saturday digging through dried, and not so dried, dog poop mixed in liberally with legions of roaches, spiders, fleas, and several snakes residing in and around 25 years worth of accumulated junk, a lot of it British cycle parts. That was 15 years ago and I'm still making use of the crusty treasure I found at a price I'm almost embarrassed to mention. I had to promise to clean up the mess, which I did, and then threw in a case of beer, which I got to drink a good portion of, after I washed my hands about 500 times.

While not the most inexpensive way, perhaps the safest way to find a good project bike is through an established dealer. Many have a good selection of candidates available for projects. Reputable dealers will be honest about the bike they are selling, both in terms of what they know and what they don't. Since a successful dealer values his reputation, he is far less apt to misrepresent a project bike and far more inclined to keep a returning customer. Many of these dealers advertise in *Walneck's Classic Cycle Trader,* another great place to hunt for parts and project bikes. If you're very new to Brit bikes and don't have a knowledgeable friend to help select a project, a dealer can actually save you a lot of money by steering you away from a project that is tragically flawed. He'll be even more receptive to a lower counteroffer if you promise to throw him a good bit of parts and service business.

The Internet

The opposite end of the safety spectrum is a booming private market that can produce wonderful projects but is also, in my personal experience, the place one is most likely to get burned. Internet fraud is rampant. I've been ripped off on three different occasions buying parts online, and the Internet is filled with con artists of all sorts selling worthless junk far more suited to scrap metal than restoration.

It is certainly possible to find good project bikes on the Internet, but I can't recommend sending any large amount of money for an uninspected project bike to a private party. When I bid on these and win, I arrange to meet with the seller before taking the money out of my wallet. It's good policy. Escrow accounts are another good protection, and if a long-distance seller won't go for either, walk away. Also, always check for a feedback rating that's good and that the seller has been doing business for a while.

Much safer, but still potentially problematic, is public auction. Many of these are now run by reputable dealers who won't even let a bike enter the auction unless it is legally titled (an important issue). The buyer can also inspect the bike on site. Generally, you won't be able to ride or test it, but you may be able to question the owner. This is getting to be a bit easier with the advent of cell phone technology. At larger auctions many owners will list a cell number for people with questions. Like any auction, a major drawback is competition. People with time limitations, though, may find an auction is the

eBay can be a parts and project bonanza, but is also a very dangerous place because many scam artists practice in cyberspace and disappear before you can find a dark corner and a baseball bat. eBay is still worth using if you are careful, however, as this truckload of parts, picked up for under $400, reveals. Most guys on-line are just honest bike freaks like us.

quickest route to a project bike and some pretty good deals do occur.

The Road Less Traveled

Brit bikes can pop up in uncommon places. I've seen them for sale in second hand stores, pawnshops, flea markets and increasingly, estate sales. If you get lucky at one of these the price is incredible. Salvage yards are also worth a look, and don't limit yourself to motorcycle salvage yards; many bikes turn up in automotive scrap yards.

PART SELECTION AND ACQUISITION

Parts is parts? No they ain't. There are good and bad parts, cheap and expensive ones, new and used ones, and some that don't even fit on your bike. So the worst you can do is to buy a bad expensive part that doesn't go on your bike, right? Sound far-fetched? Unfortunately, it happens all the time. However, if you know where you're going in Parts Land, the risk of getting expensively lost can be minimized.

When ordering parts for an old Brit motorcycle, you must realize there is a very great chance that a departure has been made from stock due to a previous repair. I've seen engines alone with parts from four different years in them, and I'll bet this isn't a record. I've built a few like this too. While there are many common parts among bikes of different age and model, there are almost innumerable small variations that can result in an incorrect restoration, an oil leak like the Exxon Valdez, or even worse. A factory parts catalog for your specific year and model is imperative, but not infallible because an aftermarket change may have taken place. For example, I couldn't understand why I kept getting the wrong parts for my 1971 BSA until it was brought to my attention that it had a 1966 engine.

If you're building your first Brit twin and don't have anyone around who knows much more than you do, it might be very wise to do business locally. Did the person at the local shop seem to know what he was talking about? If he's any good, he did. Did he seem willing to help? He should. Two affirmative answers here might well mean you'd be smart to give them a good piece of business, even if it costs a little more. Service has a price; is it available and worth it to you? Also important is that a good local shop can help you solve problems or perform a procedure that requires a special tool you don't own, perhaps for little or nothing because they appreciate your prior business.

Thanks in great part to both Triumph and BSA failing to recognize the importance of producing a good supply of replacement parts, today we still have many aftermarket manufacturers catering to both makes. In lots of cases, their products are superior or at least as good as in the original. In many other instances, this is sadly not the case at all.

The worst parts seem to come from Taiwan, but some real garbage floats out of India too. I don't know what's in Oriental rubber, but I've learned to stay away from footpeg rubber and oil seals sourced from this region. I've also bought headlight bulbs that work for five minutes, trim pieces that disintegrated on contact, and piston rings that were hell to install and never sealed well. You can recognize these rings as they have a three-part oil ring. Forget 'em. Hepolite and Hastings make good sets.

Not all Oriental parts are bad deals though and lots of Oriental parts seem more than up to the job at a fraction of OEM price. I've used Oriental pistons for years sold under the Cyclecraft brand that work well, so long as they're mated to a good set of rings.

It is generally true that English parts are quality items, and aftermarket manufacturers like SRM, MAP, Britech, and Norman Hyde are better than original, but don't think there's never a problem with original equipment parts. I bought fork boots once that practically crumbled in my hands. They sure were original, and 30 years old.

Next on the list are used parts; I love 'em, but you can get stuck here as you can with new parts, sometimes even worse. The best deal anywhere is still a complete junk bike picked up for little or nothing. Paying for a model identical to what you're working on or close to it can be a great deal if it has what you want. While I don't love the Internet when it comes to buying parts, I'm absolutely in love with it for selling. Your budget can be greatly aided by selling off what you don't want or need at a fair price.

Junkyards can be a bargain, but often aren't. A $20 cylinder head that needs $400 in machine shop work isn't a bargain. Conversely a good wheel for five bucks can't be beat. Don't be afraid to haggle with used parts guys; they expect it. Always make a lower offer and go from there.

SWAP MEET SAVVY

The mother of all parts opportunities is the swap meet. Tremendous bargains can be found amongst the piles of old boxes and greasy bits, but one has to be extremely careful. A very common occurrence, unfortunately, is putting the shop's castoff parts heap out for sale. I once spent an hour sifting through a pile of various parts, and every doggone one of them had some tragic flaw. I'd bet almost anything that each part had been rejected during service work. Lots of pure junk can be found at any swap meet.

At the opposite end of the spectrum is the bargain available because the owner didn't need the part. Value is relative to need and original cost. If the part was acquired for little or nothing and isn't needed, then letting it go for a song makes sense. Look for the guy with just a few parts sitting around; he's probably just an enthusiast looking to let go of things he just doesn't want. Conversely, be very careful around the guys with hundreds of parts sitting around in old boxes.

With any used part subject to service wear, it's absolutely imperative to bring measuring tools along when shopping. A worn-out set of cylinders can look really good after a little sandpaper and a cheap coat of paint are employed, but still be pure junk if they can't be bored again. Yes, there are sleeves available, but the expense is far greater than a good used set and a bore job.

The newcomer to parts buying is the Internet and it has tons of potential. Don't be afraid to use a reliable source, but be careful too. Everything said for the swap meet scams applies double to the Internet, where it's often absolutely impossible to tell the junk from treasure without in-person inspection. Consequently, get a return guarantee with any significant parts purchase. Honest guys won't have a problem with this.

Another way to save big is knowing what parts are common and obtainable from the original source. Items like nuts and bolts will have a Triumph or BSA part number, but that does not mean it isn't a common machine bolt. Buy one with a factory part number and you can pay three dollars for a ten-cent screw. Many bearings are also obtainable from the original manufacturer or a company specializing in bearings. Here the savings can be even bigger. Bearings generally have numbers for the inner and outer pieces which can be matched or cross referenced by a good bearing supply house.

My final advice about parts acquisition may be the most valuable, and that's where to purchase common items needed for any restoration: things like wire, consumables like sandpaper, etc. All of these can be found at the local chain auto parts store, but that's the last place you want to buy them because the markup is tremendous. The auto parts chains have a narrow profit margin on many parts they sell because they advertise to beat the competition and draw in customers. They make up for this on small items, precisely the stuff you need for a restora-

For various reasons this wreck wasn't dragged home. Both the engine and transmission were locked and the front end was rusted solid. We marveled especially at the use of an old scrap of tire tube as a bowl gasket for the monoblock carburetor. Repairs like this are often good indicators of the "quality" you can't see.

tion. You can save hundreds on any restoration by simply avoiding the chain auto parts stores and instead sourcing supplies discounted at big box hardware and electrical supply stores.

More than anything else, get educated about market prices for the parts and projects you have an interest in, and be aware of regional price differences that can be considerable. Don't be concerned with the offering price; it's the final sale price that's important. Here's where eBay can't be beat. Take your time and watch the auctions for parts and projects of interest. It's easy to do by just clicking "watch this auction." Take note of final sale prices, really what the market can bear. Remember, though, that eBay prices are generally higher than direct casual sale prices due to the competitive bidding process and competition from all corners of the world.

Finally, make all of this fun. Plan parts and project hunting vacations. Taking a trip to a place like Mid-Ohio during Vintage Motorcycle Days, where the swap meet covers 40 acres won't cost nearly as much—and be even more fun—than a trip to Disneyland. Most times, you come back with a lot more than memories.

4 *Keepin' It Legal*

OVERVIEW

While there's certainly room for trust in our lives, when cycle trading in America, it's very important to remember that wheeling and dealing can be vastly lacking in integrity. In fact, a keen awareness of the sometimes crafty and devious fringes of American business dealings calls for one very sure axiom: trust no one and verify everything. If you religiously follow this practice, it's highly doubtful you'll ever see your budget Brit being hauled away because of legal ownership issues.

Is it real or is it Memorex? Just prior to converting to OIF frames for 650 cycles, Triumph 650 and 500 frames had the Vehicle Identification Numbers (VIN) stamped on a flat plate on the primary side of the downtube. This frame area is where most Triumph numbers are generally located. Earlier years do not have the special logo protection or plate shown in the bottom frame, but missing in the top one. Earlier frames just have the VIN stamped on the tube in this same area. The reason the logo is missing on the top frame is that the number has been ground off and new ones stamped. Normally, this is very bad news, but in this instance there appears to be a legitimate reason. The number is actually one that's been reassigned by Texas DOT, which does this by using a sticker that can still be partially seen.

THE NUMBERS GAME

First of all, check the title carefully and make sure the vehicle identification number (VIN) on it matches the one on the bike. It is not at all uncommon that a title for one cycle is used for another. Unit Triumphs from the factory had matching engine and frame numbers; unit BSA twins did not until 1967. Commonly, the VIN used on the title is the one on the frame, stamped on a lug on the front left side where the engine mounts on A50/A65s until 1971. On Triumphs the VIN was most commonly stamped on the left side of the frame downtube near the triple tree. Generally, OIF BSA frames were stamped on the steering neck, as were some Triumphs, but numbers were struck on the left downtube near the neck in later OIF Triumphs.

Check the title for alterations, another old con game. Often a crook will alter a single number, like changing a "0" into an "8." Altered titles are invalid on the face and nearly all alterations can be spotted if one just looks carefully.

Once you've verified that the title is genuine, take a careful look at the bike's VIN on the engine and frame to see that it's legitimate. This chapter shows quite a few examples. If you find a VIN stamped in an area other than where it should be, like lower on the frame or in a completely different location—it's a good indication the bike's been renumbered and the old number covered up with bondo, ground off, or both.

Engine and frame numbers should be visible. Be extremely suspicious of a story about a "replacement" case or frame as the reason for no number being where it should. Replacement frames and engines were commonly stamped by dealerships and not sold to individuals as blanks. However, there are legitimate examples out there, and this chapter shows one of them. Mostly, though, frames and engines with no numbers are bad news.

One reason it can be difficult to spot a forged VIN is the haphazard way the numbers were stamped at the factory. This BSA VIN is a factory original, but looks like a nearly blind drunk did the stamping. One good clue to its originality is the casting grain pattern under the VIN, the same as the rest of the case. Be very suspicious of grain differences. This case is a '69. Early cases do not have the raised plate; later ones feature a rolled-on logo to make alterations far easier to spot. Earlier Triumphs are marked in the same location, but do not have a raised plate; later ones have the plate and logo.

This is a legitimate late Triumph 500 case. Note the logo and the stamping. Later 650s and 750s have a more-raised plate with the logo design; earlier ones—both 500s and 650s—just had the numbers stamped on the primary side of the case near the cylinder flange, and often not very neatly.

With stamped numbers there are numerous ways to hide the original, and we can detect them. A very common way to hide numbers is to put body filler over the number and then paint over it. In this case, insist on sanding at the proper number location before buying. It won't take too many passes to reveal the numbers if they still exist, or the depression and/or grinding marks if one was completely obliterated. Be suspicious of welds or brazing near VIN locations as this is a more sophisticated means of hiding the original VIN. VIN alterations are more difficult to detect on BSA frames before 1971, as the plain flat lug where the VIN is stamped almost invites fraud. Measurements taken across the lug centered over the bolt hole on two different A65 frames with known good numbers revealed a thickness of about 1.5 inches on each. A lug measuring a lot differently should be suspected of metal removal and restamping.

Speaking of obliteration, police agencies have an acid solution that can reveal ground off numbers in many cases. Lots of times the local police are very cooperative with motorcycle restorers, as many cops also have a passion for old wheels and are willing to run a check for honest collectors if you just ask them. In many cases today, the obliterated number is not carried on any hot

sheet and a document from the police taken to the local motor vehicle office can yield a replacement title. Some states will provide a new set of numbers.

COUNTERFEITS

A bit higher up on the fraud scale is the renumbering bandit. The English call them "ringers," I guess due to the sound made when stamping numbers. To spot these frauds, one has to be a bit more careful. The hardest ones to catch are on earlier bikes that have no logo stamping. In later years, both Triumph and BSA started rolling a logo over the area for VIN stamping on engines and also on some frames. Removing the VIN number removes the logo, and that makes fraud detection extremely easy: No logo=bogus number.

However, many earlier bikes do not have this protection and numbers were just stamped on a specific area. Also, the true original VIN often looks like a wino did the stamping, so irregularities in placement are frequently legitimate. To spot phonies, look for a difference in the size of the letters from a known good original. Also, cast parts like cases will have a grain, and if this isn't there or looks different, it's suspect.

PAPERWORK

Okay, now that we've played the numbers game, lets move to getting documents for a project bike that doesn't have a title, an extremely common occurrence today. Fortunately, so long as the numbers are legitimate, this is pretty easy in many places.

This is as bogus as it gets. The Triumph VIN has been partially obscured to protect the poor soul who may have bought this swap meet case or might be legitimately running the VIN on a frame somewhere. This 750 case has been filed so much the raised plate is completely missing, making it look like an earlier case. However, with an earlier case, the grain pattern will be similar to the rest of the case, not smooth like this one. Always clean around the numbers to reveal this malfeasance, as it's common for crooks to load it up with dirt and grease to hide their handiwork, which is almost always very crude like this example.

Triumph and BSA departed from the usual area for VINs on the first few years of the their OIF bikes, deciding to stamp these numbers on the headstock, as shown on this Triumph. BSA continued to locate numbers around the neck, but Triumph soon reverted to stamping them on the left downtube, now two pieces, but still on the outside of the tube near the neck like it did before.

Let's start with the easiest, the so-called title companies. I say so-called because these outfits don't really give you a title, they register it in a non-title state and then transfer ownership back to you. What happens is the company provides you with paperwork and you "sell" them your bike. After the "sale" they register it, often in either Alabama or New Hampshire, and then ownership is transferred back to you.

This practice makes use of a legal loophole caused by most states agreeing to recognize motor vehicle ownership laws of other states. It must be clearly understood that with "title" companies *you do not get a legal title and you may not be the legal owner of the bike until your state issues you a title.* Yes, you can go through a title company and still not be able to register nor legally own your bike! Here's how to make it less likely to encounter problems with "title" company paperwork.

First of all, try to have local police run a check on the VIN number before you buy any vehicle without a clear title. Most times there will be absolutely no record of the vehicle, which is good. However, if it's stolen, there may be a record, and you want to know this before you try to title the bike! Secondly, the bike may be subject to liens. Unlike most vehicle records, which are purged every so often, bank liens are assets and are often transferred to other banks. They seem to exist forever!

You also can bypass the title company completely and do the same thing they do, register the vehicle in another state not requiring titles. This is very easy in many states, some may not even require residency. Good ones to check up on are Vermont, New Hampshire, Alabama, and Maine. The Internet helps making connections.

Recently, several new businesses have advertised the ability to secure actual titles. Their rates are expensive; the following alternative methods are much cheaper.

DO-IT-YOURSELF TITLES

Lots of states have a simple appeals process that is, in my mind, the best option to get a legal title. In many cases the process is free or nearly so. For example, I titled a paperless 1969 BSA in Texas by doing the following:

1. Having the numbers checked by the Department of Transportation and getting a letter testifying they had no record of the vehicle. This cost me $3.

2. Filling out a form explaining why I didn't have the paperwork. I told the truth, "I bought it at a swap meet for cash and did not even get a receipt, just the dead motorcycle." I was required to provide a number tracing of the VIN and a wonderful picture of the wreck. Do your paperwork before doing any other work on the bike as the uglier it is, the fewer the questions. A fully restored classic, however, may raise many questions.

3. Attending a title hearing, which is a fancy name for a meeting with a county representative who looked over the application. This took two minutes. I was then walked across the hall with a title application, paid the regular title fees, and got my title in the mail four weeks later.

You might not be so fortunate. If you live in Ohio, as one example, title company documents won't fly. However, where there's a will, there's a way, and Jim Tuttle of Marion, Ohio was kind enough to share his methods.

Jim explained that the county level court of common pleas allows individuals to petition for vehicle titles. The more documentation you can provide—details like notarized bills of sale, parts receipts, written details and explanations, photographs, etc.—the better. The court requires a $50 filing fee that must be included with the details. After filing, a court date is set.

Jim reported that the actual court hearing is informal, only involving a judge and reporter, and that judge in his case was extremely helpful. After the hearing, an application for a title was issued a week later. This process, Jim explained, required taking a half-day off from work, in addition to the $50 fee. However, his efforts resulted in securing an Ohio title for his previously paperless Matchless.

What all this amounts to—in Ohio, or anywhere else—is intelligent navigation of our wonderful legal system. Jim said an Ohio attorney will do this for about $500, but that he's never used this method for "five hundred very good reasons."

Bottom line? Do the legwork, fill out the papers, answer all questions honestly, and you can get a title just about anywhere—if the only issue is missing paperwork.

The only place to find a legitimate frame VIN on A50/A65s is on this lug on the primary side where the front motor mount bolt goes through. Because the area is flat and has no logo protection, it can be very hard to spot a fake, but most restamps will be smaller numbers and letters as the stamping kits readily available generally aren't this big. Also, measure the lug thickness as described in text.

Be very suspicious of any frame or case without VIN stamping. Commonly the excuse is that it's a factory replacement. Just as commonly, it's a lie. Here's a legitimate one because the logo is still resident, so it was never stamped with a VIN. It's the real deal. Often, replacement frames were stamped with the original VIN, but some weren't, and this now allows for a lot a fairytales.

5 *Teardown*

Three Ts to Successfully Dismantling Old Brit Twins

TIME, TOOLS, TECHNIQUES

Old Brits rusting in neglect for decades frequently don't come apart like it says in the factory shop manual. Sometimes it's a matter of using an alternative tool or method and on other occasions it can be the need for remedial work to correct a previous owner's mistakes. Lots of times we have to overcome severe corrosion never imagined by the factory manual tech writers. Consequently, in this chapter we'll study another version of the Three Ts: time, tools and alternative techniques. Used together, these Ts almost always conquer rust, neglect and ham-handed abuse.

Weapons of No Destruction: This assortment of tools facilitates a damage-free teardown. Many will be shown in action in this chapter, but a few that aren't deserve mention here. Note the locked clutch plates in the foreground and the offset position of the two locking bolts. This allows this homemade tool to perform two functions: one when placed inside the clutch basket to lock the assembly, and another as a clutch hub wrench when a bar is added to aid replacing clutch hub rubber. Aluminum dowels adjacent to the propane torch are invaluable soft drifts good for removing bearings and for other duties. To the immediate left of the clutch plate tool is a special flat wrench that permits removal of fork tube nuts while the handlebars remain in place.

THE FIRST T: TIME

Restorers are much like medical doctors for machines, and the old medical maxim "First do no harm" cannot be overstressed. Snapped studs, broken cooling fins, and stripped threads do not occur on their own. Instead they are most commonly the result of diving into a project too far, too fast, with too little thought of consequences and alternatives. Patience truly is a mechanic's virtue.

With some exceptions, most crusty parts will eventually come apart without undue damage if they are given enough time to loosen up. I once waited and worked periodically for over a month on a set of exhaust pipes that were firmly stuck to the head and crossover pieces of an old Bonneville. Stuck exhaust pieces are particularly difficult to remove intact because their construction makes it impossible to use a lot of heat or shock force, as either can easily cause damage. Consequently, gentle persuasion and patience is the prescription for fragile parts.

Every three or four days, I'd soak the little stinkers in penetrating oil where they joined, and used only a moderate amount of heat from a propane torch to avoid bluing the chrome. After heating, and also when cold, I tapped them with a plastic hammer, never hard enough to make a dent, just enough to loosen up the rust a bit. Next, I wrapped a rag around the pipes in different places and pushed and pulled in moderation.

Finally, the pipes began to move.

All of this only took a few minutes each time I tried, so the actual amount of labor wasn't excessive. Even if you don't plan to reuse them, good used pipes—and these were nice—often sell for over fifty bucks and are well worth the effort for trade value alone.

BE CLEAN GENE

Not only is it a lot more pleasant to disassemble a project that's clean, it's a lot easier and avoids damage. Pressure washing is one of the best ways to clean a bike that looks like it was dumped into a vat of tar and then set on fire; most low buck projects tend to look like this.

To pressure wash, block off and protect intake and exhaust openings and remove or cover ignition and electrical parts, and then saturate the mess in a good commercial cleaner. (There are many options here. The more expensive ones are sold in spray cans; less expensive options can be purchased in bulk at stores catering to professional shops. Simple Green works surprisingly well and is very safe to work with.) After giving the cleaner some—here's that magic word again—time, spray the mess with a high-pressure washer. If you don't own a pressure washer, cart the wreck down to the local car wash.

Don't let the remains just sit and drip. Spray cleaning is just a preliminary to knock off junk and loosen other crud. Next we have to brush and wipe down the project using lots of clean rags or the extra tough paper towels they sell at auto parts and hardware stores. Follow up with a liberal coating of WD 40 to help dissolve rust, free fasteners, and remove remaining moisture. You can get WD 40 in gallon cans and then use a spray bottle to apply it; it's much cheaper than using individual pressurized containers.

It is very helpful to work with the bike at an elevated level. If you don't have a lift, you can build a simple and inexpensive work stand with scrap two-by-fours and plywood. Placing your work at a comfortable height not only makes this process much more pleasant, it's conducive to doing a better, more careful job.

Check every visible fastener and remove all hardened crud. Use a small pointed object—an ice pick works great—to dig out and clean every screw slot. Many good bolts and screws mutate into troublemakers because debris keeps a tool from fully fitting; then it slips and strips the holding slots or bolt head. A small wire wheel on an electric drill quickly cleans rusty nuts and studs.

With all external parts cleaned well, do a careful inspection and again spray every fastener

Throughout the teardown, especially with long-exposed projects and those that have gone through several reincarnations, be on the lookout for trouble beyond the ordinary. Quite commonly, problems rarely mentioned in any technical publication will arise. In this case, we have the work of a mud wasp that has blocked the oil line of this rusty Triumph. These insects are quite common in many parts of the U.S. They often build their nests farther inside passages where they aren't at all obvious. Believe it or not, these creatures apply some pretty good glue that can hold well over 100 psi. Check every oil passage with both fluid and air. If you find an impossible blockage, suspect our little friend. Cure? While mud wasp nests are resistant to high pressure, liquid drain cleaner works well; be sure to use goggles when blowing out the remains. Nature isn't the only problem, however. Many old Brits have suffered horrible "repair" and often require considerable corrective action and much vigilance to spot unusual errors. My favorite bodge? A BSA flywheel that was mounted backwards and in the wrong balance position on the crank.

with WD 40. Look for trouble with partially stripped nuts and mutilated case screws that will require extra attention and perhaps a different technique.

While all the external fasteners are soaking, it's a great time to drain ancient fluids. Don't be alarmed if nothing comes out, as a lot of projects have long since bled dry or the lubricants transformed into something you'd scrape off your shoe. If a gummy mess or nothing at all comes out, fill the oil holding cavities, such as fork tubes and transmission cases, with WD 40 to aid disassembly and later cleaning. If the spark plugs aren't frozen, remove them and flood the cylinders with WD 40 as well.

If the plugs are stuck (commonly they are) soak at least overnight before trying to remove them. If they're still resistant, use the procedure described later for frozen nuts. If your bike has externally sprung forks, pour several ounces of WD 40 into the seal holders and into the tubes for all forks. Also, soak and then loosen the bolts holding the fork tubes in the triple tree and liberally saturate the area where the tubes enter the trees.

MANUAL LABOR'S SIESTA

The next part is easy. Take a break. Let the rust busters do their work and save yourself from unnecessary aggravation. In the meantime, decide how you want to disassemble your project for inspection and plan for a way to organize and inspect the various assembly components. A failure to plan and organize will unleash the Shop Gremlin, a creature who lurks in the dark recesses of every garage to emerge silently and unseen to steal critical parts and mix others.

ORGANIZATION

You can form a gremlin-proof barrier around your project easily. Two of the best gremlin weapons are plastic storage bins and zip lock plastic bags. Used together, the bins and bags create a great system for organizing components. These are far superior to old cardboard boxes that have a nasty tendency to let go at the bottom and provide more gremlin food.

In addition to bins and bags, a small note pad, a pencil, and a good permanent marker will help avoid later confusion and mistakes. For example, a note inside a parts bag reading, "Spacer goes behind gear with chamfered side out" is an investment in time that can prevent hours of later frustration. A few pictures really can add up to thousands of words, and an inexpensive digital camera can jog a time-fogged memory and provide enormously useful information, especially if you are working on an unfamiliar bike.

When you tag and bag, do a little preliminary cleaning and inspection along the way. Knowing precisely where that stripped case screw came from, for one example, can lead to further notes as to its specific location and the possible need for something like a thread insert.

PLAN OF ATTACK

Where to begin the teardown is more a matter of personal preference and what work is to be done. I generally like to elevate and secure the bike and remove the engine side and clutch cover to expose the high-torque nuts. On BSAs I also remove the inner cover on the timing side.

I now use an air-operated impact wrench to loosen high-torque nuts, because it's quick, efficient, and does not require locking the engine. Never, however, use this tool for any installation. Since I began using an air impact wrench for teardowns 10 years ago (as opposed to the long lever method) I've yet to damage anything, although I've heard cries of danger from others. Use your judgment here.

After loosening high-torque nuts, I remove the engine, place it on a work stand, and then tear down the motor before getting to the rest of the bike. This leaves a rolling chassis that's easy to move around and also gives the forks more time to soak in WD 40. Crusty forks can be particularly nasty devils; the more soak time the better. It may be wise, though, to remove any parts on the chassis that need to be rechromed as some plating shops measure their job list by decades.

Ts TWO AND THREE: TOOLS AND TECHNIQUE WORKING TOGETHER

Owning or having access to both generic and bike-specific tools is critical to disassembling any old Brit. A set of Whitworth sockets is a definite requirement for most British bikes of the period. A propane torch is also a must-have as is a soft hammer, one that has a combination plastic and rubber head that can apply shock force without damage to working surfaces.

Be careful removing Triumph rocker boxes. Always remove the small screws before the larger bolts as valve spring force on the tiny screws alone can easily strip them.

Most head fins are damaged in attempts to dislodge a head carbon-glued to the cylinder or still held by one of the holding bolts (such as the one deep inside the BSA head). If your head is so afflicted and all the fasteners are removed, resist the urge to strike the fin surface at an angle, they're super easy to bend or break. Resist another poor option, banging on a protruding stud. Instead, get a wood dowel and hold it so that you can use it and a hammer to apply shock force to the upper part of the intake and exhaust ports. Be careful around older spigot-mount Triumph heads as it isn't hard to strip the threads holding these spigots; they may very well be damaged already. However, if they're

This small screwdriver has been ground down to fit inside the slot shown in the piston, to make it easier to remove the clips holding the wrist pin. Before using it, make sure to carefully pad out the opening in the case with clean rags if you don't plan to split the case. It's also a good idea to cut small pieces of pipe insulation to wrap around the rods to prevent accidental damage to the rods.

tight, you can use the soft hammer moderately on these.

Also extremely useful is a second "soft" hammer up the scale a bit from the plastic and rubber one. Get one made out of a softer metal like brass or aluminum. This allows a good shot of force to steel parts without causing damage. While not nearly as handy, pieces of hard wood placed between a regular hammer and the part being struck soften the blow and distribute the shock force.

If the cylinders won't come off and/or the motor won't turn over, pray that your problem is piston seizure or stuck rings. If it's soaked in WD 40 a good spell and is still frozen, you might need to use some force. Make sure you've removed the cylinder holding nuts and then try turning the engine over. Many times, the jugs will come up with the stuck pistons. When it does, support the cylinder flange with wood shims between it and the case, and then strike the pistons down with an aluminum drift. Don't worry about damage to the pistons; if they're this stuck, they're shot anyway. Continue to drive the pistons down while shimming the cylinders up with progressively thicker pieces of wood until the pistons are free. Another popular alternative is to braze a grease gun line onto an

old, hollowed out spark plug and then use the hydraulic force of the grease to move stuck pistons before removing the head.

You'll need a clutch locking tool sooner or later, and now's a good time to make one out of two junk clutch plates, one bonded and one plain. Just put these together, drill several holes through them, and then hold the pair together (see photo at the beginning of this chapter) with a couple of bolts. If you don't have access to junk plates, turn to the transmission section and check out the ones on your project. Good chance you have junk ones you don't know about.

If you use the long lever method to break high-torque nuts, you'll have to lock the engine and clutch with the tool you just made. This is easiest with the top end off so a bar or long socket extension can be placed through the rods to keep the motor from turning. Bend back any lock tabs and loosen the two nuts on the ends of the crankshaft (remember the BSA has left-handed threads on the timing side). Also loosen the clutch hub nut and the one on the timing side of the transmission shaft.

Never, ever, pry apart case halves with a screwdriver. Use a soft hammer as shown. If it resists, you've missed a fastener or gear key somewhere. A soft hammer can also be used on the crankshaft end to push apart the cases, but never strike it with a hard object or damage to the threads will result. You can also make a tool to push on the crank in imitation of an original factory tool, but this really isn't necessary.

Some mechanics remove keys like this with a screwdriver, but that method can result in launching the key to parts unknown. A more controlled method is using cutting pliers as shown.

Much can be done with simple universal pullers that allow the use of bolts to attach to parts like sprockets and cam gears that often have threaded holes for this purpose. You don't have to remove the cam gear(s) to split cases; however, you will need to do this to remove the cam(s) from the case.

TOUGH NUTS AND SCREWY FASTENERS

Just about every teardown encounters barriers. Screws will be stripped, covers will refuse to budge, and some parts will seem immovable. Remember the three Ts.

With respect to time, it's frequently advisable to give a reluctant fastener or part another day's treatment with penetrating oil before proceeding further. I like to let a bike just sit and soak for at least three days before I turn the first nut.

After a good soaking, if a nut won't turn with reasonable pressure on the wrench, use a propane torch to heat the nut; then hold a wrench on it and apply moderate torque while lightly tapping the end of the wrench with a hammer. Once the nut turns out a bit, spray again and turn it back where it was. This back and forth motion used in conjunction with penetrating oil is especially effective on frozen spark plugs and may well help you avoid a Helicoil job. The heat,

back and forth turning, and reasonable shock force works on 99 percent of the stuck parts one generally encounters. Resist the urge to greatly increase torque, as this is precisely how snapped studs and emergency room bills are born.

Reluctant screws require a hand impact wrench and sometimes the same heat treatment. Make sure you have the impact wrench set in the proper direction and held firmly against the screw in the direction you want the screw to turn. Speaking of direction, beware the left-handed threads on the Triumph cam gears and the BSA crank's timing end.

SPECIAL TOOLS AND TASKS

It can actually take more special tools to take apart a Brit twin project properly than it does to assemble one. Some substitute tools are acceptable; others invite disaster. Lets look at more tools and solutions to common problems now.

The primary assemblies on all unit BSA/Triumph twins are nearly identical, featuring a clutch basket with plain steel and bonded plates capped by a holding cover that is pushed by a rod from inside the transmission to release the clutch. If you don't have the tool to remove the cover nuts, one can be easily made by cutting a slot in the middle of a large flat blade screwdriver. The clutch cover must be removed to gain access to the high-torque clutch hub nut. Once these cover nuts are removed, you can remove the cover and usually pull out the plates and the hub that holds the cushioning rubber or use the clutch puller to free the entire assembly in one piece. Many times during this process, the roller bearings let go, so make sure you're working where these won't get lost.

The primary chain is continuous and is removed together with the basket and front sprocket. Before you can do this, the alternator rotor and stator must be removed. Gear pullers may be needed for the rotor and crank sprocket.

REMOVING CLUTCH HUBS AND PINION GEARS

All Brit twin teardowns will require a special clutch hub puller. These are relatively inexpensive. Using something like a universal puller almost invariably breaks the hub. The hub is a keyed interference fit on the transmission shaft, and sometimes even with the right tool, it won't budge. If you get a tough one, fit the tool and tighten it up, but don't apply excessive torque or you'll break the tool itself. When it's tight, first apply a little shock force to the center nut and/ the wrench putting pressure on it. No go? Next try a moderate shot with a hammer to the center nut. Still trouble? Okay, now we apply heat to the inner clutch hub after removing the outer hub that holds the rubber shock absorbers. After heating the inner hub, use light shock force on the end of the wrench used to tighten the tool and the bolt that goes into the tool. These actions almost always free the super hard ones.

Behind the clutch hub you'll find a clutch door retained by slotted screws. Sometimes these are badly chewed up, and this mess can be avoided in the first place by using a hand impact wrench to loosen the screws first. If they are mauled badly, they can be drilled out, but Sears markets a great screw removal tool that will back out chewed up screws with ease. Unless you're really good with a drill, trying to drill out busted or stripped fasteners can make matters much worse. If you lack the special tools or talent, take this problem to a pro. In the long run, you'll save both time and money.

Another real stinker is a clutch nut that is either stripped at the small holding slots or stuck to the spring, such as this one is. If the nut protrudes far enough, you can get a locking pliers on it, but if the nut is recessed, the cover can be sacrificed and cut to get a good hold on the nut for removal. Alternately, some folks drill into the nut and get it off by inserting rods into the drilled holes that then allow the nut to be turned, or they just drill out the holding bolt. If you cut into the cover, be careful not to cut into the hub or spring cup. Good used covers are inexpensive, but new after-market alloy covers are reasonably-priced and improve clutch action.

A variety of job-specific shop tools exist to remove the large nut holding the drive sprocket. The old steel-chisel method also works, although it does chew up the nut a bit. The sprocket is normally exposed after removing the screws holding the clutch door behind the clutch basket. In this photo the sprocket is shown on a BSA case after it was split so that the position of the chain and how it's held is easier to see. Note the chain around the sprocket. It's a short section held in a vise to keep the sprocket from turning. After bending back the lock tab, just position the chisel as shown and give it a good shot until the nut turns. Once it is loose, you can use a pliers and/or fingers to take the nut off the rest of the way.

Removal of the Triumph crank pinion requires the shop tool shown, but this is an unusual case, a 1972 650 that was either cast or machined incorrectly, thereby preventing the tool from fitting behind the pinion. Careful metal removal with a small rotary file made fitting the tool possible. Since it's probable that more of these exist, I used this example just in case you've got another one like it. Normally, the tool fits easily, making removal of the pinion simple.

Universal, factory, and homemade pullers shown all have many uses. The small puller in the center is my favorite, as it has many different applications; it is shown here set up to remove a BSA cam gear. It is also used to pull A50/A65 crank pinion gears in conjunction with the homemade pulling arms shown at the top. These arms were made by welding steel bar stock, previously ground as shown, to two bolts. The factory puller shown at bottom removes Triumph pinion gears.

Behind the clutch door lurks the transmission sprocket held on with a large nut. Special tools exist for these, but the nuts can be removed and installed with a steel chisel, as can just about any nut. While this method is crude and sloppy, holding a steel chisel well below the nut point and then striking the chisel with a heavy hammer seldom fails to do the job.

An easy way to remove a tough BSA pinion is shown here. These pinions can be particularly difficult and are known to resist even the factory puller or one made in imitation. The tool pictured— a pickle fork—is used to remove tie-rod ends but happens to be an excellent tool for this use. This pickle fork required slight filing to permit it to fit over the crankshaft without damage. Make sure you previously remove the crank nut, oil pump, and pump driving gear, so all that's left is the pinion. Next, heat the pinion with a propane torch and then position the tool as shown. Finally, give the pickle fork a good shot with a hammer and the pinion will either pop off completely or move out far enough to be removed by a conventional gear puller.

Both Triumphs and BSAs have a pinion gear on the timing side of the crank that can be a real dog to remove. A special tool is readily available for the Triumph and is highly recommended. The BSA equivalent has long since disappeared into the annals of time, but you can make one yourself (see photo) with a little grinding and welding. However, the BSA pinion tool attaches to relatively thin pieces on the sides of the pinion gear, and I managed to break three homemade tools on reluctant pinions before stumbling on a simple solution. It's called a pickle fork, a tool normally used to remove tie-rod ends. I had to clearance the inside of my fork a bit to fit over the crankshaft end. To remove the pinion gear, heat it with a torch and then place the fork between pinion gear and the timing-side bush. Finally, give the fork a good shot with

To expose the BSA's transmission cover, cam gear, oil pump, and crank pinion gear, the inner cover must be removed after the outer one. Prior to this photo the points plate and advance mechanism were removed. The advance unit on BSAs and Triumphs can be removed easily by threading a bolt into the center of the advance unit and then giving the bolt a light tap with a hammer. Note the shift shaft to the left of the screwdriver. There's a tiny Allen screw holding this piece, and also a return spring, on the shaft. If the return spring breaks during operation, it can cause the transmission to lock, so it's best to replace a questionable one with new. Generally, this spring and holder are pulled off after loosening the Allen screw holding it on the shaft. With these parts taken off, the cover is then removed. However, the Allen screw was snapped off, preventing removal of the spring and its holder, leading to the discovery that the cover could still be removed with the spring and holder in place by giving the cover a good yank. In this case, the shift shaft comes with it.

a hammer. This may raise a little metal on the pinion gear, but that's easy to remove with a file. There's no need to worry about the bush, as it's almost always shot and must be replaced.

All that's left before splitting the case is removing the transmission (see photos) and the nuts and bolts holding the case halves together. Never pry on the case seams. They're leak prone without any extra help. Instead, use the plastic and rubber hammer to knock apart the case halves. If the halves don't split easily, it's almost always an overlooked fastener or gear key.

BSA (shown) and Triumph 500 transmissions come out as a unit. Once the cover hardware and drive sprocket nut are removed, use a rubber or plastic hammer on the transmission shaft from the primary side to help push it out. You can split a BSA case without removing the transmission, but if you're going this far, it's best to remove the transmission for a complete inspection.

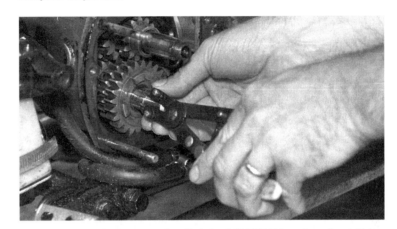

Once the transmission cover is off of the 650-750 Triumph, pull out the rod holding the shift forks in line and then fish out the forks. Next, you can begin to pull out the individual gears and shafts. On a 5-speed, however, don't forget a small retaining ring on first gear, right behind the piece that looks like a small iron cross. The clip must be removed using the tool as shown. You'll encounter both internal and external retaining rings like this on all Brit twins. This tool, sometimes called circlip pliers, can be adjusted to either expand or compress these clips.

OTHER PARTS

Stripping the rest of the cycle is mostly a matter of removing common bolts and screws. Reluctant ones should be treated as mentioned previously. The fork assembly, however, can be challenging.

Begin by securely raising the bike off the front wheel and then removing the wheel, fender, headlight, etc. Follow by removing the handlebars. With these out of the way, you can easily

Pre-71 Triumph and BSA forks feature 40 tiny bearings that just love to disappear. Collecting them with a magnetic pickup tool helps, but some of them almost always get loose. See text for another way to corral these little critters.

One of the first things to do when tearing down an old rusty relic is to remove the top nuts on the fork stem and fill the tubes with penetrating oil. Be careful with later OIF bikes because the forks are internally sprung. When the bike is supported by the front tire, the springs are under load and can launch the nut right back at you! Consequently, you must elevate the bike to take the weight off the forks before removing the cap nuts. This spring looks very clean, but many will look like one large coil of rust and will need replacement. Soaking the fork parts for several days makes them a lot easier to get apart.

get to the fork nuts and remove them and then the stem nut and other hardware that varies according to make and model (but is all pretty similar). You'll need a section of flat bar stock to remove the stem piece on some BSAs.

Now comes the fun. If you're working on a set of pre-71 forks and the steering neck hasn't received a tapered roller bearing conversion (a good idea) you'll soon be hunting 40 tiny ball bearings if you aren't careful. Having tried everything from washtubs to magnetic catch basins, I finally found a dirt simple way to keep these critters together.

Invest in a cheap poly tarp and place it so that the middle is directly under the steering neck, leaving plenty of room beyond it on all sides, as ball bearings seem to be able to fly by themselves. Wrinkle the tarp up a bit, as small ridges help prevent the bearings from bouncing.

Once the tarp is positioned, use a rubber or plastic hammer to tap the bottom of the top triple tree until it releases; then slowly lower and remove the fork assembly. Have a baggy in your pocket to collect the bearings still stuck in the

upper and lower neck and fork stem. Set the forks aside and then slowly pick up the tarp at the corners so that any loose bearings just roll into the center. A few may still be stuck on the tarp, to the fork tree or inside of the frame, but these are easy to see and grab.

If you entertain any notion of reusing the fork tubes, be careful removing them. They can be driven out of the lower tree (you already loosened and lubricated it earlier) by reattaching the top fork nut and using a wooden dowel with a hammer on the nut. If the tube is badly rusted, you may have to sand it or the rust will prevent the tube from sliding off the lower tree.

To disassemble pre-1971 fork stanchions, the fork-seal holders must be unscrewed. A special tool exists for this to fit into the two holes of the holder. This is the best option if you can afford it. However, the holders can be loosened often with little or no damage with a small aluminum drift and a hammer. Use the small drift in one of the holes that exist for this purpose to turn and loosen the holder. A strap wrench (see photo) is a great universal installation and removal tool, but you may need to start the seal holder turning with the drift first.

Unfortunately, seal holders sometimes become thoroughly frozen to the lower leg. Don't give up early, because you may have success using the soak, heat, and try again method. However, this may not work if the holder is severely rusted, and many are, since water easily accumulates inside the cup when tears occur in the rubber boot protecting it. If you encounter one of these, you'll have to use a hand hacksaw and carefully cut the seal holder where it threads into the fork leg, being careful not to cut into the leg threads. Next, use a steel chisel and hammer to spread and turn the seal holder. With the seal holder off, you can remove the fork leg, but you might need a soft hammer to get it to release the top bushing and valve assembly.

LATER FORKS

Generally, '71 and later forks are a lot easier to take apart. If you haven't already removed the internal springs, do so now. You might need to make a simple tool with a spark plug socket identical to the one that fits the standard size plug for your bike (see photo). You hold this tool in place to keep the valve assembly from turning while using an Allen wrench to remove the screw at the base of the fork leg. Once you have removed this screw, you can pull the tube and valve assembly out.

But every once in a while, the valve assembly unscrews itself inside the leg because the Allen screw is rusted tight; you can turn forever and nothing happens. Don't fret; this can be overcome. Invert the reluctant fork leg and hold it firmly in a vise between pieces of wood so the leg isn't marred. Locate a drill bit smaller than the fork leg's recessed hole but larger than the Allen head that's misbehaving. Now center the drill; it's easy, unlike a snapped stud, because of the way the Allen head is made. Begin to drill and continue until you get close, but don't cut into, the bottom of the fork leg. You just want the top of the Allen head very thin. When it is, place a small punch in the center of the screw and strike it lightly with a hammer. If it doesn't let go, drill a bit more, and strike it again with a hammer and punch, but do not increase striking force. Very soon, the valve assembly will drop and you can pull apart the fork leg for service. Remove the busted screw with a vise grip and replace it when rebuilding.

At this point you should have separated the project into major component parts and sub-assemblies. We'll look at the component parts in more detail in their respective rebuild chapters.

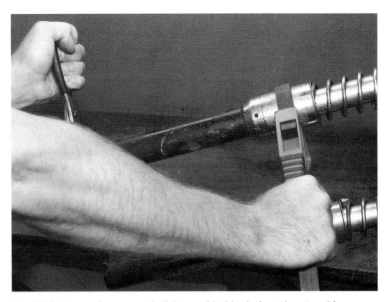

Pre-71 forks require removal of the seal holder before the stanchion can be disassembled. A special tool exists to remove it, but other alternatives will work. A universal strap wrench shown does a good job and won't damage the chrome, but you may have to loosen the seal first with a punch placed in the small hole shown in the seal holder and then strike it with a hammer. A small piece of aluminum stock works well and won't badly mar the hole.

This homemade tool is slipped into the tubes of '71 and later internally sprung Triumph and BSA forks to hold the valve assembly while removing the Allen screw at the base of the fork leg. It consists of a conventional spark plug socket and extension brazed onto a long piece of all-thread. If you have enough long extensions, that will work too.

6 *Taking It Off*

OVERVIEW

An important part of the inspection process is cleaning, since problems become more evident as junk is removed. Also, meticulously cleaned parts are required for any quality mechanical restoration. After a good soak to soften crud, every fastener thread must be cleaned and in-

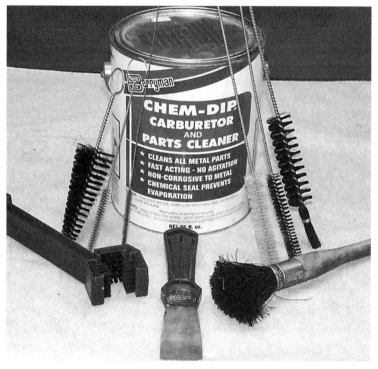

This tank dip carburetor and parts cleaner works wonders but comes with more warnings than an OSHA bureaucrat. Heed them well as this concoction can severely damage living tissue and contains known cancer-causing chemicals. Around the tank is an assortment of parts cleaning tools for both internal and external uses. Not shown, but also needed, are soft scrapers. It's good to have one in plastic and another in aluminum. You can easily make the aluminum scraper with a piece of aluminum bar stock shaped into a wedge at one end. Also important is steel wool; it can do amazing work on chrome plating that might seem hopeless. English chrome is exceptionally tough and resilient, owing to the much thicker coat of copper plating under the chrome used on our old Brits. Sometimes a lot of elbow grease and a single pad of fine steel wool can save a trip to the plating shop, a very expensive journey nowadays.

spected. Individual parts can be cleaned by dipping in solvent or by media blasting. An alternative to blasting small parts is a wire brush mounted on a bench grinder. Larger pieces can be worked on with a hand-held drill and brush attachment. Let's look at some of these cleaning methods in more detail because these time-consuming chores are extremely underemphasized and seldom explained in most shop manuals.

SOLVENTS

"What's best at cleaning parts?" I once asked my friend John, who answered without hesitation, "MEK."

"Isn't that dangerously toxic?" I continued.

"Well…" He paused then, nodded, and added a wry smile before continuing. "If you use it in California that stuff causes cancer. I don't know what the hell it'll do to you in Texas."

I left it at that, both the conversation and MEK, short for methyl ethyl ketone. For the record, he actually used a commercial parts washer containing filtered and heated mineral spirits. Pro shops have lots of high-dollar alternatives; some parts washers even use sound waves along with a solvent and heat to break up oily dirt. Weekend wrenches are more often not nearly so blessed by technology but they still enjoy a wide array of chemistry and techniques for cleaning parts. Let's look at some options and also study the risks a bit more.

Absolutely the best parts cleaning solvent I ever used came in unmarked five-gallon buckets a friend purchased at an oil field bankruptcy auction. However, even after thoroughly washing the parts in water afterwards, I always found my hands felt sticky. A doctor later told me why this occurred. "It's melting your skin," he explained.

"Can you still smell and taste something funny even after washing up?" the doc probed further.

"Yeah, now that you mention it, my wife says

she can smell something chemical on my breath for days afterwards," I replied.

The doctor grimaced. "That means whatever it is you're using is getting into your bloodstream, either through your skin or, just as likely, through your nose and lungs."

He recommended finding a new solvent and never touching any unknown cleaning solution. Many cleaning chemicals today carry cancer warnings and are labeled for use only with rubber gloves and organic solvent respirators. The warnings exist for very good reasons.

While I never did find out what the oil field stuff was, an almost equally effective gunk buster is tank-dip carburetor and parts cleaner (see photo) found in many auto parts stores. Unfortunately, it shares almost identical traits with the mystery cleaner and even has a similar smell. Be very careful using this stuff.

Nevertheless, this tank cleaner also works wonders on the carbon buildup that must be removed from the piston ring lands and valve stems. Soak the parts overnight and it turns this rock hard problem into easy-to-remove goo.

Before going further, let's eliminate another extremely foolish cleaning option: gasoline. Gas is specifically manufactured to do one thing very well: burn. It does so with very little provocation. Gas belongs in your bike, not on it.

Going down the petroleum distillate ladder a bit we come to kerosene, relatively safe and inexpensive if purchased correctly. The containers sold at most hardware stores are almost always expensive, top grade-kerosene, designed for stoves and heaters. Get solvent grade; it's way cheaper, and while still flammable, solvent kerosene isn't likely to be ignited by a stray spark.

Since solvent kerosene is exceptionally cheap in comparison to many other solvents, it is cost-effective for use in dip tanks. These can be constructed simply by using two containers, one larger than the other. In the smaller one, drill or punch holes and attach some sort of handle. Put your parts in the smaller container and dip it into the larger container filled with solvent. The containers can be big enough for an entire engine block or bench sized for small nuts and bolts. Soak time will vary greatly depending on the sort of crud involved and how deep and hard

it's gotten. There are also commercial products available to be mixed with kerosene that increase kerosene's cleaning ability.

One problem with kerosene, however, is that it leaves a residue of its own. Many other petroleum-based solvents also suffer from this problem. You can just use water as a final rinse and then wipe down the part, but rust can then become a problem if you don't dry it carefully. Another deficiency with kerosene is that it's not very good at removing gasket cements.

A two-tank approach using kerosene and lacquer thinner is a simple and effective solution. First dip the parts in a kerosene bath and work them with a cleaning brush and rag to remove most of the grease and oil; then dipping the parts in lacquer thinner finishes the job and leaves no residual film. Don't use paint-quality thinner, go for what's often called "gun wash" or primer thinner. Be advised that lacquer thinner also comes in a skull and crossbones marked can and is quite flammable. The tradeoff is that it does a great job on old gasket cement and is a super degreaser. Really tough gasket residue can be treated with paint stripper, a most effective gasket remover. A well-ventilated room is absolutely essential for all this sort of work. Always use a vapor removal fan and wear an organic solvent respirator.

BLAST OFF

Although chemical paint stripper can also be used effectively for paint removal, it's extremely nasty to work with and also biologically very hazardous. Sometimes it is advantageous in cases where many old coats of thick paint make other processes excessive or when one must remove paint from something like polished alloy.

A far less hazardous option for parts cleaning and paint removal is media blasting, spraying small abrasive particles under air pressure onto a part. It poses no health risks aside from dust that can be easily avoided by wearing a simple gauze mask and goggles or it can be contained in a blasting cabinet. To media blast you will need a good compressor and the appropriate media, which is available in many types, ranging from sand to crushed walnut shells. Glass beads are the most common media used inside of many

This bucket blaster is shown just before being used to blast a frame. You have to provide the bucket and media—in this case, fine sand.

Although crude and ugly, this homemade blasting cabinet was cheap and easy to make and the results, as you will see in other pictures, are anything but ugly. Media blasting is quick, inexpensive, and safe. It deserves serious consideration in your arsenal of cleaning techniques. The arm sleeves on my blasting cabinet are actually old pants legs with a rubber band sewn inside to keep them closed around my wrists while blasting. A hose at the bottom of the cabinet is attached to a shop vac to recover media and keep dust down for better visibility. Hose going into the right armhole is from a bucket blaster, also shown in this chapter. Duct tape covers the other holes I used originally to blast and route hoses, but sealing them and running the hose though the sleeves seemed to work better. The Plexiglas top and simple hinge are hardware store items, as was a bit of weather stripping to make the lid seal better.

The cleaned clutch hub at right looked even worse than the crusty one at left and came out of the same box of long-neglected parts. Bead blasting performed this magic in a few minutes. The cleaned hub is now enjoying another life on the road.

shops. They do a terrific job, but can cause problems of their own; really greasy parts should still be cleaned in solvent and brushed down first to speed the blasting process.

Opinions differ about whether it's a good idea to bead blast something like an engine case because of the chance for stray glass beads to remain in oil passages. While it's quite possible to plug these holes before blasting and flush out stray blasting media afterwards, you can still miss some. Polished parts and anything with chrome plating should not be blasted, as doing so will dull the finish. Walnut shells, while more expensive than glass beads, are softer and therefore much safer for parts like gears and cases as a stray particle is much less likely to cause damage. Blasting external steel parts like gas tanks, frames, and side covers with fine sand does great work as a rust and paint remover. Glass beading is great on finned alloy surfaces, like cylinder heads because it gets inside the many recesses quickly and completely.

DO-IT-YOURSELF BLAST CABINET

If you already have some of the following items, for less than the price of what many shops will charge to blast a single head, you can build your own homemade blasting set-up. All that's needed is a sheet of plywood, light bulb and socket, shop vacuum, a piece of Plexiglas, and a small bucket blaster. Bucket blasters can be purchased inexpensively from many tool companies. Take a look at the accompanying picture for a clear example and more details.

Media blasting is simple: Aim the gun; pull the trigger; check the area cleaned; move to a new location. Motorcycle frames are too big for most cabinets so they are usually done outdoors. If you place a large poly tarp on the ground you can reclaim most of the sand. Remember to clean parts very thoroughly if you plan to powder coat, as all paint must be removed prior to this process.

RUST REMOVAL

Not only must we get rid of gunk, but rust must be completely removed and neutralized. If you don't get it all, it'll come back with a vengeance. Sandpaper is slow and labor intensive, but effective for paint and rust removal on many parts. Wire brushing and media blasting are easier and much more thorough—especially media blasting—as it gets into the little pockets rust can create that sandpaper often glides over. Regardless of how careful you are cleaning, it's important to treat any part that showed rust with some sort of rust converter. There are lots of commercially sold options here. Just follow the directions on the one you choose.

There is a very inexpensive, old-school approach to rust conversion known as electrolysis that's useful on many parts, but particularly effective on gas tanks where rust is almost impossible to aggressively and completely remove in some hidden areas. See photo in this chapter and also information in tank section for complete details and more information on rust treatment in general.

STORAGE

Once all the smaller parts have been cleaned, put them back into new bags to keep them from picking up stray crud left in the used bags. If you are using a plastic bin for a larger part, clean the bin carefully before returning the part. Also, if you used media blasting, those parts must be blown clean with plain air, wiped down, and carefully inspected for stray blasting media.

No matter what you do, remember the old maxim: "There's no such thing as too clean."

All you need to neutralize rust is shown above. The plastic bottle in the center is a commercial liquid, one of many on the market. (See text for specific recommendations.) The battery charger, simple electrode, and washing soda are used for electrolysis, a very effective and super cheap rust conversion system. This small plain steel electrode is for use inside of gas tanks. A much larger one is in use in the next photo.

A simple electrolysis rig is shown in action working on a rusty side cover. The positive wire is attached to the electrode, negative wire to the part. More information is located in the tank chapter, where this technique is especially useful. A piece of wood with several nails suspends the part and electrode. Electrolyte solution is made with one tablespoon of washing soda per gallon of water. Try it; you'll like it!

7 *What's Worn, What Ain't, and What to Do Ya Ain't Sure*

OVERVIEW

Early in my mechanical apprenticeship, the importance and advantages of precision measurement were vividly demonstrated. I worked in a small Louisiana VW repair shop for a master mechanic who seldom failed to press home a technical lesson. He directed me outdoors one afternoon to listen to a faded old Beetle that nevertheless had a sweet sounding motor. The air-cooled engine, very similar to our beloved Brit twins in many mechanical respects, was built entirely out of used parts: bearings, rings, every-thing—most of it never resident together on the same motor, all of it scrounged from old used parts bins. The old Beetle had already gone 50,000 miles since its low-buck reincarnation and gave every impression it was good for more.

How was this possible? Each part was carefully inspected and measured before use and only those well-within wear specs went into the motor. The feat was greatly facilitated thanks to German engineers who are deservedly famous for meticulously detailed and well-organized wear specifications. The good folks at Triumph/BSA, however, weren't so methodical in providing critical wear limit information.

"The valve springs should be inspected for fatigue…by comparing them with a new spring or the dimensions given in general data" goes the Triumph shop manual, never bothering to give an acceptable wear limit measurement nor exactly what qualifies as an acceptable comparison. The vagaries are plentiful in both BSA and Triumph manuals. The lack of hard, specific data determining when, precisely, a part has gone beyond its useful life is often left to the individual "fitter" as the Brits say. Budget builders must overcome these obstacles, so let's study how this can be done.

DECISION MAKERS

A budget engine builder must know when to reuse a part as-is, when it needs to be machined or otherwise rebuilt, and when to pitch it because it's too worn to be of any use. Many rely on another's expertise for this evaluation, sometimes a very wise choice for beginners. Bringing your parts to someone else to check and spec is perfectly acceptable, provided the person doing the measurement and inspection is knowledgeable and trustworthy. It is far better, however, to learn how to do this yourself.

Sometimes very common shop items make great measurement tools. In this case we are using a fluorescent tube pulled from a shop light being used as a straightedge to check this fork tube. Roll the two together across a flat surface. If the fork tube is bent, you'll find a gap; if it's good, the light and fork tube will remain in contact the complete length of the tube. This one is bent. Although hard to see in this picture, there is a gap. Measure the largest gap found with a feeler gauge to determine how much it needs to be bent back into position, something we'll do in the fork chapter. Be sure to mark the high spot of the fork tube with a marker to locate where to apply force. If the tube is bent more than 5/32 of an inch, junk it. Old bent fork tubes, by the way, make great cheater bars when slipped over a wrench to provide greater leverage.

We mostly measure to determine running clearances, the distance between parts that must be kept for reliable operation. Many times we have to do a bit of math to get these numbers, but fortunately, it's a simple process of reading shop manual data tables and subtraction.

As an example, let's calculate original valve guide running clearance. Running clearance in this case is the space between the valve stem and the inside of the guide. Original clearance, by definition, is the space between moving parts when first assembled at the factory. With wear, clearances become larger, and this is often why an engine needs to be rebuilt. Excessive clearance causes things such as smoking and low oil pressure. Too little clearance, though, can cause an engine to seize. We must spec our engine to ideal clearances as designed. To do so we'll also work with two abbreviations: ID for inside diameter and OD for outside diameter.

First we need to look up the OD of the new valve stem in the shop manual. You'll see two numbers in the general data section for just about every specification, and that's due to variations in manufacturing tolerances, fairly large by modern standards.

For 650 Triumph exhaust valves, the new stem OD is between .3090 and .3095 inches. Next we need to get the ID of the new valve guide and that's between .3127 and .3137. Let's determine the minimum possible clearance first by subtracting the largest valve stem OD from the smallest guide ID to arrive at a minimum running clearance of .0032. Conversely, we can go to the opposite extreme and subtract the smallest valve stem OD from the largest guide ID to get a maximum clearance of .0047. Many mechanics would say that this clearance is already excessive.

Hughie Hancox, in his excellent video on Triumph rebuilding, recommends replacing both the guide and valve if the valve stem OD shows more than .0015 wear from new, an excellent reference figure. My two-cents? If the valve measures within Mr. Hancox's wear limit recommendation, it's reusable, but renew the guides as a matter of routine because today's classic engines usually aren't run frequently and the guides dry up completely between runs.

Telescoping gauges come in all sizes and generally are sold as a set that is fairly inexpensive. This tiny gauge allows measurement of the valve guide ID with a micrometer. To use it, just slide the gauge into the hole, keeping it straight in the bore. When it's positioned, lock the gauge and remove it for measurement with a one-inch micrometer.

Consequently, guides today often suffer more quickly from friction wear. How far do you let this go? Lots of wiggle-room here; the word "excessive" pops up a lot because most veteran Brit wrenches just rock the valve in the guide to make a decision. Still dying for a hard figure? Nicholson allows up to .003 guide wear. Using the minimum guide ID of .3127, this would mean at .3157 the guide is shot. Of course, the .003 wear limit could be applied to the largest possible original guide ID to allow a guide ID up to .3167.

As for maximum permissible clearance, .005 is borderline and .006 is as far as I've let it go, and this was for "poverty" motors where the valve seats weren't cut and the valves simply lapped in. For what it's worth, I've torn down many an old Brit head to find well over .010 guide-to-valve clearance, but the engines undoubtedly burned oil even though they still ran.

Mark Zimmerman, my vote for the best in the business when it comes to motorcycle technical advice, says that for friends he's "hammered together" a few Triumphs with .007 valve-to-guide clearance, but quickly adds that any clearance twice that of new means the assembly is shot. He strongly recommends, and I completely agree, that the best bet is to set up the head with all new hardware and use the clearance recommendation given by the valve and guide manufacturer. It's wise to do so because the parts are inexpensive and allow for very precise cutting of the valve seat, something not possible with worn guides.

When positioning rings for end-gap measurement, use a piston to make sure the rings are straight in the bore to permit accurate measurement with a feeler gauge. Note the small piece of fuel hose between the lifters. This is a very easy way to hold them in place during cylinder removal and installation. For more wear specifications and alternative ways to measure, see the Introduction to Engine and Trtansmission Building chapter.

A feeler gauge is used to measure ring gap. Analysis of bore wear can be made by using the same ring and measuring the gap in the top as shown and again at the very bottom. Always measure the ring gap on new rings; they will often need filing to provide the proper minimum gap. A failure to do so can result in a seized piston. Also measure the clearance of rings between the piston grooves to check for wear.

A larger telescoping gauge is used here to measure bore diameter. The piston at the bottom helps position the gauge perpendicular to the bore. Next, the piston will be measured with a caliper to provide an accurate measure of bore-to-piston clearance.

Of course, what's absolutely acceptable clearance with our old Brits today can vary according to intended service as well as the sort of parts involved. As just stated, it's always best to get clearance figures from the part manufacturer—such as bore-to-piston and valve-to-guide clearance—as different metal compositions will have different expansion properties. As for specific valve guide clearance, Rowe, a major manufacturer, recommends a minimum valve-to-guide clearance of .002 for exhaust guides and .001 to .0015 for intake guides. However, down here in south Texas many machinists allow additional clearance for expansion in our extreme heat; their addition of .001 to recommendations is common. Racers may also allow more clearance because of the extreme heat caused by high-performance engines running at high speeds. Way up in Canada, Mark Appleton, a former Triumph dealer and owner of British Cycle Supply, used Ampco 45 guides and built his street-use Triumph Bonneville with .0025 clearance for both intake and exhaust guides. Mark also recommends the use of a plug gauge to locate high spots on the ID of valve guides, something your machinist should have at his shop. He explains that the interference fit of the guides into the head can cause high spots inside the guide and insufficient clearance, something the plug gauge will detect and your machinist can correct if necessary. Many guides will also need to be reamed after installation to achieve proper and uniform clearance, something your machinist can do at little expense. If you intend to do this work a lot, you can buy the right size reamer at specialty tool houses for about fifty bucks.

Okay, now that we understand clearance calculations on paper, we need to break out the tools and borrow those we don't have. Even if you implicitly trust the measurement competence of someone else, it's every engine/transmission builder's responsibility to recheck measurements for human error. Not only must you check others, you must check yourself. Always measure any part subject to wear at least twice and in different places. If the numbers differ, find out why.

The reliance on "feel" understandably frustrates beginners, but this is indeed the English way. What will help you acquire this feel is knowing that both parts are within factory tolerances, or very close to it, and then observing how a good part feels in a bore, on a shaft, etc. This is an acquired skill, but it is within the ability of most people with a bit of practice.

To do quality engine work you must own more than a set of feeler gauges. If you add just a few more tools—in particular, a dial indicator and a good caliper—you're well on the way to measurement independence. Add a set of telescoping gauges and a micrometer or two, and there's very little you can't measure accurately. Let's get to it.

PISTON AND CYLINDER CLEARANCE

Because of relatively high running clearance required between pistons and cylinders in air-cooled engines and the high stress and operating temperatures within the cylinders, the bore is one of the first things to wear out. We need to measure taper of the bore, and to do so we take two readings, one near the top at right angles to the wrist pin holes and another at the very bottom of the cylinder where the piston never reaches, and where, consequently, the bore will measure the same as when new or last bored. If a difference of .005 or greater is found, it's time for a rebore. I generally measure this with telescoping gauges (see photo) and a digital caliper accurate to within .001. The very best tool, however, is a bore gauge, an instrument that reads bore differences via a dial indicator. An inside micrometer is more accurate than telescoping gauges read with a caliper.

Save yourself some time, though, if you can feel a ridge near the top of the cylinder where the top piston ring stops at TDC. Don't confuse this with the ridge of carbon formed at the very top of the bore, this one's lower. If you feel a ridge here, off to the machine shop you go; the bore's very worn. See, you're getting the "feel" of this already!

CRANKSHAFT CLEARANCES

Plastigauge is an excellent tool for accurately measuring rod bearing-to-crank clearance. Use it twice: once when you first take off the rod cap and again when doing final assembly. Save the old rod nuts on teardown to use with measurement checks, since once the new locking nuts are on, you can't take them off. Rod nuts are one-shot deals; never reuse them except for measurement checks. Make sure to mark your rods before measuring clearance as they need to go back on the way they came off.

To use Plastigauge, cut a small piece (see photo) and place it on the bare crank with a bit of oil to hold it from slipping. Gently attach the rod cap and tighten the nuts evenly, a little on each nut at a time. Also, be careful not to rotate the rod on the crank as you do this. Use a torque wrench for final tightening to 22 foot-pounds.

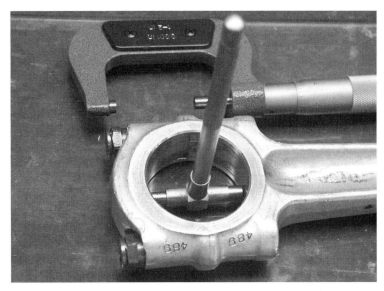

All BSA rods must be measured for the tendency to wear out-of-round, very common because of the use of an alloy rod cap. BSA only allows .0004 variance before recommending rod replacement. However, the rod can be restored at moderate cost by a competent machinist. This one is out .0015, way too much. Measure across the rod where it splits and then along the rod's axis (as shown) and compare figures. Even if the rod checks out, have a machinist recheck your measurements, as the margin for error is very small and a good machine shop will have better tools to measure very fine tolerances like this.

Plastigauge is inexpensive, accurate, and ideal for use in checking connecting rod bearing clearance. Measurement is made with a simple printed scale. Match the width of the flattened strip to the scale for precise reading. See the text for the full measurement procedure.

and then remove the nuts and cap again. Place the gauge guide up against the now flattened Plastigauge strip for a very accurate reading of clearance. Clearance of .001 or less means there's a lot of life left, but at .002 you're at the end of the line or darn near it.

Even with Plastigauge to measure rod bearing-to-crank clearance, we also measure the crank journals with a micrometer. If you aren't good at reading one, ask your machinist for help. Calipers and micrometers are both available with digital readouts that are super easy to use.

Check the crank gear-side journal on BSA and early Triumph 500s (as shown) and also the rod journals on BSA and Triumphs with a 2-inch micrometer. Measure in several places as the journals can wear out-of-round too. Wear of more than .002 inch on any journal means it needs machine work.

Digital calipers are super-easy to use and read. Once very expensive, they now can be purchased for around $20 and are well worth it. These can be used for many measurements, but aren't as accurate as a micrometer. Still, they're plenty accurate for measuring valve springs as shown. For other parts they can give quick figures that can be later checked more carefully if need be. If you don't own any precision measurement tools, a digital caliper is a good first purchase.

A crank that's been reground will generally be stamped somewhere with .010, .020, or .030 and the back of the rod bearing shells will often have this marked as well. In any event, once you know the size, measure the rod journals in different places. If any reading is .002 less than it should be, it's time to regrind the journals.

WRIST PIN CLEARANCE

Use a micrometer to measure the wrist pin diameter where it runs in the rod bush and telescoping gauges and the micrometer again to measure the inside of the small end rod bush. Subtract the pin OD from the bush ID to obtain a clearance measurement. However, this is generally another Brit feel job, as in "feel for excessive movement." Another old trick is to run your fingers along the wrist pin with your eyes closed. If you can tell by feel where it has ridden in the rod, it's very worn. Clearance between bush and pin on a new 650 Triumph is between .0005 and .0012. Replace bush/pin if excessive clearance is found.

VALVE SPRINGS

Calipers are accurate enough for measuring valve springs. BSA, at least, allows a limit of 1/16 inch of collapse for their springs, so I've always used this limit by converting into a percentage, 3%, and allow up to that in difference from original size on Triumphs. If hard redline running

or a hot cam is on the agenda, go with new or high-performance springs regardless. Also, carefully check all used springs and keepers for obvious signs of failure like cracking or chips. While it's unlikely you'll have access to one, there is a tool to measure spring pressure at given heights, the very best test.

BSA TIMING-SIDE BUSH, TRANSMISSION, AND CAMSHAFT CLEARANCE

While inside and outside micrometers are the best tools to measure clearance, they may not be available or practical. Regardless, clearances are extremely important. One of the most critical is the clearance between the crank and main bush on the A50/A65. Amazingly, this clearance figure isn't even mentioned in the BSA factory shop manual, nor the two widely distributed aftermarket manuals, Haynes and Clymer. This crank-to-bush clearance can also be measured with a dial indicator. See photo and caption on the next page for complete details.

Fortunately, we have expert clearance recommendations, thanks to SRM Engineering. These folks have experience going back to BSA's racing days and manufacture their own line of improved BSA parts as well as doing specialist work such as conversion of the timing-side bush to a roller bearing. For the record, the timing-

Clearance between a BSA main bush and the crank is measured here with a dial indicator, a very versatile tool. Various simple brackets like the one shown can be made of bent bar stock to support the instrument firmly. To measure, position the indicator on the bracket and place it in contact with the shaft, and then set the indicator dial to zero. Next, move the shaft toward the gauge as shown. In this case, we had .009 clearance, way more than the .0015 to .003 allowed. This case must be split and the bush replaced, at the very least. Inside and outside micrometers will provide more precise measurement, but the dial indicator method does not require complete disassembly and its readings are quite accurate if taken carefully. Any radial clearance, like cam-to-bush clearance, can be measured in this fashion. Crank endplay is also measured with a dial indicator using a different bracket to position the indicator at the end of the crank. Once positioned, push and pull the crank along its axis and measure the movement between extremes. Triumph 650-750s allow quite a bit of endplay, .003 to .017 but the BSA must be within .001 to .003.

side bush-to-crank clearance new is .0015. Gary Hearl, SRM director, reports that SRM reams new crank bushes for clearance at .0015 to .00175. SRM considers clearance at .003 borderline, and .004 calls for a new bush, at least. The crank must also be measured and shop manual specs call for regrinding at .002 wear.

Camshafts and the bushes in which they run must also be measured and evaluated against the shop manual for excessive wear. Cam-to-bearing clearance can be checked with a dial indicator like the crank bush. Wear in the cam lobes can be detected by measuring them with a micrometer and comparing the figures obtained to those in the shop manual data table.

Transmission parts must also be measured. You can measure the bush diameters on gears and also the mainshaft and layshaft OD on

which they run to check for excessive clearance. Again, specific wear specs aren't given and most good box builders just test by sight and feel. If you are uncertain about a given clearance, seek a second opinion, and this goes with any part subject to wear. Once you've rebuilt a few of these, however, you'll be pretty independent. We'll do more wear checks in the transmission rebuild section, and there are many other measurements that provide important data that we haven't covered, but now you can check these yourself by using the methods given here.

So why do we make all these measurements? This goes back to our opening. If you measure carefully, you can reuse what's good. This can save you a big pile of money. Get second and third opinions if you aren't sure. And remember, it costs nothing to measure and inspect.

8 Taming the Prince of Darkness

OVERVIEW

Quite frankly, in most cases, Lucas electrical parts found on most British bikes have nothing inherently wrong with them and can be solid, reliable performers. Many common problems aren't Lucas design faults but are caused by the vibratory jackhammers to which these parts were bolted.

Let's take one of the most cursed items in the whole stock set up, the Zener diode. Many Zener diodes fail when they are loosened by vibration. The Zener relies on a solid contact to ground, both to ensure proper electrical performance and also to transmit heat. When it gets loose it can't do its job, then it overheats and blows. See the relationship?

Right next to vibration-induced failures are uninformed American bikers who thought all hot wires had to be on the positive terminal. Almost all of our Brits do it differently with a positive ground, until 1979 when the change was made to negative ground. Many Lucas alternators, very reliable units normally, were rendered impotent after the battery terminals were connected backwards. According to John Healy, one of the most noted Triumph experts in the states, when the battery is connected in reverse, you turn the stator coils into "a wonderful demagnetizer." This destroys the rotor and Joe Biker starts cursing Lucas.

I do fault Lucas, and maybe the industry in general, for providing confusing technical instructions. I can remember reading some electrical testing instructions a dozen times, and then thinking to myself, "Now what the hell does that mean?" A lack of photographs and an excess of complicated but unnecessary tests add to the confusion. In this book, we'll stick to just the basic tests we need to locate problems. We'll also keep to more common terminology. However, in contrast to the lack of specific figures for many BSA and Triumph parts, Lucas offers an abundance of specifics and tests, so if you're an electrical engineer, it's technical heaven. Common guys like us can at least refer to exact figures for fault finding and diagnosis.

THE TEST RIG

Many tests require the use of a one-ohm resistor wired in parallel to the testing rig. The terminology confused me for years. What this means is you have to connect the two parallel test leads across the resistor. Picture an H. The little crosspiece is the resistor. The two upper bars of the H go to what's being tested; the two lower bars connect to the testing instrument, like a volt meter. Also see photos that show the test rigs clearly.

This is a simple load and measurement circuit needed to perform charging tests. In this case the AC voltmeter has a one-ohm resistor across the test leads, with each lead going to one of the alternator wires. Alternator output is therefore tested with a one-ohm resistor load. This same testing rig is used with a DC voltmeter to measure the rectifier output under load, and also to test the battery's high-rate discharge.

Test rig is shown here with larger resistor (300 watt) in place and set up to conduct a high-rate discharge test. Note the simple "H" pattern with the top leads going to the tested part (the battery) and the bottom to the meter. The resistor is connected across these leads to put the system under load, as required for many tests.

A second problem is locating the right resistor. Heavy duty resistors aren't commonly found, and making one as described in the manual takes a lot of time and requires materials you don't have or can't find.

There are two simple alternatives. Both are shown in use in this book. One is a Radio Shack one-ohm resistor rated at 10-watts. It will get hot enough to burn you because it is being overloaded when used for Lucas testing, but I've checked the results against a 300-watt resistor and found no appreciable difference in test figures. Just be careful if you use the small resistor as you can fry it if it is left connected too long, but this isn't necessary for testing. If you would prefer to use a resistor appropriately rated, a great inexpensive source is Surplus Sales of Nebraska. They can be reached by phone at 402-346-4750 and on the web at www.surplussales.com. Tech specs call for a resistor that can handle 15 amps, which for a one-ohm resistance equates to 225 watts minimum rating.

GROUND ZERO

Many novices fail to appreciate or understand the importance of a good ground (frame) connection. Simply stated, electricity needs to flow in a complete circuit around your motorcycle. In a positive ground system, electricity flows from the negative battery connection to a component, like your headlight or coil, and then it needs to get back to the battery through the "ground," normally the frame, that is attached (grounded) to the positive side of the battery. Poor frame contact can cause all sorts of weird and troublesome problems. Make sure that all frame contacts are connected securely to bare metal. Newly painted frames must be sanded to bare metal at the contact point before a ground wire is attached. Dielectric grease and lock washers are highly recommended for all connectors and a bit of dielectric grease should be used for all push-on electrical connectors to inhibit corrosion. While dielectric grease is non-conductive, the grease is pushed off the metal-to-metal contact surface when making a tight connection and then surrounds it to prevent moisture from reaching and then corroding the contact surface. Many times, just cleaning and tightening frame connections at the battery and various component ground connections will cure charging and ignition problems completely. Consequently, this is a good first step when encountering problems and before testing components.

MAKING CONNECTIONS

Although I can already hear the howls of condemnation, I have absolutely no problems recommending commonly available (and inexpensive) crimp-on electrical connectors for budget builders. I base this on simple experience: I have yet to have one fail me in service if it was properly installed. Failures are caused by either over- or under-crimping or using the incorrect tool. A proper crimp should not cut into the wire and you can tell if it does by the crunching sound the wire makes and also by visual inspection. Conversely, under-crimping means the connector does not tightly grasp the wire. Always pull very hard on the wire after each crimp. If you can

Anytime you remove a female tab connection like this it's a good idea to back-crimp it as shown, at the end of the connector nearest the wire. Don't try to do this at the end of the connector where it attaches to the male tab connector, because then you won't be able to easily reattach it. If you tighten up the connector like this it won't come off until you decide to remove it.

move the connector or it pulls off, it wasn't on tight. Also, if you need to pull apart a spade connection for service work, use a needle nose pliers on the upper part of the connector closest to the wire. Back-crimping tightens the connector and prevents it from slipping off. A dab of clear silicone will waterproof connections that are exposed to the elements. Also, any signs of dirt and corrosion must be removed before attaching any connector.

MAJOR COMPONENTS

The Alternator

Alternators are found on all BSA and Triumph unit-construction engines. Unlike generators, alternators produce much more current at relatively low rpm, and when mounted inside the primary drive on the crankshaft, seldom create problems. Failed bearings are things of the past because, unlike magnetos and generators, alternators have none. The rotor (a magnet) is mounted on the crank and surrounded by the stationary stator (electrical coils).

Lately, I've read a lot about how Lucas alternators do not produce enough electricity and that the battery discharges when the lights are on at idle. I don't know about that, but I do know you can run the entire stock system with the lights on at idle without a battery if you use a capacitor. The 60/55 watt H4 halogen bulb I generally use to improve Brit headlights does draw more current than a stock bulb. However, I have not

This neat test is as effective as it is simple. If the alternator rotor can hold its own weight on a toolbox at each magnetic point, it's okay. Make sure the insert is tight, as they can become loose and make a weird knocking sound. If It falls either test, junk it. Good used rotors are easy to find and inexpensive.

found that it overtaxes the stock charging system if it works properly, even when used with a lot of stop and go driving.

The Rectifier

Unlike a generator, an alternator sends out current on both directions, alternating the direction of current flow many times per second. However, a battery can't accommodate the switch back and forth, so engineers incorporated an electronic device—the rectifier—to work like a one-way valve. Early rectifiers sim-

This test circuit is set up to check rectifier output, using a DC voltmeter and resistor as shown. See text for test figures.

This closeup shot of a Lucas rectifier shows fingers on the wires coming from the alternator. Center wire is the output and must be removed for testing. Note the center bolt. This must be held tightly when the bottom nut is installed or removed. It must not be turned. If the center bolt rotates, the rectifier plates often rotate with it, destroying the rectifier. Many rectifiers were ruined this way. The unused connection in the center is for an optional capacitor.

The infamous Zener diode lives inside the breather box on OIF bikes and many other places, depending on the particular year and model. If it doesn't test out, junk the stock Zener diode/rectifier system and replace it with a solid-state unit that often costs less than the Zener diode alone and is much more reliable and efficient.

ply suppressed that half flowing in the "wrong" direction to produce current flowing in the "right" direction only. Later rectifiers used both halves of current flow and are much more efficient. These are called, respectively, half-wave and full-wave rectifiers. Both types of rectifiers are easy to damage, especially the earlier ones made with selenium.

Zener Diode

This creature (pronounced ZEE-ner) serves as the alternator's voltage regulator. It is designed to pass off excess current by converting it to heat, but when it's not working properly it only makes the owner hot. Rectifiers and Zener diodes can be replaced, often at much less expense, with solid state electronic units that do the job better and seldom fail to do so. However, budget builders may want to keep what's working. Also, a lot of guys just throw away perfectly good Lucas parts so you can get good used ones cheap.

Aftermarket Alternatives

Several manufacturers make modern replacements for the rectifier and diode combination that work better and are less expensive than new stock replacement. I've used Podtronics, Tympanium, and Sparx units and found all three work well. Nearly all Brit dealers carry one or all of these.

The Coil

A coil's job is to produce high voltage, sometimes as much as 100,000 volts, that is then sent via a thick wire to the spark plug(s). An electromagnet of sorts but also an inductor, a coil is made up of two separate wire windings, called the primary and secondary windings. Current in the primary winding is turned on and off by the ignition points (or by an electronic ignition system). The secondary winding is connected to the spark plug. The secondary commonly has hundreds of times more windings than the primary. The crux of a coil's operation is what happens when the current in the primary winding is interrupted, either by ignition points opening or through timing by an electronic ignition system. In either case, the primary coil's field collapses and this induces a very high-voltage current in the secondary winding to fire the spark plug.

The Battery

Virtually all motorcycles and cars use some form of an old invention, the lead-acid storage battery. It makes use of simple chemistry to produce and store electricity by exchanging electrons in an acid solution between plates of lead and lead dioxide. This exchange is reversible when current is applied from an external source, and that's what happens when you charge your

This bike has the full enchilada: Podtronics regulator, Boyer ignition box, and new wires and coils. Super reliable. Some builders don't like crimp-on connectors like these, but if they are properly installed and of good quality, they rarely fail. Be sure to use a bit of dielectric grease on each wire end when installing connectors. The non-conducting grease will be displaced during the crimping process to allow good metal-to-metal contact in the connector and will prevent moisture from reaching the connection, corroding it, and causing an electrical fault. Don't overcrimp, cutting the wire inside, or undercrimp, making it possible for the wire to eventually slip out. Always pull a new connection to make sure it's on tight. If you're wondering what the big fat "wires" are at the top and bottom, they are two ends of a spare clutch cable, wise insurance to carry on any bike.

battery. Eventually the battery loses its ability to swap electrons and dies by increments. Sometimes the battery can give up the ghost all at once, too. When it does this on the road, you're cooked, so it's best to change the battery every other year as part of regular maintenance. A relatively new component—the gel battery—is completely sealed and requires no maintenance. It won't vent battery acid all over your newly painted frame or fender, so it's well worth considering if you need a replacement. Gel batteries, however, do not have the same storage capacity as a conventional battery of the same physical size, so this may be a consideration.

Capacitor

Some motorcycle systems run without a battery and use only a capacitor, an electronic device that briefly stores up a charge until triggered to release it, and some run a battery with the capacitor as a backup. The are a number of units—the Mity-Max for one example—that also regulate voltage and can replace the entire Lucas charging system and battery (except the alternator).

TROUBLESHOOTING THE PRINCE OF DARKNESS

All right, now that we have the basics and know the names of the players, let's check the electrical system systematically.

We'll start with emergency troubleshooting, the sort of stuff you can do on the side of the road with a few tools and spare fuses if you're prepared, and if riding old Brit bikes is your passion, you'd better be. Fortunately one can find and quickly fix most road problems. See photo for simple kit particulars, and add a small flashlight if night riding's on the menu.

If the bike suddenly stops, check to see if the lights work. If not, suspect a blown fuse. Turn the ignition switch off and check the fuse. If it's blown, root around the bike and look for obvious problems. Although it happens, fuses seldom just up and blow; it's almost always a wire touching the frame or fender when it shouldn't. Common places for these are around the triple tree where wires pass from frame to headlight, any place where wires run through the frame or fender, and in and around any switch. Also, look under the seat and around major electrical devices, especially the brake light switch, a very common troublemaker because it's so exposed. Also, any hotwire connector can get loose and touch something that conducts electricity.

If no physical problem is apparent, try isolating the problem to a smaller part of the wiring. Make sure all lights and ignition are off and then replace the fuse. Turn the ignition key to the position allowing the bike to run without lights. If your bike isn't wired this way, change it ASAP as it makes this sort of troubleshooting much easier. Otherwise, you'll have to pull or cut the hot

Here's another inexpensive Taiwanese option, a replacement ignition switch that is very reliable and, unlike some switches, has two switch positions to allow you to energize one or both of the two output terminals. This kind of switch allows wiring the bike to run with or without power to the lighting circuit. This is not only very handy for emergency troubleshooting, but may allow a sort of electrical reserve if you find yourself trying to get home on an almost dead battery.

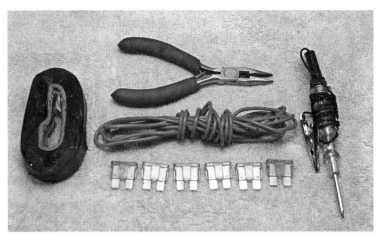

Don't leave home without it: This simple electrical kit is all you need to get home after most electrical failures. Modern fuses are better options and a good upgrade from the older tubular fuses, but carry a half-dozen of whatever kind you use, so they can be sacrificed to help locate problems. Make sure the piece of spare wire runs the length of the frame and a little more. Small needle-nose pliers can cut and strip wire, as well as recrimp loose connectors. A small test light can serve as a crude voltage tester and check for current at suspect locations.

wire on the ignition switch going to the lights for this test. If the fuse doesn't blow on "ignition-only," try starting the bike.

It runs? Good. Now turn the ignition switch to the "lighting" position or reconnect the lights wire, but with the light switch off. Fuse blew? Suspect a short in the light switch—quite common, especially with a lot of cheap aftermarket switches—or the hot wire to it. Things still okay? Try the light switch now. Fuse blew? Check for a short in the headlight bucket or the hot wire going from the light switch to the headlight and taillight. Everything still okay? Try the brake, front and back separately if you have switches for both. If the fuse blows, you know where to look. Disconnect that circuit in order to get home.

If, however, the fuse blows with the ignition switch in the "lights off" or "completely off" position, check for ground faults in wiring from the battery to the ignition switch. If you find nothing, suspect a shorted ignition switch. Disconnect the hot wire to the switch, replace the fuse, and then run a jumper wire from the battery to the ignition system to bypass the switch completely. If all's well now, try starting the bike. If the fuse blows again, check around the other ignition pieces like the coils. Generally, though,

if you run the test this far, you almost always find the problem and can get back on the road. If it's night and you have a shorted light switch, just cut the hotwire to the switch and run another hot wire directly to one beam of the headlight.

If the fuse is okay but you have no power, use the test light across the battery poles. You want a nice bright light. If the test light fails completely or only glows a faint yellow, it's walking time. Many times, though, it's something as simple as a loose connector on the battery. If the battery is strong, use your test light and find out where the continuity break is and correct it. If you find a weak battery and no obvious reason for it, it's time to spend an afternoon in the shop checking the entire charging/ignition system. Let's do this now.

ELECTRICAL TESTING

Since the battery is the shortest-lived component of the charging system it should be the first component tested. Also, many test figures are based on readings with a fully charged battery and such conditions must be met for accurate analysis.

A charged battery should produce 12.4 volts

The joke T-shirts showing the Lucas switch reading "Off-Dim-Flicker" have roots in truth, but aside from switch problems, the method of attaching the headlight bulb with a connector like this leaves a lot to be desired. These connections are often the cause of the flicker problem or even total blackout. The mating bulb also has a soft lead connector that indents and creates more problems over time. This connector can usually be made to work by cleaning the contacts and pulling out the springs behind them. A more reliable remedy is to replace the entire reflector/bulb/plug assembly with a more modern three-prong plug.

or more for a 12-volt unit, topping out at about 13.6 volts. Even if it tests out for volts (use a simple voltmeter set for DC, across the terminals) remove the battery anyway and check to see that it is clean and filled to the appropriate marking line. Use distilled water only for topping off low batteries.

There can be a dramatic difference in charging rate caused by only a moderate change in electrolyte level. Topping off the battery shown in this book doubled the rate of charge the battery took even though none of the cells were below the minimum level mark.

Even a good battery loses about one-percent of its charge daily when not in use, and if it seems to be losing more than that or resists charging, junk it. Specific gravity tests that point to bad cells are useful, and a simple hydrometer to measure specific gravity can be purchased for about five bucks. You can buy a special piece of equipment to put a battery under load to check it out—the best test—but if you don't do a lot of cycle work, this really isn't necessary because you can make a simple high-rate discharge tester that works pretty well.

HIGH-RATE DISCHARGE TESTING

To test the battery you'll need a DC voltmeter and the test rig described at the beginning of this chapter. Make sure the battery is fully charged before testing. Most of the small batteries in our Brits charge up well in a couple of hours on a small automotive charger running at about one to two amps.

To test, place your leads on the positive and negative terminals and hold in position for 15 seconds. Keep your eye on the DC voltmeter as you do. If after 15 seconds, the charge is above nine and one-half volts and does not begin to drop off, your battery should be okay.

Even if all tests come out okay, remember most batteries for old Brits are relatively cheap, so if there's any doubt, replace one before doing any other testing. I've yet to have anyone explain this to me satisfactorily, but considerable experience has proven that old batteries can behave mysteriously and cause many problems that appear to be related to other components but aren't, even though the battery seems to check out. If faced with extreme poverty and a questionable battery, borrow a good one for testing.

IS THE JUICE ON THE LOOSE?

After checking, charging and/or replacing the battery, install the now-proven battery and check for adequate voltage at various points in the cycle. There should be no appreciable voltage drop anywhere in the system. Make specific tests at areas of concern, like hot wires to coils and lighting equipment. No voltage anywhere means something's broken between the switch and the battery, at the switch itself, or in the wires leading from the switch. Bad ground wires are frequent culprits, too. Let's find out.

Use the voltmeter or a simple test light from the ignition switch hotwire to a grounded point on the frame. If voltage is found, check the terminal(s) leading back to the electrical component that isn't working. If no voltage is found when the switch is on, the problem is a dead switch. Lucas was especially adept at constructing switches that only served ornamental purposes or provided sparks and smoke at very inconvenient times. Budget builders can make great use of the plentiful used switches found on junk Japanese motorcycles. (I use an ignition switch from a Honda 50 on my Trident. Makes me smile every time I start the bike; it has worked perfectly for years.)

Sometimes older switches can be coaxed back to life by simply turning them on and off for a while because internal corrosion has caused a break in continuity. Contact cleaner or lacquer thinner can fix a few too. Still, I recommend that you replace balky switches ASAP just for insurance purposes if it's a Lucas original. Many weren't that good even when new and it is one Lucas legacy of failure I do fully acknowledge.

If the switch terminal delivering power to the other devices has voltage but there still is no current going to various parts, suspect a broken wire or loose connector to or at the part in question. Same goes for no voltage coming in to the switch.

In factory wiring, one will find a bundled mass of wires routed all over creation and bound in a loom that makes checking individual wires extremely time consuming. See the photo and caption for a shortcut. Regardless of the method used, one must isolate the offending wire or connector and repair it. Replacing the entire harness on older bikes solves many problems and prevents others from arising.

It's also very easy to rewire older British bikes yourself by making your own simple loom from scratch with plain wire and connectors. You can also buy a re-pop loom for about a hundred bucks. See illustration in this chapter for a very simple wiring diagram anyone can follow. See the Boyer section (last chapter) if you want to convert to electronic ignition or you already have this ignition system and need to test it.

Budget builders who wire their own bikes can do so for about ten bucks in wire and connectors and, I think, gain a special advantage because they will have a complete mental picture of their wiring system from end to end. Quite frankly, I didn't fully understand what was going on electrically in my cycle until I personally made all the connections myself.

However, a factory loom will be necessary if you are aiming at show points for originality; re-pop looms are fine too. If you plan to use either,

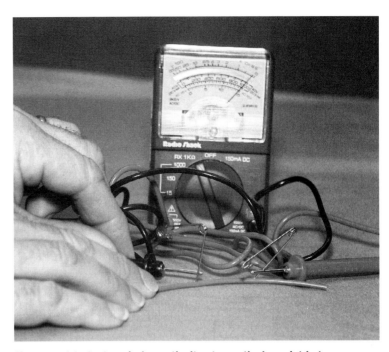

If you want to test a wire's continuity at a particular point between contacts, insert a couple of small needles or pins into the wire and test with an ohmmeter. This only leaves a tiny hole and does not damage the wire. Use a dab of silicone sealant on the hole sites after testing.

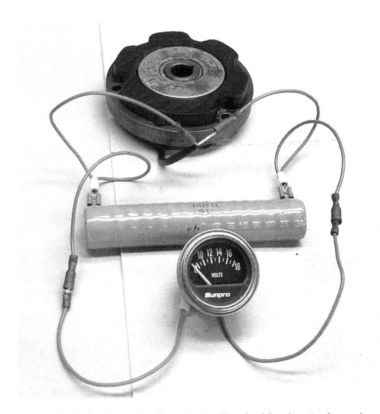

A test circuit is shown for alternator testing. An AC voltmeter is used with a load resistor as shown.

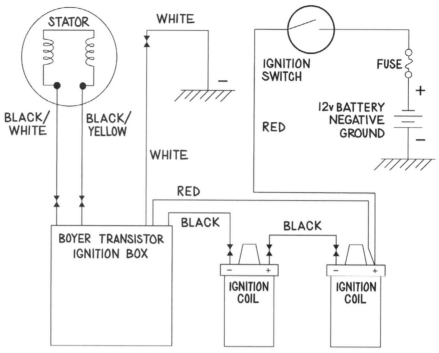

NEGATIVE GROUND MODELS (eg. 1979 & Later Triumphs)

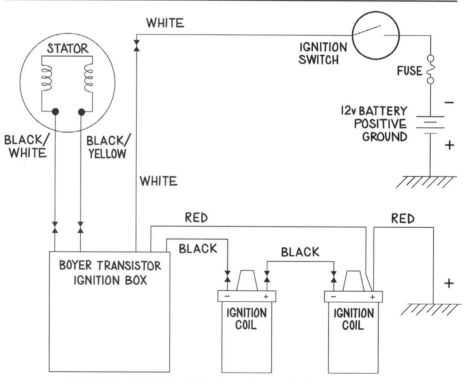

POSITIVE GROUND MODELS (Most British Bikes)

Boyer electronic ignition systems are easy to install and provide much more reliable performance than traditional points systems. Note that the coils are wired in series, causing both cylinders to fire together.

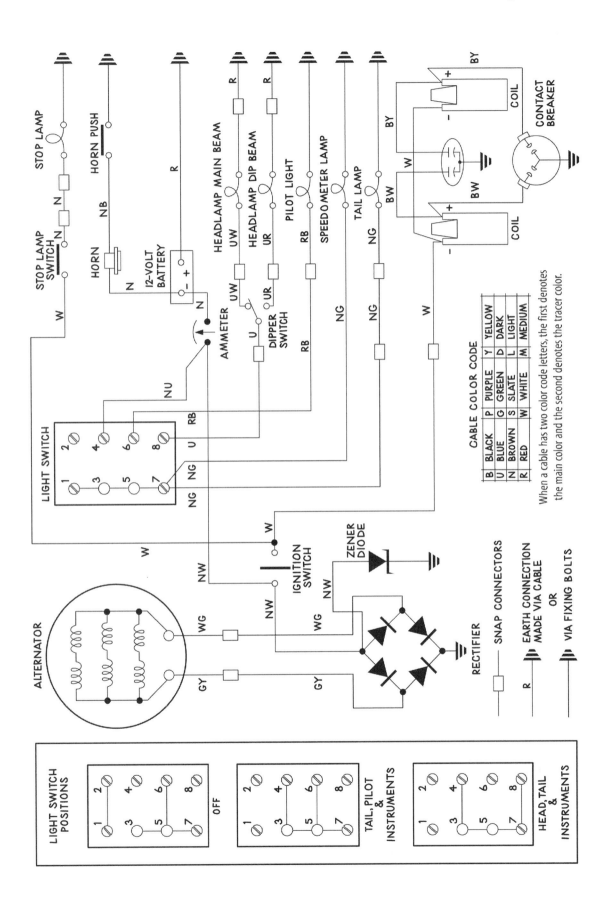

This simple diagram is representative of wiring on many Brit twins. It is very easy to understand and implement.

A mockup test circuit is shown for Zener diode testing. The switch in the foreground represents a hot wire from either ignition switch or battery, whichever wire ran to the diode originally. The ammeter runs in series on this connection in the foreground. A second wire runs from diode to DC voltmeter and then to ground.

it makes good sense to carefully take apart and label all original connections with masking tape or wired tags using corresponding numbers on the loom and electrical connection points. Then, place the old and new loom next to each other and transfer the tags. Lots of digital pictures will help avoid mistakes.

GETTING A CHARGE OUT OF LIFE

Once we've determined that our delivery system is okay, we can then go forth and check specific components of the ignition and charging systems. Let's start with charging.

The first step in checking the charging system is to measure the charging rate back to the battery. Disconnect the negative lead from the battery and then the lead to the Zener diode. Tape the diode lead because it's hot and you don't want the wire to short out. Now connect an ammeter between the wire you disconnected from the battery and the negative battery terminal. Start the bike and hold it at 3,000 rpm. With the headlight off, you should get 4 to 5 amps, with it on, about one. If you don't, we have more checking to do.

Alternators can be checked with the same wire and resistor rig you used to check the battery load, but this time with an AC voltmeter. Disconnect the alternators leads and then connect your test leads to them. With the most com-

mon two-wire Lucas alternator, you want to find over nine volts at 3,000 rpm. Lower readings point to a demagnetized rotor. I use a multimeter set for 10 volts AC and let this rest on the ground as I run the bike. This way, I don't have to read the fine markings; I just watch the needle peg out at maximum, and this is easy to see and provides the needed information.

Check the alternator for shorts by using an ohmmeter from the alternator wires to ground. There should be no reading at all. If you don't find a ground fault and have no voltage or weak charge, it's quite possible that one or both wires coming from the alternator inside the primary case are simply broken. Pull the primary cover, check, and remedy. Malfunctioning stators aren't repairable and must be replaced. Same goes for alternator rotors, as there's no practical way to remagnetize the rotor.

If the alternator checks out, measure the voltage with a DC voltmeter from the center terminal on the rectifier. Attach the negative terminal of a DC voltmeter with resistor (same rig as the load test for the battery) to the center rectifier terminal and attach the positive side of the voltmeter to a good ground. If no voltage or low voltage is evident (less than 7.5 volts at 3,000 rpm) junk the rectifier/Zener diode system and replace with solid state. It's actually cheaper than replacing it with OEM equipment and works even better.

ZENER DIODE TESTING

If your problem is overcharging, this is generally evidenced in two ways: bulbs keep blowing and/ or the battery is overcharging and sending excessive fluid out the vent tube. Here's when we suspect the Zener diode.

To test, remove the resistor from the DC voltmeter test rig and run two plain wire leads instead. (Remember the H? Just remove the resistor crosspiece.) Remove the Zener diode female spade connector and tape it to prevent shorting. Attach to the Zener diode another large female spade connector with two wire leads coming from it. You should now have a new spade connection with long wire leads coming from the diode. On one lead from the new connection attach the positive terminal of the ammeter and run the negative connection of the ammeter to the female connector you took off the diode. You can just wrap the bare wire around the connector and tape it, or you can also make an easy connection by using a male terminal on one lead coming from the diode. On the other test lead coming from the Zener diode, attach the negative end of the voltmeter and then attach the positive side to a ground on the frame. Also, make sure before testing that the diode itself is on tight and solidly connects to the frame.

With everything in place, start the bike. It often helps to have an assistant for this test as it's tough to juggle the wires and two gauges while starting and running the bike.

With the bike running, check the voltmeter and ammeter simultaneously. Increase the rpm to 3,000 and when the voltage gets to about 13.5 volts, you should start to get a reading on the ammeter indicating excess current is being dumped through the diode. At around 13.75 to 15 volts there should be around 2 amps of current through the ammeter, and consequently, the Zener diode. If readings aren't close to these limits, junk the diode/rectifier system and install a modern replacement as recommended earlier in this chapter.

IGNITION SYSTEM

"Man that hurts!"–Wiseguy shop assistant tricked into holding finger in high-tension spark plug wire.

A lack of spark in a conventional points ignition system where the charging and battery system are okay can have numerous causes. The most common is a loose or broken wire or connector to the coil or coils, followed closely by malfunctioning points.

Checking for spark is simple, just remove the spark plug and ground its body on the engine while turning the engine over a few times with the ignition switched on. Be advised that Boyer units won't produce a spark at a slow turn like points will. The pickup unit must be spun at least 200 rpm, equivalent to a good kick. If you suspect the Boyer unit, check the Boyer section in the back of this book.

With points, make sure they're clean, un-

A coil's primary winding is being checked here. Resistance should be relatively low; about 3 ohms is common. Resistance in the secondary winding is much higher. Also check for a short circuit between terminals and case, and check for no continuity at all, meaning that something's broken inside. Regardless of your test results, never rely on these measurements absolutely. This coil showed correct resistance on the bench but failed in operation. It was replaced during service work to fix a misfire that occurred only when the coil got warm, after about 30 minutes of riding. You can check for a hot spark from the coil on the bike by kicking the engine over with the ignition on and holding a known-good plug wire with a bare end close to the case. A hot blue spark should jump. A yellow one means it's weak.

burned, and correctly set and adjusted. If a heavy spark occurs between the points, that's a sign of a bad condenser. Generally, it's best to replace the condenser when you replace a points set.

TESTING COILS, PLUGS, AND WIRES

If attending to the points fails to produce a good hot spark, and the coil is getting electricity, suspect the coil. Usually, though, it's a bad plug wire or plug. Try different ones and see if there's a difference. If not, remove the hot wire from the coil and test the primary (low-voltage) coil winding. Around three ohms is good.

A very simple test is to analyze the color of the spark at the plug. A good coil will produce a strong white/blue spark. A weak coil will make a yellow spark and will often misfire the engine when it's under load. Just be sure you use a good spark plug for this test.

There are many other tests we can perform, but coils are deceptive animals. They just love to work one moment, and then quit when hot or misfire randomly at inopportune times even after testing okay. Substitution is often easier and quicker. For example, if one plug fires and another doesn't, swap the coils. If the problem moves with the coil, you've found the bad coil. If not, look elsewhere.

If you have an intermittent problem that may be heat related, like cutting out or hard starting after running, substitution can also help isolate isolate the offender. Substitute and road test.

Nicholson's super easy test for Zener diode leakage is shown. Turn the ignition on but do not start the bike. Remove the connector and try to get a spark to jump to the diode blade. If you can get a spark to jump, the Zener is shot and further testing unnecessary.

▶ BERNIE'S ELECTRICAL BRILLIANCE

Lucas alternator rotors are very durable items if they aren't demagnetized by connecting the battery cables backwards or by reverse current caused by a faulty rectifier. However, they do frequently suffer from a mechanical failure when the steel insert loosens up inside of the alloy rotor housing. At one time, I'd just pitch the rotor, but according to *Modern Motorcycle Mechanics,* this isn't always necessary: "Just a trace of backlash between the rotor and hub its hub does not necessitate replacement. This can sometimes be overcome by punch-locking." (See photos for details.)

Nicholson also has a super easy test for Zener diode leakage that does not require a single bit of test equipment. To test, simply turn the ignition on and remove the connector to the diode. If bringing the connector close to the diode causes a spark, it's leaking and must be replaced. Nicholson also recommends using threadlock on the diode threads because only 2 ft-lbs of torque should be used on the attaching nut. In absence of a tiny torque wrench, something Nicholson recognizes as likely, he recommends using a very small wrench and only light pressure.

Use a center punch as shown, close to but not quite touching the rotor insert. Work around the insert and then retest for movement before installing.

If you can move the insert inside of a Lucas rotor, it needs fixing. So long as the backlash isn't too severe, punch-locking can be employed.

▶ SPARKING DISCOVERY

BY MIKE BROWN

If I had a dollar for every "bad" sparkplug I threw away over the years I might be able to retire while Social Security was still solvent. Oh well, at least I eventually learned that most times poorly performing plugs can be put back into top notch service, and no longer test my throwing arm when plugs fail to provide adequate spark.

Although sparkplugs do eventually wear out, more commonly they produce problems because they're fouled by fuel, oil, carbon, or all three together. I'm not going to pretend to understand the physics behind sparkplug misbehavior, but I do want to share a few observations and the results of experimentation.

What brought me to sparkplug enlightenment was a set of Mikuni carbs running way on the rich side. As I tinkered with jetting, I frequently found new and nearly new plugs once fuel fouled failed to work correctly afterwards, even when carefully cleaned with a wire brush so that all evidence of fouling, at least what I could see, was removed.

I was down to my last set of good plugs, and still running too rich. Earlier that day, I'd bead-blasted a BSA head, and got to wonder how that might work on a set of fouled plugs. I quickly discovered that bead blasting worked where other techniques didn't. I still don't know why, but it is what it is, and since that time this is how I handle plug cleaning.

With bead blasting, it's imperative you follow up the blast job by carefully blowing out the plug with plain compressed air to remove any traces of glass beads as one does not want this inside of a combustion chamber. After that, check and/or reset the gap and you're good to go.

Recently I picked up the unit shown that is specifically for plug cleaning. JC Whitney carries it. It arrived with directions written in a language only faintly resembling English and a small package of coarse abrasive. With one compressor down and my other only capable of making 85 psi, I couldn't get it to work. However, when I ditched the abrasive the tool came with and substituted finer glass beads, the little dickens worked to perfection at lower pressures.

Also of relevance here is that a plug can fire nicely when it's tested out of the cylinder and then refuse to work under compression, when it must, or sporadically, under different loads. If you have a plug like that, try the blast treatment; it frequently cures the problem. Then again, you might want to practice your fastball.

This fouled plug refused to fire correctly and shows signs of rich mixture.

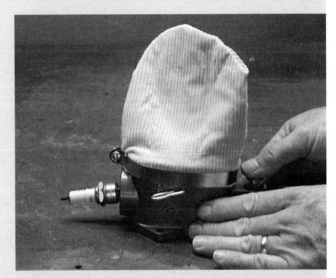

Plug cleaner in operation. Blast media is contained inside and the plug is held by a rubber washer in the far end.

Here's the cleaned plug. It worked perfectly and took all of five seconds to clean.

9 Ahh... Fork It!

OVERVIEW

Once you get the rusty things apart, rebuilding your Brit forks is fairly easy and well within the ability of most anyone. Damage repair is a bit more involved, but still not rocket science. You can also make your old Brit forks work even better than new with a few modern upgrades, something not in the shop manuals. Nor are many other useful DIY repair strategies we'll cover here. Let's do it.

FORKS BEFORE 1971

We'll start with the earlier externally-sprung forks and assume you've already removed, dismantled, and cleaned the fork legs as explained in the teardown.

If the tubes stand any chance of being used again, hold them for service work in a vise with soft jaws made of two pieces of aluminum angle stock. Use a vise grip to unscrew the hydraulic valve assemblies for cleaning and be sure they have the circlips in place. Very early BSA and Triumph forks have a long rod and more complicated damping pieces.

After the valves have been removed, check the top bushing for clearance on the tube. You can measure the ID/OD of the bush and tube and compare with new specs in the manual data table or just feel for play. Check the bottom bush as well for play in the fork leg. If one's worn, replace them both; they're not expensive. To remove the bottom bush, twist it off after locking a vise grip on it.

Check the tube for straightness (as shown in the measurement chapter) and also for rust pitting, heavy wear, and seize marks. If the tube is badly damaged by rust, wear and/or seize marks, it will have to be replaced. However, sometimes the rust pits aren't extensive, but the forks will still leak like a Texas oil well if these pits aren't filled. Epoxy to the rescue!

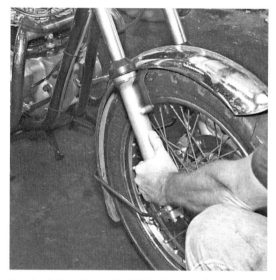

To check for play in the triple-tree bearings before and after rebuilding, push and pull on the lower fork legs as shown. You should feel no front-to-rear movement. The play you feel before rebuilding can also come from worn bushes or fork legs.

Light pitting can be repaired by smearing a thin layer of epoxy over the pitted areas and then sanding, first with 125 grit sandpaper followed by 220 and 400 wet sanding. This is just like fine bodywork, meaning you may have to apply several skim coats and resand each time. If you can get the tubes so they feel absolutely smooth where they were previously pitted, they'll work, but don't fool yourself. If you can feel any irregularity on the surface, don't use them; they'll leak.

REPAIRING BENT PARTS

Forget the heavy mallet shown in the BSA manual being used to straighten fork tubes; if you have to straighten bent fork tubes the only way to do so is with hydraulics. A press large enough to place the tube across it is the easiest way, but a ten-buck bottle jack and heavy vehicle will do the job. Most passenger cars aren't heavy enough, but a big truck axle can't be beat. See photo and caption for more details.

After you're sure the tubes are straight, use them to check the lower trees that can also be bent. Place the tubes and tree on the workbench and make sure both tubes are parallel with each other. A great tool to check for problems is an old chopper tweak bar. You can get old, crusty tweak bars for next to nothing at most swap meets. These bars were designed to minimize flexing in extended fork tubes and are often found by themselves or very commonly attached to the extended fork tubes of an old chopper. Loosened up just a bit, the tweak bar should slide up and down the fork tubes if everything's okay. If it hangs up somewhere, something's bent.

To straighten lower tree misalignment, the manual recommends holding one leg in a soft-jaw vise and putting a long cheater bar on the fork tube on the bent tree side. The idea is to use leverage force to bend the tree back into alignment. Heating the tree a bit helps, too. However, I hate to apply this kind of force to good fork tubes. It's much better to use rejected ones for this job and then check alignment with the good tubes. You can also get a better grip in the vise without the soft jaws required for good tubes.

REBUILDING SEAL HOLDERS

Once the tubes and trees pass muster, attend to the seal holders. They may need rechroming, and if they do, make sure the plater keeps the chrome off the fine threads inside or they'll be hell to install.

Before plating and cleaning, we have to remove the fork seal by inserting a drift or old screwdriver in the bottom of the seal holder so that it rests on the seal and then knock the seal out with a hammer on the drift. Sometimes the top bush is stuck inside too and this can be removed the same way, except from the top or by pulling it out with pliers.

Once the seal holder's perfectly cleaned and/or replated, the new seal must be driven in. Also replace the rubber O-rings. Be very careful not to damage the main seal during installation. Use a homemade seal driver or a commercial one to gently seat the seal straight into the holder. If you see any crimps or bends in the seal afterwards, you've ruined it and must replace it with another.

This fork tube is being straightened with the help of a bottle jack and truck weight. Be sure to find a nice level surface like this concrete slab and hold the tube to keep the high side up. Old chopper tweak bars are great for this and other fork service. Note the piece of flat aluminum bar stock taped to the tube to prevent damage to the tube. A metal bar and feeler gauges are used to measure how far the tube needs to be straightened.

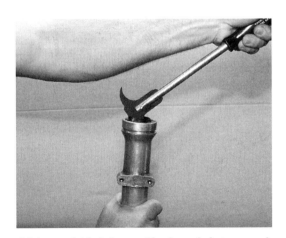

A later-model fork leg seal is shown being removed with an inexpensive commercial seal puller, a far better tool than a screwdriver for this job. Regardless of the tool you use, be very careful not to mar the soft alloy leg where the seal rests. Work your way slowly around the seal and keep the tool on and in the seal, not directly on the leg.

Our early-model fork tube is shown with the new bottom bush and plastic tube installed. The cleaned valve assembly is about to be screwed into the tube.

The fork seal holder is installed after the top bush is gently driven into place on the top of the fork leg.

To allow modern caged roller bearings to be installed on an earlier BSA frame, a new race is being driven in with a plastic hammer to avoid damaging the race.

FORK TUBE REBUILDING

Begin rebuilding the tube by first inserting the plastic tube; then install the bottom bush by driving it on with a plastic hammer or equivalent. Next, install the cleaned valve assembly (see photo) and tighten with a vise grip.

If you haven't already slid on the top bush do so now and then lubricate the fork seals, bushes, and tubes with either fork oil or automatic transmission fluid (ATF). Now insert the tube into the lower leg; it should be a close fit with the new bush. Use a plastic hammer to drive the top bush into the top of the fork leg or use a piece of PVC pipe slid over the fork tube for this. Finally, slide the well-lubricated fork seal holder carefully down the tube to prevent damage to the seal. Tighten the holder as much as you can by hand and then use a strap wrench or special factory tool until it's tight.

We have one more job to do on the seal holder. Use the strap wrench or factory tool again and turn the seal holder back one full turn. Now coat the top few exposed leg threads with a thin coat of good gasket sealant (Hondabond #4 works great), and then retighten the holder and wipe off any excess sealant. If you lack the special service tool for final tightening, use a soft aluminum drift in one of the holes to move the holder a bit more after using the strap wrench to be sure it's really tight. The use of modern sealant replaces the WW II era manual's suggestion for using a piece of string to seal the threads. All that's left now is to slide on the fork spring, upper cork washer, top spring holder (if it had one to begin with) and boot and then offer the assembly up into the triple tree. Check your parts book for respective model/make/year as there are many variations in required bits. Make sure you've checked and/or replaced the springs, and even better, upgraded to modern progressively wound springs. If your boots take clamps, don't forget to put them on loosely before inserting the fork leg into the triple tree.

If you have cleaned out the triple tree holes carefully and removed any stray paint and rust, you can usually get the legs to slide into the bottom tree and far enough into the top tree to start the cap nut on the fork tube. Tighten the nuts to draw up the legs. If you encounter resistance from the bottom of the tree, spread the holes apart more by using a wedge in the slots. A little WD 40 on the tubes helps too.

Every once in a while, you have problems getting the tubes up high enough to reach the fork cap nut. The manual shows the shop tool used to overcome this problem, but you can make an equivalent one by grinding the top of an old fork tube cap nut so that it will pass through the top triple tree holes. You then weld a large piece of all-thread onto the nut. Afterwards, double-lock two nuts higher up on the all-thread and use them to screw the ground-down fork nut into the tube. Once the old nut is well inside the fork tube, remove the locked-on nuts. Now you can offer the tube up into the hole and drop a short piece of pipe or a deep socket, with a diameter larger than the tree hole, over the all-thread. The all-thread must stick out over the top of a pipe or deep socket. Now place a large washer over the all-thread and pipe and then attach and tighten one of the nuts on the all-thread to pull the tube into position. You can also use this tool to drive tubes out of the trees by striking the top of the all-thread. Attach a nut on the all-thread to protect the threads when using it this way.

Another option that involves no special tool construction is to use a soft hammer to drive reluctant tubes into the trees after the tree's been mounted on the bike and then rebuilding the tubes on the bike. If you take this route, be sure to attach anything like the fork ears holding the headlights first or you'll just have to remove the stanchions again.

Either way, we have to remount the triple tree after replacing the bearings. Just to save my sanity, I almost always convert early loose bearings to modern cup and cone like '71 and later forks.

If you do consider reusing the loose ball bearings, check the top and bottom races in the frame and the ones on the tree for roughness and pitting, and the bearing balls themselves for flat spots. If you find any problems, you should replace the entire assembly with an upgrade kit, but you can get the stock races too. The bearings are plain 1/4 inch balls that are a lot cheaper generically at the bearing house. You'll have to grease the bearings and races a lot to hold the lit-

Fit and operation of new steering stem bearings are being checked and adjusted on this BSA. Bearing adjustment on pre '71 Beezers will require use of a piece of flat stock as shown to tighten steering stem.

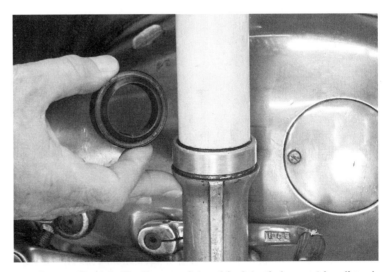

Interference-fit seals like the one pictured for later forks must be aligned properly or they'll wear quickly and leak terribly. The seal is installed after the tube is inside the leg; it is driven in squarely with inch-and-a-half diameter thick-wall PVC pipe placed over fork tube as shown. Special seals that float in the leg are easier to install and provide better, longer lasting leak protection but are more expensive.

tle stinkers together for installation. Be very careful inserting the fork stem because even with grease it's still easy to dislodge a ball or two during installation.

Removing the races from the frame is simply a matter of using a long punch and knocking them out from the inside. Tap the new ones in with a soft hammer (see photo) and be sure they are fully in. You can grind down the outside of the old races a bit to use as a driver to make the job easier.

The bottom race on the tree, however, can be a snot to remove. Make sure you've removed all rust from the stem as this can prevent the race from sliding off. If it resists prying, and it often does, heat it with a propane torch and drive a chisel between the race and tree to free the race. We'll cover final adjustments later in this chapter, as it's basically the same procedure for newer forks.

Old and new external forks springs are shown. Use of worn springs like the one at right will result in less than satisfactory performance in any suspension system. New springs aren't very expensive; and modern progressive springs are also reasonably priced and improve stock performance. Wise investments.

LATE MODEL FORKS

There's less work to do with '71 and later forks because there aren't any bushes; the tube runs in the alloy fork leg. If you find too much clearance, the entire leg must be replaced. Also, any surface damage to late-model tubes means they either need to be replated or replaced. You can straighten them, however, the same as early tubes. If you replace the tubes, you may find you have bought stainless steel tubes instead of the original hard chrome plated steel. These are great, but they come without an important warning about the nature of stainless steel and the tendency for galling. You can easily ruin a brand new stainless fork tube if you fail to use anti-seize on the threads.

We do need to replace the fork seal. You can make a simple removal tool from a notched piece of bar stock, or use a commercial tool, but be careful with either. It's way too easy to gouge up the soft alloy surface of the leg around the seal and this can cause terrific leaks. If you have a fork leg that is otherwise serviceable but has a chewed up seal surface, sand down the high spots where the seal goes and fill the scratches with epoxy. Finish the seal surface as described for early fork tubes. An improved aftermarket seal exists for these units, but it floats in the leg, so the surface area must be perfect.

There's an aluminum nut at the bottom of each fork tube. Hold the tube in a vise with soft jaws and unscrew the nut to remove the valve assembly. Aside from careful cleaning, the only

Carefully check studs on both early and later forks for damage.

A later-model valve assembly is shown with a new anti-stiction seal that replaces the rubber O-ring, greatly improving performance. Pry off the old seal with a small screwdriver and gently install a new seal, being very careful not to stretch it too far; it's very easy to damage it on installation.

thing you need to do with the valve assembly is to remove the tiny rubber O-ring and replace it with an anti-stiction seal. This is a great improvement over stock and eliminates a big problem with these units. If you add a set of modern progressive fork springs, you'll have a very smooth and reliable assembly, much better than stock. Finally, lubricate the valve assembly with ATF and return it to the fork tube.

FORK ASSEMBLY

Let's turn our attention again to the fork leg. If the little sealing washer at the very bottom inside of the alloy fork leg didn't come out during cleaning, use a long piece of stiff wire—welding rod works well—and pry it out. Replace the old washer with a new one on which you've put a bit of grease to make it stick in place. This washer rests in a recess at the bottom of the fork leg and can be guided into place by using stiff wire. Insert the wire and let it poke out of the bottom of the leg to act as a great guide for the washer.

Now we can insert the fork tube into the leg with the socket tool we used (detailed in teardown chapter) to take it apart inside the tube. Use a little thread sealer on the Allen bolt, insert it into the hole at the base of the fork leg, and screw it into the valve assembly while you hold it with the tool to keep the valve inside the leg from turning.

Next put a piece of plastic sandwich wrap on the top of the fork tube to protect the seal, and then slide the ATF-lubricated seal down the fork tube so it rests squarely on the top of the leg. A piece of inch-and-a-half schedule 40 PVC pipe makes a great installation tool. Make sure the tube is square on the seal and drive it in with a hammer on the plastic pipe. The rebuilt legs can now be installed into the tree after first installing a new dust boot over the tube and pushing it into the holding groove on top of the leg. You can drop the springs in now or after the tubes are in the trees.

ADJUSTING THE FORKS

Once the legs are in the trees on the bike, adjust the tree bearings. Make sure you've cleaned, inspected and repacked them with new grease. Be gentle tightening the fork stem nut or you can ruin the bearings. You want the stem nut just tight enough so there's absolutely no play in the forks, but loose enough so the forks fall by their own weight. The forks must also feel perfectly smooth when turning, or something's wrong.

Install the wheel and fender now (early forks too) but leave everything just hand tight because we have to align the forks. To do so, apply the front brake and bounce the forks up and down. This can be done without brakes by positioning the front wheel against an immovable object. After bouncing the forks, tighten only the right axle cap nuts, bounce again, and then tighten the left ones. Do not over-torque the nuts, especially on later models, as you can crack the alloy easily; and yes, there's supposed to be a gap there, and on old style steel axle caps too.

Okay? Now bounce the forks again, tighten the fender nuts, bounce and then tighten the lower fork clamp nuts, and then the upper ones if you have them. Finally, bounce again and finish off by filling the fork legs with ATF and tightening the top tube nuts.

All right! Now we got the forkin' things fixed. Let's go fix a wheel to use on 'em.

10 *Wheel Building*

OVERVIEW

The shop manuals tell you next to nothing about wheel building, other than to say it's a job for specialists, and that's bunk. However, wheel building does take time to learn, and truing a wheel has driven many an amateur to the brink of emotional collapse. Patience is required. If you do become frustrated truing a wheel, calm down and keep trying until you get it right, or bring the assembled wheel to a good shop for truing after you put it together. You'll still save money doing the basic lacing, providing you don't blow your cool and ruin parts through excessive use of force. Throwing the entire wheel across the shop in a fit of anger should also be avoided. Okay?

WHEEL INSPECTION

The most common reason for rebuilding a wheel is that the rim is rusty and the only way to repair it is to either replace the rim or have it rechromed. Either way, the spokes and hub must be removed. Considering the cost of plating today, and the ready availability of quality new rims, I recommend that you go for the new rim, as it will be much easier to work with and not much more expensive than chroming your old one. Stainless steel and alloy rims are also viable options.

Wheel damage, side-to-side movement, or out-of-round movement also call for wheel work. Some old wheels are so bad they resemble a Bourbon Street tourist after midnight, wobbling unpredictably all over the place and certainly not roadworthy. When a wheel gets this bad, it can be almost impossible to bring it back into alignment, but many a goofy wheel can be trued up and made completely serviceable. However, we can forget about perfection with an old used rim. We'll be happy with getting lateral (side to side) and radial (up and down) runout to .032 inch or less. You should expect new rims to be much more accurate.

There are several things worth observing in this picture to help you remove or mount a tire. The homemade stand shown here makes this job a hundred percent easier than wrestling with a wheel on the ground or working with one on a bench. The centerless stand constructed of scrap wood allows use of your legs and knees for force and also keeps the wheel flat and stable. Also, forget screwdrivers; use the real deal, motorcycle tire irons like those shown. With alloy rims it's best to use alloy tools. Any rim can be protected from damage by cutting pieces of hose lengthwise and slipping these in place over the rim edge where the lever will be used. The longer lever being held provides additional leverage helpful to begin this task and will be positioned under the brake lever to keep the tire from popping back into the rim while the two smaller ones are worked around the wheel. If you can't break the bead by using just your knees, put the rim and tire in a vise to break the seal.

If this is your first shot at wheel building, be sure to clear the day's agenda, and I do mean day. By the time you make the tools you'll need, disassemble the wheel, and then rebuild and true it, you'll blow the whole day. If you plan to reuse the spokes and the used rim, we're most likely not talking about an eight-hour day either. When a master wheel builder does his thing, he's super fast and makes it look simple. Don't expect the same when you do it. If time is critical and money not a major concern, give the job to a pro.

You might also want to see a live demonstration before doing a wheel. If you don't know anyone who does this, Cycle Works Inc. puts out a very good video and is the original source for a lot of the neat low-buck tips included here.

INITIAL STEPS

Ahh, so you do want to have a go at it mate? Good for you. I felt like the reincarnation of Jack Wilson the first time I did a wheel and it came out right. If you believe the shop books that say you can't do this yourself, you'll miss out on a powerful feeling of accomplishment when you get an old wobbly wheel running true again.

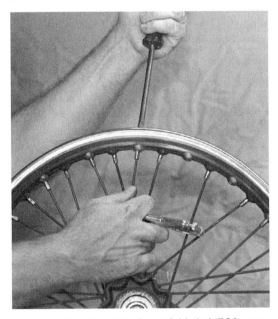

Some spokes, like these in a crinkle-hub BSA, may have to be held with a vise grip to keep them from turning while the nipple is turned. After nipples are loosened with a spoke wrench, using a screwdriver the rest of the way speeds removal considerably.

On bikes that have been sitting for a long time, it is very easy to wreck a perfectly good rim when removing an ancient tire. What happens is the tire gets hard—some are almost like rocks after only five years—and then the force of removing it distorts the rim badly. This is doubly true with alloy rims. If you have an age-hardened tire, cut it off with something like a power saw. Get close to the rim and then cut the rest of the way by hand.

Next, remove the rim strip and break out the can of rust fighter. Liberally spray the nipples and let them soak overnight before attacking your project. This applies only if you plan to reuse spokes and nipples. If you have the money for a new set, go for stainless replacements and break out the bolt cutter. Use it to cut out the old spokes and cut down the job time considerably. You might still have to cut some spokes off anyway, as rust can make some impossible to remove without damage.

SPOKE PATTERNS

But wait! Be awfully sure you know your spoke pattern—there are lots of them, and different kinds of spokes too. It's imperative to record what goes where. A failure at this point can doom a lacing project! Fortunately, the Brit wheels covered in this book are all laced basically the same with two spokes crossing each other on one side of the rim, and another two crossing spokes on the other side. The two sets of crossing spokes are offset slightly and form a 4-spoke repeating pattern around the wheel. One set of spokes will be on one side of the hub, and second set on the opposite side. However, the angle of crossing and respective holes in the hub and rim vary a lot from wheel to wheel, so marking the pattern is very important for a successful rebuild.

My favorite reference option is a rusty junk wheel, of which I have plenty. A set of good photographs taken from both sides on the wheel and at different angles will definitely do the job, but a three-dimensional model is far superior.

Even with a visual representation, you still want to do some marking before disassembling the wheel. Get a bottle of nail polish and mark both the hub and rim for spoke placement. Also mark the hub and rim for left/right side so you can put it back together the same way it was before. You don't have to mark each spoke, just the initial pattern. Here's how. Spokes are laced in a repeating pattern. Discover yours and mark accordingly. If, for example, you have four different placements repeating themselves (as is most common) mark the first spoke in the series with a single dot on the rim and hub, the second with two dots and so fourth. If you replace your rim, keep the old one and then line it up with the new one and transfer your dot patterns to it.

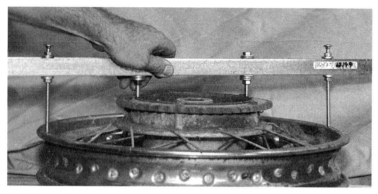

Here's our homemade offset tool being set to measure a conical hub wheel.

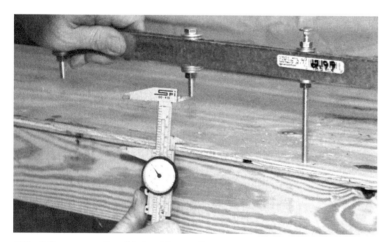

Offset figures can be obtained by setting the tool as shown in the upper photo and then measuring the distance with a caliper. The tool can also be set this way with figures provided for the wheel. The following are some offset figures for general reference only, taken from common Brit twin wheels with stock steel rims: Triumph/BSA conical front, .624; Triumph/BSA conical rear, 1.916; Triumph/BSA '69–'70 twin-leading-shoe front, none, even with rim; 500 twin leading shoe, .231; '69 Triumph rear, 1.890; '65 BSA single-leading-shoe front, .595. Since the BSA quick-detach rear wheel is laced without the brake drum, the offset was measured from the top of the splined shaft at .762.

Okay, now we have another variable on our program, and that's offset: the axial distance between the hub/brake drum and rim when measured from the side of the wheel. You can see this clearly by looking at the photos in this chapter. Offset varies a lot depending on bike model/year and wheel type.

We can make a dirt-simple tool to measure offset from two pieces of flat bar stock about 25 inches long and four bolts (see photo). Place two bolts with washers between the two bars on each side at a distance that will allow the bolts to sit on the outside edge of the brake drum. Tighten the bolts when so positioned. Now use the other two bolts (I used quarter inch carriage bolts on the outer end and 5/16 in the middle) and place the outer bolts at opposite ends of the bar stock so they touch the wheel rim. You'll have to play around a bit with the bolts but it isn't hard. What you want is the entire assembly resting flat across the wheel. When it does, lock the bolts and remove the tool. Now place the tool on a flat surface and measure the distance from the center bolts to the flat surface. That's your offset.

If you trust the current dimensions of your wheel, you can just set the tool up on the wheel before taking it apart and skip measurement. Otherwise you'll need specs for the wheel. Some common ones taken from measuring old stock wheels are provided in the photo captions, but there are many variables. For example, a change in rim type can change the offset. Always ask about specs when buying a new rim or spokes; buy elsewhere if you can't get them. Buchanan's Spoke and Rim is an excellent source for information and wheel supplies for your Brit. Another good source is Britech. Once you have offset figures, adjust the tool to these specs for use when you true the wheel. (See Resources appendix for contact information.)

MORE TOOLS

We're almost ready to take the wheel apart, but before we do, we need to make a truing stand. There are lots of ways to do this, but the least expensive is to drill a hole a bit smaller than the wheel axle in the center of a small block of wood. Cut the wood lengthwise up the center and place the two halves and your axle in a vise

Skip buying a special wheel truing stand and save your money for something like a new rim. An old block of wood drilled, split down the middle, and held with the axle in a vise like this does the job well for next to nothing. A junk fork leg is another good low-buck truing stand alternative.

Both a small vise grip and a spoke wrench make wheel building easier.

and tighten. Slide the wheel on the axle, and volia! You have a great budget truing stand.

The last tool we need to make is one that let's us see and measure radial and lateral runout. In a perfect world we don't want any runout at all, but if we get close, it's really imperceptible to the eye and on the road where it counts.

To get a rough measure of runout, cut down a fifty-cent T-brace available in any hardware store and mount it on a magnetic base dial indicator holder (see photo). You can rig this up lots of other ways, too, but the commercial stand does make the job lots easier. You can get one for about 15 bucks at most discount tool stores compliments of those wonderful Chinese folks.

INITIAL CHECKS AND DISASSEMBLY

It's not a bad idea before you start taking apart the wheel to check it for truth. Most pictured here were incorrigible liars and in need of serious correction, but repairable. If you find something like a big dent, forget it; you'll never true a wheel like this. Pitch the rim and get a new or good used one. Sometimes minor flat spots can be hammered out of alloy wheels after heating them up with a propane torch, but you can easily do more damage.

If you're reusing the spokes, each one will have to be removed individually. A spoke wrench helps a lot but isn't absolutely necessary, and you may need a small locking pliers to keep the spokes from turning in some hubs. Once you get a spoke a little loose, work on the other ones sequentially. If you hit a tough one, skip it and go on. After the wheel tension is relieved, you can go back and usually it's easy then to loosen and remove. If everything fails, cut the bad one out and get a replacement spoke and nipple. Here's where that junk rim can have other uses, like being a parts donor. Also, with the spokes loose, it's a lot faster to use a screwdriver on the nipple to take apart the spokes.

With all the spokes loose but still on the wheel, it's time to organize. You'll need a container for each spoke type; check your parts book to be sure because some spokes look identical and they're really not. The '69 A65 quick-detach rear wheel shown in some photos called for only two types, a left hand and right hand. Consequently, I labeled two clean cans accordingly, and made sure each spoke went in its respective can. Regardless, make sure you have a separate container for each spoke type.

When the wheel starts to get really loose, take it off the truing stand and disassemble the rest of the spokes with the wheel flat on a workbench.

If reusing the spokes, check each one for good threads and straightness, and replace any bad ones with good used or new replacements. For one example here, I cleaned each spoke on a wire wheel. And yes, this took a long time.

Poverty cases and cheapskates can make an old spoke look almost new with a little silver or imitation cadmium paint. Spray either on a rag

Our BSA wheel is completely apart. Note the individual cans for spokes to avoid mix-ups.

A junk reference rim is at left and our project rim at right has been laced for the first spoke pattern plus the first spoke in the second pattern.

Now we have one side done and will flip the wheel and repeat the process.

and then wipe down each cleaned spoke with the paint covered rag. This seems to do a much better job than directly painting each spoke in terms of imitating cad plating, and looks almost identical if done correctly. Keep the paint off the spoke threads, however.

If reusing the same rim, take a wire wheel inside of the rim to remove any built-up surface rust in the rim holes so that each spoke will seat well in its hole. Finally take the cleaned rim, hub and spokes and set them down on the workbench right next to your model or photographs.

All wheel builds require at least a check of the wheel bearings and repacking them with clean grease. If this is an old rusty and unknown wheel, remove the bearings to clean, inspect, repack, or replace them. Many bearings may be upgraded to sealed versions. Most wheel bearings have common dimensions that can be sourced generically. Make sure also that your hub looks good. It's very easy to powder coat, paint and or polish now; almost impossible once the wheel is assembled.

LACING

Having an identical wheel handy for reference makes lacing simple and error-free. You'll want to do one side at a time on a flat surface, putting inside spokes on first and then doing the outer ones. After that, flip the rim and repeat. Make absolutely sure you've first referenced the hub and rim appropriately by checking the marks you made earlier. Once referenced, it's a simple process. Just get each spoke in its hole and run the nipple up with a screwdriver so that it almost touches the rim. You don't want to tighten anything yet. We're just going for correct placement.

Install each spoke type on one side in series. This means that the first spoke in the series will be installed, followed by the next first spoke in the same series. The rim shown being laced in this chapter was a four pattern series, and the first of the pattern was done around the wheel on one side, followed by the second. This is easy if you've marked the rim as mentioned previously.

It's important to remember that the pattern on all wheels repeats. For example, if you have a four-spoke pattern, the correct spoke can be found for the correct hole in the wheel and hub by simply counting 1, 2, 3, 4 and then repeating. All number 2s get the 2 spoke, 3s the 3 spoke and so forth. Just make sure you pull the proper spoke out of the cans you clearly labeled and organized earlier.

ADJUSTING THE RIM

After you have all the spokes in the right holes, place the rim back on your truing stand. It'll be loose and wobbly, but that's okay. Begin to tighten each spoke as equally as you can by eye and feel. Put very little tension on the spokes now because you will want lots of room for adjustment later. Work in sequence and gradually tighten the spokes with about the same turn each until the wheel begins to firm up. Now we go for our tools.

Position the runout tool as shown in the photos and spin the wheel. It'll have a lot of side to side and up and down movement, and that's okay. Now get your locked offset tool and position it on the wheel. What you find now will dictate the next move.

You have two options. You can find the closest place laterally on the rim and bring the rest of the rim up to it, or the farthest place from the offset tool and move the rest of the rim over to match it. The direction you go in will depend on the offset. If you need more offset tighten the spokes on the opposite side of the rim from the hub to pull the rim away from the drum. If you need less, work on the other side. Take your time and just go quarter- or half-turns on the spokes and keep checking both measuring tools as you go. When things firm up a bit more, put the runout tool as close to the rim as you can so that it scrapes on the closest spots radially and laterally, permitting the use of both seeing and hearing.

Remember to keep track of both radial and lateral movement as you work. Start by finding the highest point of the rim, and bringing that point down some by tightening the spokes on both sides of the rim at and around the high point. Again, adjust your tool so that it just barely scrapes on the highest spots and adjust as necessary.

Generally, beginners will have to dink around

Once the spokes are laced about finger tight onto the rim, it's time to put the rim on the stand as shown to begin truing it. Tilt the stand slightly so that the wheel maintains a consistent lateral position and does not fall off the axle.

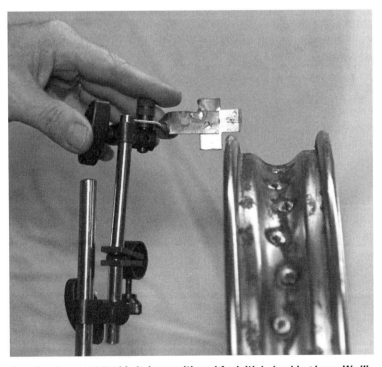

Our simple runout tool is being positioned for initial checking here. We'll move it closer soon so that it gently scrapes the high/close spots as the wheel is rotated.

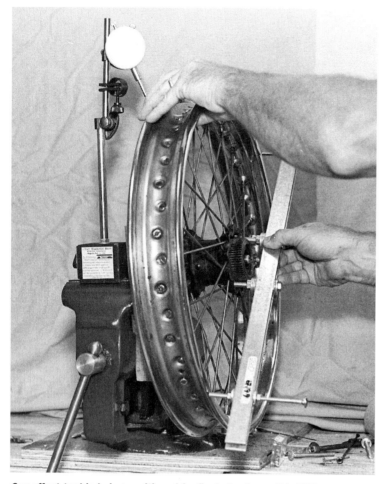

Our offest tool is being positioned for final checks on this BSA rear wheel. It is almost done now.

Fine adjustment of radial runout is being done here on a twin-leading-shoe Triumph wheel that needed only a bit of correction.

with the spokes for quite a while, but eventually it'll be possible to adjust the rim until runout is within tolerable specs. With a used rim, don't expect perfection, just get as close and you can. You may find the spokes become tight but you still have unacceptable runout. Don't play Hercules here; you'll only break a spoke. You may well have to loosen the whole wheel and start over, but you can loosen opposing spokes and gain working room too.

Eyeballs are very helpful. If you can see the rim jump up and down, it has too much radial runout. If it wobbles side to side, too much lateral runout. If it looks good both ways, you're pretty darn close and probably better than most older spoke rims on the road now.

Finally, you'll want to tighten the spokes as evenly as possible to about 40 to 70 inch-pounds, depending on spoke type; the upper limit is for stainless that requires tighter specs. Always ask for specs like torque when you buy new spokes as this varies a lot based on manufacturer and composition. Also with stainless, it's necessary to use anti-seize compound to prevent galling. It's a good idea to use anti-seize with steel spokes as well. Just dip the threads in the compound before you lace the rim. If you can't get specs, go with 40 inch-pounds for plated brass nipples, 70 for stainless.

If you're wondering how to measure torque, it's pretty easy. Some wheel shops use a special spoke torque wrench, but you can get by with a pull type fishing scale on the end of your wrench. Measure the distance across the wrench from the spoke nipple to the scale in inches, and multiply that by the number of pounds reading on the scale as you pull on it. For example, if the distance is three inches and the scale reads 10 pounds, multiply the 10 x 3 to get 30 inch-pounds.

If you try to do this for each spoke, you'll go nuts. Most people just get one or two right and go by feel and sound after that. Hit the spoke you measured with a light wrench and listen to the ring. Tighten and ring as you go around the wheel.

Before final tightening of the spokes, remove the homemade measuring tool and measure runout with a dial indicator. A feeler gauge can be used with the homemade tool too. Either way, make final adjustments as necessary. A lot of good wheel builders, though, don't even use the indicator and rely more on eye and feel. With a dial indicator and new rim, you get really close, right down to a few thousandths of an inch. It will never be perfectly true, however, because there's always a jump where the rim was welded when manufactured.

Another good use for a dial indicator is to check the brake drum after lacing. If it's out-of-round after truing, you'll have to get it turned at a machine shop that does this sort of work.

At this point we're nearly through. All we need to do now is grind off any spoke ends that protrude past its nipple. Don't grind into the nipple; just make sure the spoke is flush with it so you won't puncture a tube.

Now we can install a new rim strip and tire. Plain old duct tape substitutes fine as a rim strip. Tire alternatives would need a book unto itself. Much depends on intended service use, but make darn sure whatever tire you use is in good shape and accompanied by a new tube.

Finally, set your wheel stand up with the tire attached, or you can even wait and do this on the bike. You'll have to balance the front wheel at least, and many guys do both front and rear wheels.

To balance a wheel, make sure the axle is parallel to the ground and then spin the wheel. Use a small piece of chalk to mark the bottom point where the tire stops and do this several times to be sure you've actually found the heavy side. Once this is known, go to the opposite side of the rim and attach weight to a spoke. Solid core solder is very easy to wrap around a spoke and has been used for years as balance weight, but commercial weights are available too.

Regardless of what you use for weight, experiment until you find the proper counterbalance. You'll know this is achieved when spinning the rim causes the wheel to stop in different places randomly.

Whew, that was a lot of work, huh? Next time it'll be easier, and progressively so the more you practice motorcycle's version of Truth or Consequences.

► RECOVERING BENT RIMS

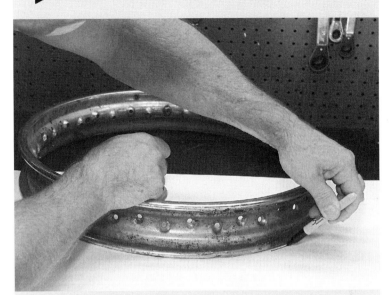

If you have a steel rim with good chrome but it has a flat spot caused by some sort of collision or pothole, it's possible to get it back into usable shape with this old school method. First of all, make a template of the good part of the rim (upper photo). Trace the rim with a sharpie marker as shown onto a piece of cardboard. Next, you can either cut a template with a razor knife using the line as a guide or just use the line itself behind the rim as a guide. Either way, you want to bend out the flat spot until it follows the template or line. To bend the rim, support it between two blocks of wood as shown (lower photo) and apply force to the rim with a soft heavy hammer made with lead shot that is covered in rubber. A hard hammer can also be employed if the rim is protected from damage with a block of wood.

11 *Shocking Revelations*

OVERVIEW

Among the best components of your old Brit twin are the Girling shocks. These units were vastly superior to the period competition, so much so that racers competing on Oriental bikes often ditched their stock shocks in favor of Girling units. The Girling company was bought out by Alf Hagon, who manufactures units today almost identical in appearance and quality. Inexpensive replacements are available from YSS, a Thailand company that produces a pretty good product for the budget-minded. Aside from simple adjustment, the manuals don't say much about shocks, and in this case, it makes sense because they're sealed units and really can't be rebuilt economically. You can, however, make an old one look almost new, so we'll concentrate our efforts here.

SPRING REMOVAL

If you aren't a strongman, you'll need a partner to help remove and install the spring. Before you do this make sure the adjuster is set at the lowest setting to ease installation and removal. Adjustment is made by turning the ring at the base of the shock. If you don't have a shock adjusting tool, a large vise grip works well. Just wrap the shock in a rag first to keep from marring the surface. If you do nick it up a bit after painting, just retouch the small scrapes on the shock with a little black paint applied with a small hobby brush.

To remove the spring, one set of hands has to pull down on the spring while another set pulls out the two keepers. Installation is simply the reverse. If you're hunting for used shocks, always remove the springs to check for operation as you really can't tell much with the spring in place.

Once the spring has been removed, push and pull on the shock to test for strong and smooth hydraulic resistance. Also, inspect the shaft that goes into the shock itself for rust and pitting. Finally, inspect the eyes for a tight fitting rubber bushing. These can be replaced, but if the rubber's shot, it's likely the rest of the shock is too.

COSMETICS

Everything okay? Cool, let's pretty her up a bit. Clean the shocks, springs, and keepers and then sand the shock and keepers prior to painting.

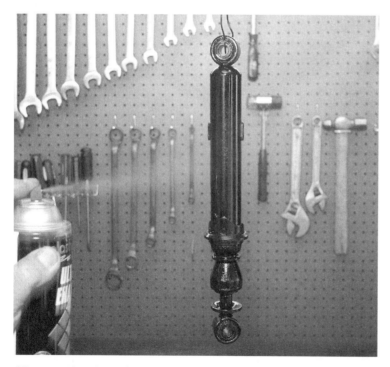

After removing the spring, the shock can be tested for hydraulic action and then cleaned and painted as shown.

Cleaning and polishing the inner part of the spring is accomplished by using fine steel wool as shown.

Old- and new-style shocks are shown. The new-style shock in the foreground has been cosmetically restored; it looked worse than the old one before restoration.

Gloss black rattle can enamel works fine, but some builders use wrinkle black paint that does look pretty trick.

Early style covered shocks will also need to have the covers painted. Later models with exposed chrome springs present other issues. If the chrome is pitted and flaking, you're in trouble because rechroming the springs can be almost as expensive as a new shock, so it's not usually a prudent expense. However, if the rust is only on the inside part of the spring, we have a neat corrective trick.

Use steel wool to clean up the inside part of the spring and polish the outside. Next, spray silver paint all over the spring, but right afterwards, use a rag moistened in lacquer thinner to remove the paint on the outside parts of the spring where the chrome is still good, leaving only the rusted inner part of the spring painted. This really looks good if done well.

Once the paint is dry, reinstall the springs and you're good to go! Shocking, ain't it?

Unless you have a spring compressor that fits, removing and installing the shock spring is a team job. Here one person compresses the spring by pulling down on it so that the keepers can be dropped in by the other person.

▶ DAVE QUINN

AVOIDING COMMON PITFALLS WITH SHOCKS

Dave Quinn of Dave Quinn Motorcycles, a leading dealer in Hagon shocks and long-time Brit bike parts dealer and mechanic, was glad to offer his expert advice on how to avoid common errors related to shocks. He said one of the biggest mistakes is over-tightening the shock bolt on installation.

"The shock needs to rotate on the bolt," he explained, "otherwise it's trying to fold itself in half." Another common misperception is blaming the shock spring for a too-stiff ride when in reality this is often caused by too much compression damping. Dave assembles Hagon shocks to order for all Brit twins after completing a detailed build sheet that takes into account rider weight, intended use, and more.

"The really bad voodoo," Dave said, "happens when a shock isn't being used." He said the best way to get long life is to keep the shock in frequent operation. He also cautions against using WD 40 on some shocks as this can attack seals as does rust on the shaft itself.

Only tighten the shock enough to eliminate side play. The shock must be able to rotate on the bolt. Also, take care not to collapse the bushing or bracket on installation.

12 *Tanks A Lot*

OVERVIEW

The shop manuals are mute with respect to tank repair but do contain useful mounting instructions and drawings of brackets and rubber insulating pieces commonly missing on many older Brit projects today. Even with the correct factory mounting parts, vibration cracks on gas tanks plagued both Triumph and BSA and were never fully resolved. Consequently, failing to correctly mount a tank is guaranteed to cause damage eventually. Direct frame-to-tank contact can crack what was a perfectly good tank in as little as 50 miles. The lesson here is to use every mounting part called for if you want your tank repairs to last, or construct your own similar pieces that employ lots of rubber insulation.

It also deserves mention that professionals utilize a great deal of metalworking skill along with special tools and equipment to achieve results that are as good as, if not better than, factory original work. Due to these factors and the time-consuming nature of the process, gas tank restoration is very expensive to job out. This chapter describes far more affordable procedures that are well within the range of skills possessed by the average home restorer. Certain tanks, however, are best left to professional hands entirely, as many of the following fixes will employ some plastic body filler which will not allow chrome plating as used on many BSA tanks. However, many budget builders choose to paint damaged chrome tanks and these can look really nice if done well.

SAFETY FIRST

For some cycle repairs, if you do them wrong, you just won't be happy with the results. With gas tank repair, if you do it wrong, you can be very dead, very fast. Please don't ever forget this: you are working on a volatile liquid storage container. The reader assumes all responsibility for

the possibilities. As they say down at the lawyer's office, you do the following at your own risk and are solely responsible for the results.

Clean It

Okay, with that warning on the table, if you do decide to use any sort of heat on a gas tank, it must be scrupulously cleaned and flushed first. Use a strong detergent and lots of water pressure to flush the tank after the petcocks have been removed. Afterwards, let the tank sit until it's perfectly dry. Although it seems redundant, flush it again and allow for a second drying. If the interior has been plastic coated, the coating must be removed before the multiple flushing. Acetone or MEK will remove most commercial coatings. Caustic soda is also used to remove tank coatings.

One of the easiest ways to flush any given tank is at a high-pressure car wash. Use the soap setting for this. If you have a pressure washer, this is good too. Having a radiator shop boil out the tank before repair is also highly recommended. Many pros do all this and then use inert gas inside the tank to prevent explosion while they work.

Ventilate It!

All repairs requiring heat on fuel tanks discussed here were done with the petcocks removed and the gas cap off to prevent pressure buildup inside the tank.

EVALUATING A USED TANK

To begin we must decide whether or not to work on an old tank or buy a good replacement. Either way, the following should help you determine whether to buy a prospective tank or fix the one you have.

Factory stock paint on a used tank is good news. This will almost always mean that no repair work has been done and there aren't 50 pounds of Bondo hidden somewhere. A tank stripped down to bare metal is also a good prospect as it's much easier to evaluate. Small chips and dings are easy fixes; damage more than a 1/4 inch deep will require a lot more work and this should be considered in your analysis.

You can check for plastic filler on a painted steel tank easily with a magnet wrapped in a clean cloth. Slide the magnet over the tank. When filler is encountered, you'll feel little or no pull.

If the tank meets your standards so far, pop the gas cap and take a good look inside using a flashlight. Almost all old tanks will have some light surface rust, but an accumulation of fine powder at the base of the tank should raise concerns. Big rusty pieces of loose rust are very bad news. Both of these conditions indicate a serious rust problem.

With a tank showing lots of rust, use a small nail to check the bottom. Poke it around all over. With a rusty piece of junk, before you get too far you'll poke right through the tank. If this doesn't happen, you most likely have enough good steel to work with. If you do poke through, walk away unless you have no other alternative.

Of course, gas tanks shouldn't leak, but you can't tell without testing. Assume the tank does leak unless you can prove otherwise. Remember, gas is thinner than water, so just because a tank holds water, do not assume it won't leak gas. Kerosene is a good test fluid.

PRESSURE TESTING

A great way to pinpoint leaks is to pressurize the tank. But speaking of pressurizing, forget about using high air pressure to pop out dents. It won't work. Same goes for filling a tank with water and freezing it; you'll just rupture the seams or otherwise deform the tank. You only need moderate pressure—I use 20 psi—introduced to the tank most easily through the petcock hole (most air hoses have the same thread pattern and will screw right in) or through the petcock itself by rigging up a connection with fuel line and a couple of hose clamps.

Block the second petcock hole and tighten the gas cap. It will leak some around the cap because it's designed to vent, but that's okay. Make sure you have the compressor regulator set to maintain constant but moderate pressure inside the tank.

Locate a bucket and small paintbrush. In the bucket put a 50/50 mixture of dish soap and water. Now use the brush all over the tank and pay especially close attention to any welded seam and all over the bottom of the tank where most rust holes occur. Even tiny leaks will be easy to locate as they will produce soap bubbles.

At this point you can either mark the areas needing repair and skip to the Cheap Trix section, or just mentally note the problems. In either case, a second test will be done after working on the tank to ensure that new leaks didn't spring up during repair work.

If your tank passed all the above tests, you have a pretty good one. If not, let's go about fixing common problems.

TAKE IT OFF—TAKE IT ALL OFF

A good pro always strips the tank down to bare metal because he can't afford surprises on a top-dollar paint job. Sand or glass-bead blasting works great to remove paint and old filler. Chemical paint strippers work too but involve extremely nasty chemistry that can leave a film if not carefully cleaned afterward. The residual film left by chemical stripping has been known to damage new paint.

This tank makes the best case I have seen for going down to bare metal. I found evidence of six different repairs, one of which started leaking again. It's a mess, but fixable. One previous repair job on the holding studs will have to be removed by cutting the bracket with the tool shown. Then I'll be able to get to the leak. Note that it's been marked with a Sharpie marker, a good tool to use when pinpointing problems. There was a time when I'd pitch a tank like this, but with skyrocketing prices for original old tanks, it's prudent to try to fix even the rough ones if there's enough good metal left.

OUTER DAMAGE REPAIR

Dents more than a quarter-inch in depth must be worked out of the tank if a long service life is expected. Beware of the swap meet hustlers and eBay crooks who don't care how long a repair holds and just want to make a fast buck. These guys will fill huge dents with layers of thick Bondo. Then they'll do a quick sanding job over the half-assed repair and hit the tank with a coat of cheap primer. Finally, they'll hang a sign on the tank saying "Ready for Your Paint." I know a guy who bought one of these and fuel capacity was reduced by more than half a gallon because of all the space taken up by dents! Even without the loss of fuel capacity, too thick filler will soon shrink and/or crack and ruin a good paint job. Conversely, properly used filler will generally outlast the paint job and need not be feared or considered a shoddy repair.

The basic problem with gas tank dents is that there's no easy way to get behind the dent to knock it back into shape as one would with something like a fender. Many times, the only way to get access to the dent is to cut a section out of the tank. Some pros use curved hammers to good effect, but these methods require quite bit of metalworking skill. If you're up to this, go for it. If not, here's a much easier alternative: pull the dent from outside the tank.

Pull It

Pulling a tank dent is relatively simple and only requires one specialized tool: an inexpensive slap hammer/puller. You can find one for about five bucks at almost any auto parts store. You'll also need a means for attaching the puller to the dent. A commercial tool that spot welds a special device to pull on is available, and if you have the skills and welding tools, this is a great option. Any small spot weld will work fine too if you have the tools and talent.

We'll use an old school tool, an extremely versatile piece of shop equipment and one many hobbyists already have around, an acetylene welding torch. With it we'll employ brass; it's amazingly strong but melts well before steel does.

If you haven't been around brass much, practicing on an old tank or piece of sheet metal is

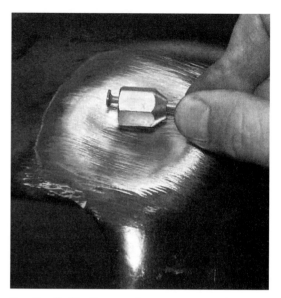

Small nails like these make great anchors for a deep dent. This one was caused by a fork tube, fairly common damage in old tanks.

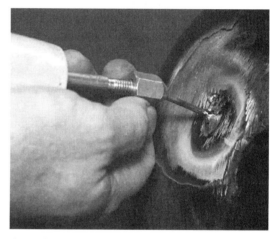

Our nail anchor is brazed to the bottom of the dent and then attached to the slap hammer.

highly advisable. The idea is to get the tank hot enough to flow brass, but not so hot that it burns though steel. This gets pretty easy with a bit of practice, and even if you do actually burn though the tank, the hole will be at the bottom of the dent being pulled and easy to fill with brass rod.

To pull a dent, first analyze the damage, as you will want to employ reverse force much as it was first used to damage the metal. Lots of objects sit around most shops that will make suitable anchors to attach to the puller tool, such as screws, nails, small bolts, etc.

The easiest way to place an anchor in initial position is to have a helper hold it with pliers while you lay down a spot of brass or weld to keep it in place. Several large hose clamps put together and placed around the tank will also serve to position anchors prior to attachment if a helper isn't available.

Once your puller is secure, concentrate the torch heat on the thicker part first, usually the anchor, and then move the torch a bit to the tank area and then back again to anchor. You don't have to flow a lot of brass; look at the pictures to get an idea. Use as little heat as possible to minimize metal distortion.

Once the puller is secured, attach the slap hammer and hold the tank securely while you work the weight briskly back against the tool handle. Don't be afraid to use a good deal of force; you'll need it to pull out the metal, and the brass will hold. Speaking of force, don't try to use the dent pullers sold down at the local auto parts store to pull old Brit cycle tank dents. These tools are designed for use on modern, super-thin sheet metal and do not have the metal pulling power to work on thicker steel.

Continue to work your pulling tool until the dent is less than a quarter inch at it's deepest, but don't be afraid to pull too far, either, because high spots can be lowered with a few moderate shots with a body hammer.

When the dent is pulled to your satisfaction, you can remove the brazed-on anchor. To do so, grip the anchor with a pair of locking pliers while you heat the brass. Very soon it will become plastic and you can just bend the anchor and then pull it right off. At this time you can puddle the leftover brass so it's easily covered with filler. Small anchors are easy to just cut off and then grind smooth if you don't want to reheat the tank.

Welding/Brazing/Soldering

Unfortunately, many older tanks are so far gone that they can't be repaired by conventional sealers. The best way to proceed with these cases is to remove any bad metal and then weld the leak area completely. A good weld restores the damaged tank area to better than new. Really bad tanks can require entire sections to be welded into the tank.

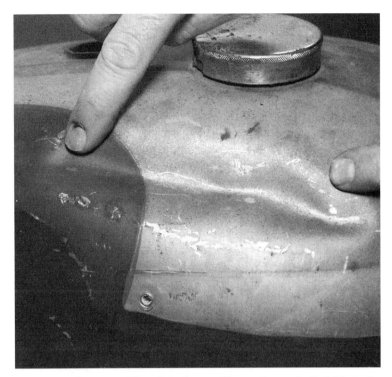

There's good news and there's bad news. The good news is that this tank is wearing stock paint, so we shouldn't have any hidden surprises. The bad news is that this nasty dent is way too deep for filler. We have to knock it out from the inside or pull it from the outside. We'll pull this one.

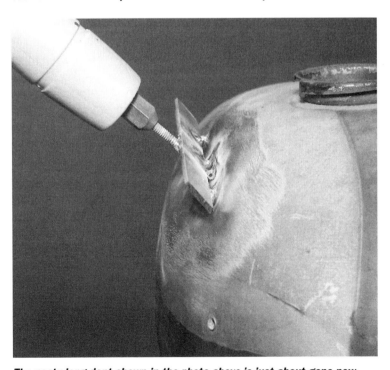

The nasty long dent shown in the photo above is just about gone now. We have a few more shots and then we'll remove our anchor. In this instance, we used a piece of bar stock attached at the lowest points of a long dent. Next, we'll heat the brass and pull off the anchor.

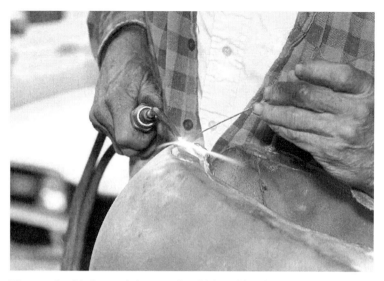

The very best hole repair is a good weld, but this takes exceptional skill and good equipment. In our case, there was too much old brass from a previous repair to get a weld to take, so we went back to brass.

Quite frankly, welding sheet metal without destroying it is an acquired art that takes a great deal of practice to acquire. I learned by practicing on junk tanks until I felt comfortable enough to try one for real.

Brazing is a bit easier than welding because the temperatures are lower and the likelihood of burning through the tank is decreased. Brass is also a lot easier to shape and grind if a final finish is needed in an exposed area. Fortunately, most leaks are on the underside of a tank no one will see, so perfection grinding isn't necessary.

To fill a hole, either with steel or brass, you have to make concentric circles around the hole, each one progressively smaller until the entire hole is filled. Make sure you've removed all bad metal around the hole before welding or brazing.

A tank can be soldered, too, but I don't like to use this in a stress area, and the heat required isn't all that much less than with brass. Several kinds of solder are used on tanks. Silver solder, frequently used in boiler construction, is high strength but expensive. It can be very useful where brass has been used before but the repair still leaks. Solder with a high tin content, like that commonly used for radiator repair, can also be used to good effect.

For both brass and solder, the idea is to get the base metal hot enough so that the rod metal flows smoothly. If it balls up, you aren't using enough heat. Both solder and brass require flux and absolutely clean metal surfaces. The smallest amount of contaminant, like an oil smear for example, will cause a poor bond and a failed leak repair.

RUST BUSTIN'

Rust is like cancer and needs to be treated with the same degree of vigor. If it isn't, you'll soon be having the Rusty Mess Blues all over again, either in the form of leaks, bubbling paint, or both. And like cancer, rust is often terminal if left to go too far.

Gas tanks present special problems because the rust can be located in areas impossible to reach by most conventional means. On the exterior, rust removal is easy and media blasting is the best way to remove all of it.

Internal rust presents a bigger problem. The first task is to loosen what you can and remove it before further treatment. Pieces of chain, nuts and bolts, small rocks, etc. can be placed in the tank and shaken around. Some recommend marbles to prevent stray sparks, but you should always completely clean any tank before working on it anyway as explained earlier, so there's nothing flammable to ignite. Doing your dent pulling and welding before final rust treatment also aids in the process as all the heat and pounding helps loosen up the crud inside.

Chemical Rust Conversion

Once you've removed all loose rust, you can neutralize what's left. The most common method is to use one of many commercial solutions according to the manufacturer's directions. The least expensive ones are available at stores specializing in paint and auto body supplies. The most expensive are part of tank coating kits. Message: Just buy the tank coating separately and get the rust converter elsewhere. Por-15 and Eastwood's Fast Etch are commonly used rust converters and readily available. Chemical conversion is the quickest and easiest rust treatment, hence it's most commonly used. In most cases, you dilute the rust converter, a mild acid, and then either brush it on the external surface, or let it soak inside the tank. The amount of time

This oil-in-frame tank was seriously rusted inside. Here it is undergoing electrolysis to convert residual rust and loosen some we may have missed with the nuts and bolts treatment. See text and next photo for details.

it takes depends on the solution used and the amount of rust in or on the tank.

Electrolytic Rust Conversion

If you have a small battery charger, for about two bucks you can use electrolysis to kill and convert rust. Electrolysis actually turns the rust process backwards and does not remove any good metal as blasting and sanding can. It is both a chemical and electrical process, sort of like plating in reverse. Electrolysis has a second advantage over purely chemical processes in that it works from inside out and will actually loosen rust that's almost impossible to get to otherwise. The electrolysis process creates many tiny bubbles and these dislodge loose rust. Consequently, I use this as the second step in the treatment process. Once I remove as much rust as I can with the chain/bolts method, I let electrolysis go to work. After 24 hours, I drain the tank, and again work to remove the rust loosened by the electrolysis before flushing and then treating what might be left with a chemical converter. This may be overdoing it, but I find the multi-pronged attack works extremely well.

To use electrolysis, you'll need a small box of washing soda; you can get it at most big grocery stores and it's commonly marketed by Arm and Hammer. If you can't find washing soda, you can convert regular baking soda into washing soda by spreading the baking soda out on a

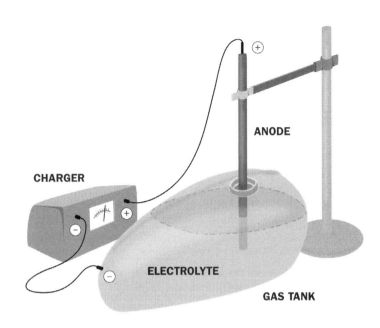

Set your electrolysis connections as shown in this diagram; the positive terminal is attached to the electrode inside the tank and the negative terminal is attached to the tank.

cookie sheet and baking it in an oven at 300 degrees F for an hour. To make a rust solution—actually an electrolyte—use one tablespoon of washing soda for each gallon of tank capacity. Block the petcock holes and fill the tank right up to the filler neck with this mixture so that all inside metal is covered with the water/soda solution.

Next, construct a simple electrode out of just about anything steel, a large washer, piece of flat bar stock, etc. Just be sure it's small enough to fit into the tank filler neck. *Do not use stainless steel as it makes the solution toxic.*

Connect a wire to this setup and be sure it is insulated above the electrode because you don't want the wire to short out against the tank. Suspend the electrode inside the tank and be sure it does not touch any part of the tank. Connect the electrode wire to the positive side of the battery charger. Connect the negative side to the tank, an easy place being to the metal plug you used to block off the petcock holes.

Shortly after turning on the charger, you'll start to see bubbles form and these will soon take on a brown cast, which is rust that's been lifted from the tank. No poisonous gasses are given off in this process—another benefit. However, hydrogen gas is a byproduct, so do this in a well-ventilated area free of open flames. Periodically, it helps to clean off the electrode to get peak efficiency. Just how long the complete rust transformation process takes depends on the size of the tank, amperage used, and the severity of the rust problem. A three-amp charger was used for the process detailed here; it worked at about one amp. The process is also self-limiting and will stop once the conversion is complete, so careful monitoring isn't necessary. I usually set this up and let it run overnight.

Once rust is converted, it leaves a glossy blackish surface very suitable for coating or painting. With either the chemical or electro-chemical process, you'll have to remove all water/moisture and immediately treat with either acetone or MEK. Both of these destroy paint quickly, so either cover the tank with thick plastic or do all of this work prior to painting, the wisest method.

Right after the acetone treatment, it's time to seal-coat the tank. If you followed these directions, you have an ideal surface for the sealant.

TANK COATING

Coating with a commercial sealant is simple once the rust has been removed. Step one requires a wash in acetone to remove any traces of water and to prepare the surface for good adhesion of the sealant. This process will require sealing the tank opening and petcock holes and also inverting the tank, and this will invariably cause some fluid to leak around the filler hole onto the outer surface of the tank. Should you be working on a tank that has good paint, you can avoid damaging it by wrapping the tank carefully in thick plastic that's at least twice the thickness of conventional garbage bags. The really thick bags used by contractors to haul waste make excellent tank protectors. Also, make a gasket of plastic for the gas cap and secure the gas cap over the gasket and tank opening. This area will leak a little when inverting the tank but the small drips will fall harmlessly on the plastic covering the tank, and not on a painted surface. Drain the acetone through the petcock holes and then again plug the arrangement.

After the acetone treatment, repeat the process with the sealer. Make sure you turn the tank in all directions so that the sealant covers everything inside. Afterwards, drain the sealant into a clean receptacle, because you can reuse it for at least one more tank instead of wasting it. Remove the gas cap and blocking plugs and let the coating dry for 24 hours at least, maybe longer, depending on temperature. When the sealant is completely dry, remove the plastic mask if you used one. That's it!

As for sealant, I've used Kreme for years and it's yet to fail in service. Most coating failures I'm familiar with were caused by poor surface preparation and not the respective sealant used.

EXTERIOR SURFACE PREPARATION AND PAINTING

While I do not personally know anyone who's been seriously injured working on a gas tank, I can't say the same for painting. Modern paints contain a number of very nasty chemicals, isocyanates topping the list. Isocyanates are close cousins to cyanide, a deadly poison, and are used in two-part paints, the kind that requires a catalyst to cure. These paints are now used more often than any other paint due to the relative ease of application and extremely durable finish. While the paint may be durable, I'm not so sure about the painters. I know several who have serious respiratory problems attributed to isocyanate exposure.

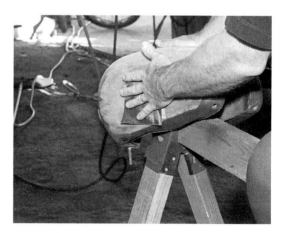

Primer is being hand-sanded, a tedious but most important part of the painting process. If the base surface isn't perfect, the final paint job will be disappointing.

Official industry standards call for only positive ventilation masks and fully protective suits when working with isocaynate paints, yet many painters still use only cartridge masks, and I confess this is what I used too when I worked with two-part paint. But after seeing what this paint did to people I know, I can't recommend using it and consequently, I won't tell you how, because in the great majority of cases you won't have access to the proper breathing apparatus and would be tempted, as I was, to take risks. In good conscience I can't encourage this. Let's instead cover what can be done safely in the average home garage.

Sandpaper and Elbow Grease

Poor prep work will cause a most disappointing final finish after hours of labor restoring an old tank. This is highly ironic because as far as skill goes, preparing a surface to paint is one of the easiest processes to get right or to correct if it isn't. However, surface preparation is labor intensive and fairly boring, and that's exactly why people frequently rush through it, and wish later they hadn't.

Refinishing a tank when it's down to bare metal is the best way, but if the original surface isn't rusted, it's okay to leave some old paint, providing it's still securely adhered to the tank. Just be sure there's no evidence of peeling, flaking, or rust bubbles.

First, you will need to complete all filler work as this has to be finished before the overall tank sanding so that everything blends in.

Next, the entire surface must be sanded carefully with progressively finer sandpaper. How fine to start with depends on the surface being worked and the paint used, but with lots of cruddy old tanks I begin with a grit of around 120 and then go to 240, which gives a good surface for most primers.

Body Filler

Let's talk a bit about filler now and please understand this is also a hotly debated subject. Feel free to get a "second opinion" as they say.

Good auto body filler today is light years better than a lot of junk used in the past that gave easy-to-use fillers a bad name. That being

It pays to watch a pro work. Here, John begins masking this BSA tank for painting. Note how he holds the tape in his right hand. This way his hand works like a dispenser, making the job easier and more accurate.

said, there's still a lot of cheap filler mass marketed, so to find out what works, check with a pro and use the same stuff. Pick up some spot putty at the same time that's recommended for use with the filler.

Even the right filler won't work well if it isn't mixed correctly. If you use too much catalyst the filler will be prone to cracking and hard to work. Just a little bit will do. Practice with it before tackling your real project.

Filler should be spread in one direction only in thin layers to avoid air pockets. Once it begins to set up you can use a body file to rough shape it. Coarse sandpaper works well too and is easier to use on rounded tank surfaces.

Once the shape is just about right, go down to finer sandpaper, ending with 240 grit. I like to check filler with a shot of fast-drying rattle can red oxide primer and then take a close look. The filler should be invisible and seamless. If you do see any outline or imperfect surface, you've got more sanding to do. Conversely, if you have dark spots, that generally means a low area that needs more filler. Tiny pinholes can be filled with spot

This homemade tank holder makes painting a lot easier than using an old saw horse. Part can be rotated during the job for better vision and gun control. All you need to make your own is a couple of pieces of pipe in two different diameters, a piece of all-thread and a nut. Form a T out of the larger diameter pipe, and then drill a hole in the upper part. Next, weld a nut over the hole and make a T-handle out of the all-thread to screw into the nut to hold the cross pipe in place or loosen it to change the position of the cross pipe.

putty. Continue this process of filling, sanding, inspecting, and spot patching until you achieve perfection, and this you must, because if you can see any irregularity through the primer, it will be magnified a hundred times, it seems, by the final coat. Don't kid yourself otherwise. Once things look perfect with filler, it's time for one more sanding, this time with 400 grit wet/dry paper. Finer grits are sometimes employed depending on the paint used, and there are many opinions as to just what's right. Ask for recommendations where automotive/motorcycle paint is applied or sold.

Painting Options

Earl Schieb and many other discount paint shops may be the best option for budget builders today. Most will be willing to shoot your tank and other parts inexpensively and the final product—in 99 out of 100 cases—will be much better than what an inexperienced hand would produce. Shop your parts around and get esti-

mates after you complete interior and exterior surface preparations. Be advised, however, that a lot of very good painters won't work this way because they won't trust your surface preparation and they have a reputation to protect. Some, however, will take your job so it doesn't hurt to ask.

You might have noticed the pictures of my friend John Rorerich, a custom pro painter doing me a favor by painting a chrome BSA tank. This was done outdoors ten years ago when it was still legal in Texas to sell lacquer paint. Lacquer is a very forgiving paint and not nearly as toxic as two-part systems. It can be safely applied using a conventional cartridge mask. A second major advantage is an extremely rapid drying time. Actually, if it isn't mixed right, lacquer will dry as it shoots out of the gun! Lacquer makes outdoor and home garage painting very possible. Alas, those days are over for many.

You can, however, still get lacquer in some states and in aerosol cans in most. I've seen some surprisingly good jobs done the rattle can way, although this too takes some practice. If you don't have equipment or cash, this may be your only option, so let's end with this.

As with all painting, you must have a perfect surface to get a decent job. Sandable red oxide primer is readily available and easy to use. Apply the primer, sand with 220 paper, and continue the process of application and sanding until the surface is perfectly smooth and seamless. Apply the color coat over the primed surface and then let it dry completely. Once it has, lacquer requires color sanding with 400 grit paper gently to avoid sanding through the color coat. The surface will be dull, but that's okay; the clear coat will bring out the shine. Some folks recommend sanding the clear coat with 600 and then 1200 grit, and this does work, but depending on how well you applied the clear coat, final sanding may not be necessary. Rubbing out the final coat with compound is also common.

I've also seen some admirable jobs done with enamel, and this is still readily available, in both rattle can and for use in a regular or HVLP spray gun. With a rattle can enamel job, however, the paint will be very soft for a long time, like a month, and will scratch if you so much as spit on

Here's a close look at one of our finished products. We can stripe it now or use it as-is. Not too shabby for a garage job, but a paint booth provides a cleaner environment if you can gain access to one.

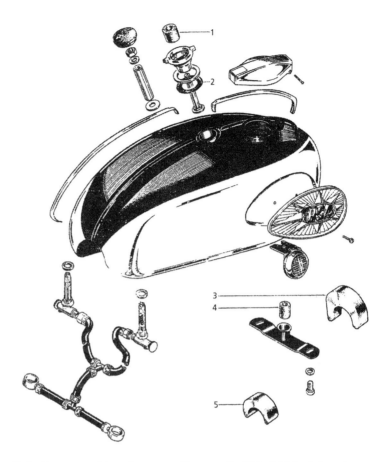

Note the many rubber pieces used in mounting this BSA tank (numbers 1, 2, 3, 4, and 5). Also note the bracket that goes under the tank, also with a rubber bushing. All of these pieces are there for a purpose, mostly to keep the tank from cracking due to vibration. All Brit twin tanks use similar fittings. While not completely effective, both BSA and Triumph fought the cracking issue for years, mounting a tank without the correct hardware or replacements made in imitation, almost assures the tank will soon fail in service. (Illustration used by permission and courtesy of BSA Regal Group Ltd.)

it before it fully cures. Lacquer also takes a long time to fully cure. Even the best two-part paint today can be damaged by today's gas, so be very careful at the pump. If you are, that great paint job will last for years.

CHEAP TRIX

Maybe you're in a hurry and/or don't have the skills for some of these processes. In this case, epoxy is your best friend. I've had epoxy leak repair jobs last for ten years, so I have no reservations about its use if applied correctly and the circumstances dictate this method. Correct epoxy application requires bare, rust-free metal and a clean surface around the leak area. Once this condition is met, mix the epoxy and push it into the leak area. Allow the epoxy to dry overnight before sanding smooth. You must also rust treat your tank as previously described and carefully prepare the exterior for paint.

13

Those Anal Amals: Bringing the Concentric Carburetor Back to Life

OVERVIEW

Damn those Amals. Sound familiar? I'll bet it does, because these may be the most cursed carburetors on the planet. The main problem with both concentric and monoblock carburetors is the zinc/aluminum alloy from which they are manufactured. This relatively soft alloy causes several problems. One is rapid slide-to-body wear caused by use of the same metal up against itself in the slide and body. Once worn to a significant degree (and we will get into these particulars soon), there is no way in creation to make the Amal idle properly.

Another direct problem caused by the soft alloy is the tendency for the carburetor to warp, either in the body, causing the nasty habit of sticking at open throttle, or at the flange where all sorts of evil running problems can occur. Then we have warping of the float bowl that can cause the poor Amal to urinate high test all over the engine and subsequently piss off the owner who runs out and buys a set of Mikunis.

While the Mikuni is a fine carburetor and is competitively priced, it's extremely important to understand that it has several distinct liabilities when used as alternative equipment. For one, it just won't fit right on lots of applications originally designed to run Amals. And if you think tinkering around with Amals can be frustrating, try it on a set of Mikunis. These have a huge assortment of jets, needles, and slides and setting them up correctly requires considerable expertise. If you're a super tuner and/or into racing and want the most horsepower possible, then the Mikuni may well be the carburetor for you. For many of us, though, the simple Amal can be a lot easier to live with, and often dirt cheap to pick up

in rebuildable condition. The lowly low-buck Amal carb begins to look a lot better in this light.

A newcomer to the field, a version of the PWK Keihin, is currently available for Triumph and BSA use. It's fitted with a flange that allows a direct bolt-on application. Reports on these have been most positive and the price, about $225 for a pair as of this writing, makes them worth considering for budget builders who find terminal issues with their Amal carburetors.

The shop manual and parts books contains excellent exploded diagrams that list each part and orient these to their respective location on the carburetor. Since you need to know the names of the players before you get into the game, familiarize yourself with the diagrams and parts list. The manual also contains a pretty good section on fault finding, instructions for dismantling and assembly, and a clear description of operation. What's totally missing, however, is how to repair and remedy the most common problems associated with age and wear, so this is where I'll focus needed attention.

EVALUATION AND INSPECTION

Our first step is to separate carburetors with rebuild possibilities from those that are either terminal or much more expensive to fix. The most expensive proposition is repairing a worn slide/body combination. This is a specialist's job, and there are a number of concerns that can perform this task. What they do is rebore the carb body to remove problems caused by wear and then install a steel or chrome-plated brass sleeve on the slide. This repair makes the slide-to-body arrangement better than new, and what is often misunderstood is the advantage of this repair as opposed to just buying a new carburetor.

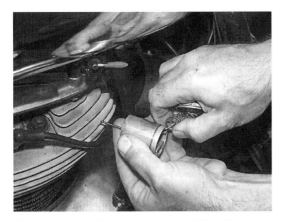

Once you take off the two screws holding the top cover of the carburetor, pull back and hold the return spring and then invert the slide as shown so that the needle and clip fall out. After that, compress the spring even more to get the cable out by pushing it out of its hole and into the larger one in the slide where the needle rests. This spring can be held back against the top cover with a small vise grip to aid removal and installation of these parts.

The 900 series slide at left shows signs of light seizing but wasn't badly worn and is reusable. The smaller 600 series slide at right, however, has worn the guide block almost into a point and can't be reused as-is, but it is repairable by specialist work as part of the sleeving process.

A well-sleeved carburetor will generally out-last a new one by about twice the service time. For example, it's common to find Amals fully worn at the slide/body area after less than 10,000 miles, while many sleeved Amals are performing perfectly after well over 20,000. Of course, service life involves many variables. Regardless, a sleeve job can make your Amal better than new, barring other problems.

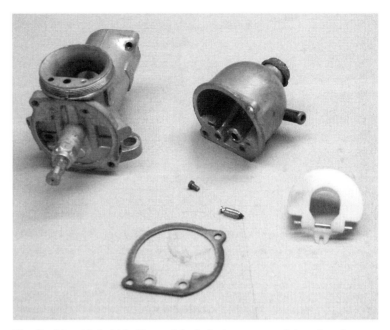

The float bowl is held to the carb body by two screws. Internal parts are shown, along with the external pilot jet taken from the body that some of these carburetors will have. Note the float needle in the center. This is a Vinton tipped float needle, far superior to the stock plastic needle and a good upgrade during any rebuild.

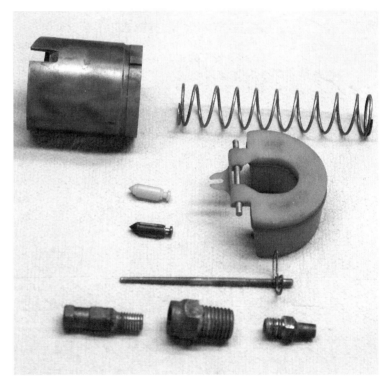

Pictured here are the major internal carburetor components: the throttle slide and its return spring are at top; below it are the float and two types of float needles; below that are the main needle jet and its associated jet components.

This sort of corrosion is terminal cancer to a carburetor. It was caused by water that crept in on a bike that sat outdoors unattended. There is no way to fix this; the carburator is junk.

SEVERE CORROSION

Severe corrosion is also the kiss of death. If taking apart the carb reveals a great deal of fine white powder (see photo) and much evidence of pitting, the carb body, at least, is junk.

When an old carburetor is left to the elements, either on or off the bike, it can become filled with water. This can also happen if the bike is flooded in a natural disaster or accidentally submerged in water. Gasoline in the carburetor that dried out during the Carter administration can have similar effect.

If water is allowed to sit inside the carburetor for any length of time and then dries, extreme corrosion sets in. The easiest way to detect this is to inspect the float bowl. If it's filled with white powder, this is extreme oxidation. While you can remove most of it in the bowl, it probably exists inside the various passages in the carb body. Check the body where the pilot passage is located. If this area is white and flaky too, it's trouble. It is very difficult to clean this junk out completely, and once oxidation sets in, it also creates pitting which plays further hell, along with tiny pieces of oxidized material letting loose under operation.

If you do accidentally submerge a carburetor in water, completely disassemble it immediately and blow out all passages with air and then WD 40 to remove any remaining water and prevent corrosion. Even waiting a day before doing this can ruin your carburetor.

CLEARANCE CHECKS

To determine whether or not your carb might benefit from sleeving, you must evaluate the slide/body clearance in some way. Here are a few methods:

1. If the carb is still on the bike, raise and lower the slide by twisting the throttle. If you hear a distinct clinking sound, that's often the worn slide hitting against the inside of the body. If it's really bad you can often hear the slides rattle when running.

2. If the bike runs, check for slide sticking. Warm it up on a good ride, but do not use much over half-throttle, unless you like to live dangerously. Once the bike is good and warm, return it to its place of residence and shut it off. Now turn the throttle wide-open and hold it open for about 10 seconds. If a slide sticks, this is an indicator of irregular wear or warpage, both good cases for a sleeve job. It costs about $90 per carburetor for this service, so factor this into your purchase/repair decision. This test must be done with the engine fully warm because a lot of worn slides don't stick when they're cold.

3. If the carb's on the bench, put a finger on the front and back of the slide and try to rock it back and forth. You'll feel only a very slight movement on a good slide/body, but noticeable sloppiness on one that's worn.

4. Grab the entire carburetor and shake it like you would a baby rattle. If it jingles enough to be used in a Christmas carol, it needs sleeving. I'd like to be more descriptive, but this is a very good test if you know what to listen for.

5. It would seem best to measure the slide/body clearance with a feeler gauge. The problem with this is the lack of reliable wear specs and the irregular way these carburetors wear. There are no figures I know of indicating the point of no return for wear. Andy Hardan, who now operates Lund Machine, a well-respected Amal repair and sleeving shop, reports that you can measure a worn Amal and get a lot of different figures depending on measurement location, but the tendency is for worn-out carbs to be tight on top and very loose on the bottom. He added that he has had to bore some out to .060 to correct this problem and that he sets the ones he

repairs to a .005 clearance, a good reference number if one is desired.

If you find a problem with sticking slides but believe the slide/body clearance isn't too bad, you can try fixing this problem yourself as detailed later, but if that doesn't work and/or you still have poor idling issue after freeing the pilot system, it's a sleeve job you need.

PILOT SYSTEM

The second big problem with concentric carburetors, but not the monoblock, is the pilot jet system. The monoblock has a much better pilot system. The concentric was not really an improvement; it was a cost-cutting measure owing to the monoblock design requiring more parts and machine operations to produce. The monoblock is back in production, but it's consequently expensive. A major advantage of the monoblock is the easy accessibility and removal of the pilot jet, but it suffers from the same wear issues as the concentric.

The concentric pilot design problem was further compounded when Amal began using an internal bush to replace the jet that was initially screwed into the bottom of the carburetor body. Lots of books will tell you what year this change was made, but they are often wrong for a number of reasons, ranging from inaccurate information to later modifications by the owner. Consequently, you will have to carefully inspect your carb to determine what you have and what you need.

For example, I've found a few carbs that had both the bush and jet resident, some that had neither. You can usually see the tiny brass bush after the carb is cleaned by focusing light into the pilot air hole after you remove the adjustment screw. Regardless of what is or isn't there, you have to test to see that all fuel/air passages are properly open.

Pilot Check 1

Get a can of spray carburetor cleaner with a plastic spray tube. You can also use a spray can of WD 40. With the carburetor on your workbench, remove all detachable parts and then put the plastic tube into the pilot air adjustment hole so that it fits snugly against the bottom. Next,

The pilot air adjustment screw is removed for all service. Check the seat inside (see text for details); if it is damaged, the carb is junk. Screws can be found on different sides to allow left- or right-hand application.

Check the pilot system by spraying into the air adjustment passage and blocking the air intake hole with a finger as shown. If nothing or very little comes out of the pilot fuel intake passage, the upper right hole in the carburetor base in this photo, you will have to unclog the system. A close view of this location is shown in the photo on the next page. This location may not have a jet and will just be a threaded hole.

place your finger over the smaller hole at the outside mouth of the carburetor where the air cleaner fits. You should see three holes: A big one in the middle, one that's been plugged, and a smaller one on the outside (see bottom photo on page 96). You want to place your finger over the small hole that isn't plugged.

Now spray the cleaner into the pilot air adjustment hole as shown in photo above. You should get three shots of cleaner out of the carb; two of them will be inside at the base, one just inside of the slide and the other just outside of it. Do this test with the slide removed. You can also check

Some concentric carbs will have an external pilot fuel jet, as shown. Concentric carbs may be threaded for a jet, but that does not mean it's required. Many will have an internal bush that replaced the external jet. In either case, this is the location to watch for flow when testing the pilot system. See text for more details.

flow with compressed air by putting your finger inside the body, blocking the small air hole at the opening of the carb and using the air gun up against the pilot air adjustment passage. With 50 pounds of pressure you should feel two strong but fine (these are very small holes) jets of air against your finger. The hole just inside of the throttle slide is the pilot bypass and the one just outside is the pilot outlet.

Most often, these two holes are free, but the same cannot be said for the pilot fuel intake, which as we said, may or may not have a jet screwed into it. Even with carbs utilizing the inside bush, this passage will still be threaded for a jet, so don't be misled. This is actually a good thing as we can use it to our advantage if major surgery is required later to free the pilot system.

After checking the two inside passages, pay close attention to the pilot fuel intake hole (see photo above with external jet installed) and retest. Some tech pieces say a "dribble" of liquid emerging from the hole is sufficient, but this can be completely wrong or misleading. Of course, the amount that comes out is also dependent on how the carburetor is positioned for this test and the amount of spray and pressure used.

Although the photo for this test is shown with the carb on its side, this was to show the test holes clearly. For your actual test, block the hole on the outside of the carb and hold the body as it would be attached on the cycle. Now spray away; you should get a good shot out of the pilot intake passage even in systems with the internal bush. If you don't get anything, or very little, there's some sort of blockage.

Here's a very important message: Do not pay to have a carb sleeved until you've made the pilot system work properly. You'll just be wasting a lot of money! The carburetor will not run right without a properly functioning pilot system; its impact is often under appreciated. This system greatly affects starting, idling, and running at partial throttle at the smaller slide openings where most operation occurs.

Freeing the Pilot System

After stripping down a carb with a blocked pilot system, soak the bare body at least overnight in a can of commercial carb cleaner. The powerful stuff may not be available in your state because of the extremely toxic nature (it comes with almost as many health warnings as an old Russian nuclear device). Read and heed the warnings in the cleaning chapter if you value your health.

However, one last warning is in order. The gallon cans of cleaner often build up considerable pressure when sealed in hotter weather, so always open one with the end away from your eyes and wear goggles even at that. If you happen to be in a region where this product is restricted, there are alternatives. While not as good, lacquer thinner will also work.

After soaking, rinse the body in water and then spray it down with WD 40. Before retesting, spray compressed air through all passages, and be careful not to accidentally spray something into your eyes. Use safety goggles to protect your eyes.

With a little luck, you have free passages now. Unfortunately, the pilot system may still be jammed up.

Our next trick is manual cleaning, something many tech books tell you never to do. Disregard this. You can clean jets and free obstructions without ruining jets, although it is fairly easy to cause damage if you use the wrong tools.

If compressed air fails to dislodge a blocked

pilot jet (and this is extremely common and the reason why lots of Amal carbs are unnecessarily junked), locate a section of stranded copper wire of about 14 gauge and strip off the insulation. Unbraid the wire and then cut off a small section longer than the width of the carburetor. Now measure the small piece of wire. You want a piece about .014 in diameter. The standard pilot jet is .016. This is a very fine piece of wire and since it's copper it won't be very rigid either. The soft copper wire will minimize the possibility of damage to the pilot bush.

Now poke your fine wire into the hole where the air adjustment screw was removed. On your first few attempts you might not hit the jet hole but sort of dance the wire around the outer edge of the bush. Just keep trying until you get the wire to go into the hole. You'll be able to tell when this happens because the wire will go past the mid-point of the carb body and hit the opposite side. When it does this, move the wire in a circular motion to help clean out the obstruction. Now remove the wire, blow out the passage with compressed air, and retest.

Sometimes this won't work because the obstruction is still rock hard, too hard for the soft piece of copper wire to move it. In this case, we have a few options.

Sometimes it takes more than a day in a carb tank to soften obstructions. I've left both carbs and pistons in chemical cleaning tanks for up to five days with no ill effects, so don't be afraid to try a several-day soak. Actually, I rarely have to resort to more involved procedures to clean pilot systems because I just throw the troublemakers back into the tank for another day or two and retry the wire method. Generally, the solution eventually softens the obstruction enough.

Micro Surgery

However, sometimes you have a super tough hombre that refuses to free up. Now it's time for the big guns, or rather, very tiny ones.

For operation one, drilling out the pilot bush, you need a #78 drill bit. This tiny #78 drill bit corresponds almost exactly to the diameter of the pilot bush hole. You can get the bits inexpensively at www.ehobbytools.com or locally if you have a source.

If a long soak in the dip tank and compressed air fail to unclog the pilot system, a small piece of copper wire of about .014 diameter inserted though the pilot air hole often does the trick.

If a piece of wire fails to clean out the pilot air path, drilling out the pilot jet obstruction with the tool shown is the next step. Pictured is the tiny #78 drill bit inserted into a 1/8-inch wooden dowel. Use the drill bit in a pin vise, also shown, to drill a hole into the center of the dowel and then use a little smear of glue or epoxy on the bit shank and insert it into the hole in the dowel. After the glue or epoxy dries, insert this tool into the pilot screw opening and rotate it with your fingers to permit the drill to cut through the pilot jet obstruction. Be careful; this is very delicate work.

Sometimes, to get the pilot system working properly, it's necessary to clean out the passage behind it. This requires a drill press on which the carburetor is securely mounted as shown. Once the plug is removed, you can clean the passage with a small piece of wire and liberal use of carb cleaner.

A hole is tapped for an Allen set screw to replace the old plug.

Here's the finished job. threadlock can be used to make the plug permanent or it can just be tightened to allow for removal later if necessary.

Secure the carb in a regular vise with soft jaws so that the pilot air screw hole is facing up. Construct a drill bit holder as shown and explained in the photo on page 95. Place the tool inside the hole so that it contacts the pilot bush and then rotate the tool clockwise with your fingers to drill out the obstruction.

Sometimes the problem is an accumulation of crud in the blanked-off passage of the carburetor behind the pilot bush. This can be evidenced by restricted flow even after freeing the pilot jet or drilling it out, or problems occurring later that again plug the pilot system.

In this case, we need to go into the blocked passage to clean it out. For this task you'll need a 9/64 drill bit and a #10-24 tap. Drill into the center of the plug and it will become loose enough to pull out or just run right up the drill bit as you work. Now you can clean this passage carefully and then thread the hole about 1/4 inch deep with the #10-24 tap. Finally, insert a matching Allen head set screw with a bit of threadlock to block off the passage again. Photos 17-20 show this operation from start to finish.

We have one more issue to deal with in our pilot system, and that's the condition of the airscrew and its seat.

The tip of the airscrew sits in a tapered seat in the carburetor body. It's not uncommon to find a seat that's badly deformed from some hammerhead trying to screw it too tightly. You can often see this damage by looking inside the hole while shining a light source into it. I don't know of a way to fix this damage. If the seat isn't damaged, you should always replace the little rubber grommet on the adjusting screw if it is cracked or shrunken. The same applies to the screw on the opposite of the carburetor that adjusts the slide height.

Another worthwhile check of the pilot air system is to see if the correct airscrew is installed, as it is not unheard of to find one that's too short. You need to have the carburetor mounted on a running bike for this check or some way to create a vacuum. First, remove the air cleaner and put your finger over the small outside hole. You should feel vacuum when the bike is running. Now, gently turn the screw into the carb until it fully seats. When it does, you should no longer feel any vacuum through this hole. If you do, you either have a too short screw or a damaged seat.

FURTHER INSPECTION AND CURES

Main Jet and Needle

After checking and clearing the pilot system and evaluating slide-to-body clearance, it's time to look at other issues. If you haven't already done so, remove the jet block that sticks out from the base of the body into the float bowl. Make sure the main jet is clean and the hole is unobstructed. If it isn't, and compressed air fails to dislodge the obstruction (common on older used carbs), find an appropriate cleaning tool. I've found that many Amal main jets can be easily cleaned with a piece of broom straw as it's close to the right diameter for many jets and soft enough not to cause damage.

Now closely inspect the needle and needle jet. Make sure the needle isn't bent or scratched; if it is, you'll have to replace it. Also check the clip and grooves it fits into at the top of the needle for damage. Many people commonly replace the needle and clip during a major overhaul, but the economy minded may want to try reusing the old needle first as it doesn't wear nearly as fast as the needle jet.

Many needle jets, though, are getting pretty worn after 10,000 miles or so. If your bike stumbles a bit right off idle, take a good look at the jet, especially the cross drilling in it. If this is plugged, free it and this may well cure the stumble problem. If you notice a considerable decline in gas mileage and rich running, this may also be cured with a new needle jet. Older needle jets won't be cross drilled; replacing them with new will improve performance.

Body Corrections

A very common problem with older Amals is a warped mounting flange. This is due to a combination of factors: the soft metal of the flange and the thick insulating block used for mounting. What happens is the flange bends when overtightened, and this does not take much force. This warping can, and frequently does, warp the carburetor body as well and causes slide sticking. It's a solid idea to use mounting nuts that are

The jet block and the jet itself can be removed and installed with a common wrench, as shown. For thorough cleaning and careful inspection, completely disassemble the carburetor and then soak the metal parts and body in carb cleaner. Don't soak plastic and rubber pieces, since they can be damaged by cleaning solvents.

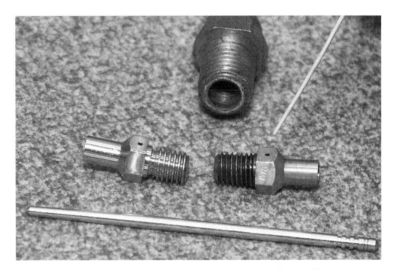

The top of a jet block, an old and new needle jet, and a needle are shown. Make sure the indicated cross-drilling is unobstructed, and if your needle jet isn't cross-drilled, upgrade to one that is for improved performance. While it can't be seen in this picture, this needle is scored and will be replaced, as will the jet it to which it was mated.

self locking and tightened only as much as you must to get the carb flat on the insulating block and the rubber O-ring properly seated to prevent leaks. You can check for leaking by spraying a good combustible starting fluid near the flange while the bike is idling or running just over that. If the rpm increases, you've got a leaking flange. The leak may also be caused by a poorly installed or worn out O-ring, so check this too. This is a cheap part and wise insurance to replace as a matter of routine any time the carb is removed for service.

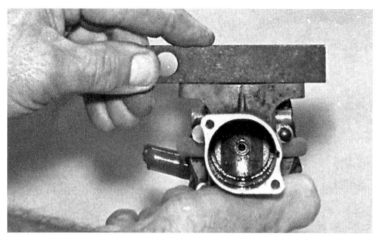

Check the mounting flange with a good straightedge. Many flanges are warped like this one.

To check for warping, use a straightedge across the flange from mounting hole to mounting hole and then hold the flange up to light, which isn't necessary for very badly warped flanges but can reveal ones that aren't as obvious.

To fix this problem, you'll need a thick pane of glass, some fine sandpaper or emery paper, and a can of spray glue or equivalent. Some recommend using 600 grit paper but I've used as coarse as 220 and it worked okay and was probably a bit quicker. Spray the back of the sandpaper with glue and attach it to the pane of glass. What this makes is a very flat cutting surface to reface the warped flange.

A warped mounting flange is corrected by resurfacing on a flat pane of glass on which a piece of fine (240 to 600 grit) sandpaper is glued. This process also works well on warped float bowls and can even correct minor head warping, all quite common problems with old Brit twins.

Move the carburetor in semi-circular motions over this surface and check regularly. Be sure to hold the carb at right angles to the flange and don't use a whole lot of pressure, as we want to take off as little metal as possible. Check the flange mating surface regularly and stop when you see evidence that every surface part has been lightly cut. You should now have a nice flat flange that will seal perfectly after you replace the old O-ring. Grease the new O-ring a bit so that it will hold nicely in the groove cut for it in the flange and not drop or shift during installation. If you had to do this work, it's not a bad idea to replace the insulating gasket at the same time. And whatever you do, use care reattaching the carburetor or you'll just be right back where you started with another warped flange.

Full Throttle Follies: The Stuck Slide Blues

Now we'll tackle a stuck slide. This can be exceptionally aggravating and time consuming, and if you're short tempered or pressed for time and have this problem, go for the sleeving which cures slide sticking 100 percent of the time.

Sticking throttle slides are not only a nuisance, they're dangerous and need to be fixed for safety as well as performance. The problem with correcting slide sticking lies in the very irregular wear one almost always finds. You can easily be put in a "damned if you do; damned if you don't" position trying to remedy tight spots while preserving as much metal as possible. It's not at all difficult to remove too much metal or take it from the wrong place and turn what was at least a good running carburetor, except for sticking at wide-open-throttle, to one that won't work well at all.

Your first mission is to determine whether or not the carb is worth dinking around with. If the wear is severe, there's no sense spending a lot of time reworking the slide because even if you get it to stop sticking, you'll never get the carb to run right.

Aside from checking the slide-to-body clearance, take a look at the rectangular protrusion on the slide that positions it in the body. If this piece is badly worn, it will need a specialist's attention. Lund Machine offers this service in addition to the sleeving process.

After polishing the slide, reinsert it into the body and move it up and down several times. Remove the slide and check for light seize marks, as shown.

Remove seize marks using 1200 grit paper; remove only enough metal to eliminate the marks. Overzealous sanding can ruin the slide.

Some people like to call Amals the "6,000-mile carburetor" and it's understandable because at this minimal mileage, or less, it can start to pull stunts like slide sticking. I happen to know the precise mileage on the one used for some of the photos shown here as I bought it new, and had 6,500 miles on it when it started to stick at wide-open-throttle. However, the body-to-slide clearance wasn't excessive and it ran and idled perfectly.

After you've evaluated the carb, clean it well, using the dip tank if at all possible. While sticking is rarely caused by crud buildup, you still want to rule this out and also be able to look for signs of seizure inside the body and on the slide.

Our next step involves the use of a polishing kit. If you're an old bike freak, you need to own one! The polishing buffer and various compounds are widely available.

Set your polishing wheel up and use the black stick for compound. Polish the slide until it shines almost like chrome and so few, if any, seize marks remain.

Next, insert the slide back into the cleaned body. Most likely it will still hang up somewhere near the top of the carburetor. Run the slide up and down a few times, as it would normally travel under operation and then remove the slide for inspection.

The nicely polished slide will clearly reveal the exact spots that need work by showing new light seize marks. You will also need to work on the corresponding part inside the carb body.

For this next step you need 1200 grit wet/dry sandpaper. Sand both the slide and body only in the area showing seize marks. We want to remove as little metal as possible since the more you take off, the shorter the service life of the slide and body before major repairs are needed. I also generally give the entire inside of the carb body a light once over with 1200 paper to make a very smooth surface after removing the seize marks found in specific areas. I've also used a small polishing wheel and the compound inside the carb body to better reveal seize marks and after sanding to assure a very smooth working surface.

Continue this process until you can achieve perfectly smooth slide operation. To bench test, place the slide inside the body so that it bottoms out. Now, turn the carburetor over. The slide should fall out on its own. If it doesn't, continue the above steps until this is achieved. You'll often be surprised how little metal you have to remove to achieve a smoothly operating slide, so little that you won't detect any change in clearance.

As a final step, polish the slide one more time and then clean it and the inside of the carb body with a good solvent like lacquer thinner to remove the compound wax and any stray metal powder.

With slide, flange, and pilot system issues settled, you can now reassemble the carburetor with a new gasket kit. Make sure you have good cables too as bad ones can create problems as well.

The final test involves the same one you used in the beginning: running the bike until it gets hot and then shutting it off and holding it at wide-open-throttle for ten seconds. If it still sticks, it's back to the bench you go. If all's well, you'll have thousands of more miles of good service.

We'll tune the rebuilt carbs in the last chapter.

14 *Them's the Brakes*

OVERVIEW

Our Brit twin brakes are simple and very reliable units that require very little maintenance. Depending on model and year you will have all drum brakes, disk and drum, or all disk. BSA never made it into the disk brake world; Triumph started with a front disk in 1973 and switched to dual disks when it also changed to left-side shifting. Reliable sources say a few 1972 650 Triumphs managed to pop up from the factory with front disk brakes, and it's quite possible older bikes have front disk brakes installed by previous owners—it is an extremely popular conversion, so always check what you have and don't rely 100 percent on the parts book and manual. Lots of Japanese forks, wheels, and brakes show up too.

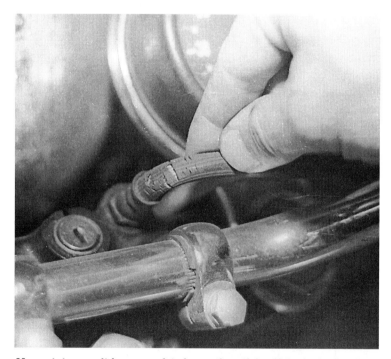

Many states won't issue a safety inspection sticker if the brake line is weather cracked like this, and you wouldn't want to ride the bike like this anyway. It will have to be replaced.

DISK BRAKES

For effective stopping power, the disk brake is the clear winner, but like most technological improvements, the cost is greater complexity. There are more things to go wrong, and with an older bike, especially one that's been sitting a long time, hydraulic problems must be expected.

Nevertheless, disk conversions are enormously popular and it's a simple direct swap to put a '73 and later disk brake fork unit on a 71–72 conical drum brake 650 Triumph or BSA. Using a Trident conversion bushing (PN 97-4145) will allow easy fitment of the disk brake front end to pre-OIF Triumph frames.

Most common with "barn fresh" budget bikes with disk brakes is that the brake fluid has long since dried, allowing the seals to crack and shrink, and then rust sets in. Remaining fluid congeals into tar-like goo guaranteed to cause headaches. If you have disk brakes, assume that you'll have to replace the master cylinder(s), all rubber lines, and perhaps the clogged metal ones too, and do a rebuild on the brake caliper(s). Rusted and pitted rotors will need to be replaced also or at least plated again. If there's still fluid inside and the master cylinder/caliper units aren't frozen, you may be in luck, but don't count on it. Also, while the calipers are most often rebuildable, the master cylinders are rarely worth the time to take apart, even if you can.

TWIN-LEADING-SHOE BRAKES

These problems may explain why I have a greater love for Triumph/BSA's late 60s and early 70s twin-leading-shoe brakes. Not only is the design capable of being a great stopper when properly serviced and adjusted, it's durable and can be quite serviceable even after sitting for 20 years in Farmer Bob's chicken shed. Still, you need to take each unit apart to inspect and repack the bearings and at least clean the drums and brake shoes.

CONICAL HUB BRAKES

In contrast to the twin-leading-shoe brakes just mentioned, many drum systems aren't nearly as effective as others and range from barely adequate to ridiculous. The worst brake of our subject period is the tiny conical hub unit on the early 70s 500 oil-in-frame Triumph/BSA that can't stop a tricycle. Don't pitch it though, as you can get good money for the 21-inch wheel and tiny brake from chopper builders.

The full-sized Triumph/BSA comical, err, I mean, conical hub unit, although better than the tiny brakes on the 500s, also provides limited stopping power but can be improved with careful adjustment and simple modification. Mechanical brakes utilize leverage to apply the stopping force to the brake shoes. The core problem with conical hubs is the lack of leverage. You can fix this by cutting the brake levers and then welding in an extra extending section, effectively increasing the leverage and making a profound difference in stopping power. Extended levers are also on the market. But even stock, the brake can be made to work adequately if it is properly adjusted and isn't worn out, so let's look at routine service now.

DRUM BRAKE SERVICE

After removing the wheel, the first step for front wheels is to remove the nut holding the brake plate; this is covered in the wheel building chapter. For the rear units, remove the axle and the brake plate should pull right off. If the axle is stuck, use a drift to knock it out of the hub.

With the nut or axle off, you can remove the brake plate and inspect the drum and shoes. Often, all that's necessary to restore braking performance is a good cleaning with a stiff bristle brush and a can of commercial brake parts cleaner, which does a good job and leaves no oily residue. Whatever you do, don't use compressed air to clean brake parts! Asbestos, used in a lot of old Brit brakes, is a known carcinogen, so you want to keep the dust down to a minimum. A dust mask is a very good idea anytime you work on brake shoes or disk pads.

Inspect the drum for scoring but don't worry about a little light rust. Out-of-round drums and those badly scored can be machined, but usually all that's needed is a little fine emory cloth and elbow grease.

To achieve full effectiveness from drum brakes you must ensure that the shoes make full contact with the drum. After some wear, most brake shoes no longer make full contact, and this adversely affects performance. To correct this condition, cut strips of medium to coarse sandpaper the width of the brake drum where shoes run and glue them to the drum (see photo). Rubber cement works great and is easy to remove. Replace the brake plate now and put the wheel in the stand you made for lacing. Rotate the drum while keeping slight pressure on the brake lever(s) so that the brake shoes make contact with the sandpaper. Definitely use a dust mask as you'll be sanding an asbestos lining. Periodically remove the brake plate to inspect until you see that the sandpaper has lightly sanded into about 90 percent of the brake lining surface. When it has, you're done. You may find you can't

Brake shoes that have seen lots of miles will wear so that the braking surface no longer makes complete contact with the drum. Loss of stopping power results. Lining the drum as shown with sandpaper and then inserting the brake plate to reshape the shoes can restore the contact surface. See text for further details. Wear a breathing mask to protect yourself from asbestos dust if you try this trick.

Snap rings must be removed before the bearings can be knocked out for service.

A punch will remove and install the bearing cover if you don't have the shop tool. Don't forget; most bearing covers are left-hand threaded (turn clockwise to remove them).

refit the brake plate into the drum with the sandpaper in place; this is actually a good thing as it means you have barely worn drum and brake shoes. In this case, just scuff up the brake surface with sandpaper (using a dust mask) or you can remove the shoe and move it in contact with sandpaper glued to the drum.

If the brake shoe lining is too thin and close to the holding rivets, pull off the brake shoes and remove the two return springs. Hold the shoe in a vise, and use a sharp chisel to cut off the soft metal rivets sticking out on the inside of the shoe. Replace with new lining and rivets using a blunt punch on the rivet when it's backed up with a hard object like another dull punch held in a vise. Use a small C-clamp to hold the new lining tightly to the shoe as you work. This is really old school, though. Relatively inexpensive replacement shoes are available with the lining glued to the shoes with modern adhesives that have made rivets obsolete.

BEARING SERVICE

As you are renewing the brakes, you should also inspect and replace or repack all wheel bearings. These wheel bearings are tough hombres and give many miles of service if you keep them greased.

To get at the bearings, most wheels require removing a left-hand threaded cover, meaning you remove it by turning clockwise. Same goes for speedometer drive rings on the rear wheel that must be removed to access the bearings. The bearing covers for disk brakes have right-hand threads, but the speedometer ring is left-hand threaded. You don't need the special tool shown in the shop manual to remove these covers; just use a dull punch to tap it to turn and remove. Check also for retaining clips and remove these as well. The speedometer ring can be removed easily with a piece of steel bar stock.

Once all retaining parts are removed, drive the bearings out with whatever drift you have available. You may be able to use the axle as a drift, but you generally don't need the stepped drifts shown in lots of manuals. When driving the bearings in or out, *drive only on the outside race,* as pounding on the inner one can easily wreck the bearing. Sometimes, though, you have no choice but to drive on the inner race. If you must do so, carefully check the bearing and seriously consider replacing it.

Once the bearings are out, inspect for rough rolling, heat discoloration, and any evidence of metal particles. If everything checks out, clean the bearing in solvent and dry it with a soft cloth, then repack with bearing grease and reinstall. If you do need new bearings, get the sealed ones; you can then pitch the grease retaining covers in the stock drum.

Front drum brakes rely on a good cable. Braking will suffer considerably when an old cable like this begins to loosen up and compress like an accordion under pressure.

BRAKE CABLES

No matter how good your drum brakes are, rotten cables that compress on the outer case when pressure is applied will negate much of your hard work. While a lot of old cables are perfectly serviceable after lubrication, many need to be replaced. You can actually watch a bad cable compress as it's worked. Brake arms and levers also need to be adjusted properly. Many opt to change the handlebar brake lever to one that's longer or pivots at a different point so that it also increases the leverage force. Carefully inspect both ends of the cable. Even if you find just one tiny strand of the cable is broken or beginning to unwind, replace the entire cable; it's shot and will soon let go.

DISK BRAKE SERVICE

Okay disk brakers, it's your turn. We'll assume you're working on a total disaster, so if you're just doing a partial job, omit the inappropriate steps. Regardless, I recommend highly that you do a complete hydraulic overhaul for a long-lasting, trouble-free service.

Remove the entire hydraulic system, which means both front and rear master cylinders, calipers, and lines. Check the rubber lines for cracking and replace them if this is evident. Inspect the metal lines for kinks, holes and rust. Use compressed air to blow out all lines.

While the master cylinders are supposedly rebuildable, 99 times out of a 100 all the curse words and efforts only reveal damage too severe for repair. However, if the piston moves; there's hope for the frugal. Stainless steel replacement hydraulic cylinders are a good upgrade and readily available. You may need to heat and soak the cylinder in WD 40 to get it to unscrew from its holding threads.

You can save a bundle on disk brake lines down at the cycle junkyard, but most of what you'll find will be metric. No problem, because with adapters like the one shown here you can make use of perfectly good lines taken from late model wrecks.

If your budget is extremely limited, you can take the front brake line and connections down to the nearest bike bone yard and shop for a good used master cylinder and replacement lines. Use your old lines to compare with suitable replacements. Get a return guarantee that the master cylinder will work, and then find a master cylinder/brake lever arrangement that fits. A number of Yamaha units from 400cc and up (see photo) work perfectly on Triumphs for less than 10 percent of what it costs to buy a stock replacement. The banjo bolt from the Yamaha master cylinder fits the Triumph hose and must be used to match the master cylinder's metric thread. You can also get metric to SAE conversion brake parts that allow you to rig almost anything up; many auto parts stores will make up custom brake lines for a lot less than OEM parts. Rear master cylinders call for the stock replacement unless you're into quite a bit of fabrication work.

Unlike master cylinders, calipers are usually an easy rebuild and well worth the time and minor expense. It's also getting mighty difficult to source OEM calipers.

Begin by removing the two cotter pins holding the brake pads. Discard the pins and always replace with news ones. Mark the pads for position so you can replace them the same way they came out if you decide they're still serviceable.

Compressed air can be used to remove the caliper pistons. Do not remove the bolts holding the caliper together; this isn't necessary and could cause the pistons to stick later.

Use compressed air in the brake line hole to pop out the pistons. They often shoot out of their bores at a pretty good clip, so it's wise to put a strip of cushioning material in the center of the caliper to soften the impact. Sometime both pistons come out together, and sometimes it's necessary to hold one piston just deep enough with a small C-clamp to build up sufficient air pressure to pop off the other one.

Inspect the pistons for corrosion. Replace if any pitting or scoring is evident. With the pistons removed, both rubber sealing rings can be removed with a small screwdriver. Be careful not to gouge any sealing surface upon removal. Coat new seals in brake fluid and install in the grooves cut in the caliper bore. Now coat the piston in brake fluid also, and gently work it back into its respective bore, being careful to push the piston in straight.

Inspect the rotors for scoring and wear. While some bikes have rotors thick enough to allow for machining, the Triumph/BSA unit is awfully thin to begin with; replacement may be the only alternative. Clean off any crud and mount a dial indicator gauge so that it barely touches the ro-

tor. Spin and check for side-to-side run out; replace the rotor if necessary.

Reassemble the entire hydraulic system carefully to avoid twisting rubber lines or cross-threading connections. At this point flush the entire system several times to remove any possible contaminants, moisture, etc. Don't reuse brake fluid just because "it looks okay." It's false economy and may have you doing the job all over again in short order. Brake fluid absorbs moisture from the air, so always use a fresh unopened bottle to avoid future headaches.

You can flush and bleed the easy way or the hard way; which one do you prefer? The old pump and bleed folks will have to work the front and rear master cylinders until they build up a good sweat. You'll have to pump quite a bit and bleed off the air until pressure begins to build. Open the bleed screw only when the master cylinder piston moves as far inward as possible, and then close the screw and release the master cylinder. You can also bleed into a container filled with fluid. Continue until no evidence or air bubbles can be seen at the bleed hole and the pedal/lever feels firm. Be careful not to run out

Vacuum bleeding makes a pain-in-the-neck job easy and is especially useful on many rear-disk Triumphs like the own shown. If not for this tool, we would have to remove the axle and lower the bracket.

of fluid in the master cylinder reservoir during this process, or you'll have to start all over again. Also, be very careful about getting brake fluid on any painted surface; you'll find that it's one of the best paint removers around.

A far easier way to flush and bleed any hydraulic system is to use a vacuum pump with a brake attachment kit. Not only is it much less work, it's far quicker and cleaner. And if you happen to own a Triumph with the disk caliper mounted on the lower part of the wheel, you have an added incentive to cough up the bucks for a vacuum unit. Thanks to less than brilliant design, the caliper is held so that the air bleed hole is at the bottom. Air naturally collects at the top of the caliper, which then requires removing the axle and sliding the bracket down to correctly position the bleed hole to the top, as the shop manual instructs. But if you use a vacuum unit, the relative position of the bleed hole doesn't matter, so you can bleed the brake with the caliper in any position and leave the wheel and axle alone.

As with any brake job, be extra careful to check all connections for tightness, leakage, etc., and then road test. With new pads or shoes, don't go around town jamming the brakes like mad because you'll just glaze them over and they'll never operate efficiently. Just take it easy and let them bed in by themselves.

▶ BAR-B-Q BRAKE

I rolled out of a tent one morning at a bike rally and before I had my first cup of coffee I smelled the worst cooking I ever encountered, and I've eaten at Denny's.

Seems this fella was cooking his brake shoes over a small charcoal grill. I asked him if he planned to have them on toast, but I realized that he was employing an ancient trick.

As it turned out, my neighbor had been a bit too enthusiastic about chain lubrication and managed to contaminate his shoes with oil. Grease, fork oil, and brake fluid will do the same thing to brake shoes and pads, with brake fluid being the worst because it can attack the brake lining and destroy it. In all cases, contaminated shoes are mighty poor stoppers. The right fix is to replace the shoe lining or pads, but there are situations when knowing this trick will get you home in one piece.

You can use just about any flammable liquid, but it's a lot safer to use something like kerosene or charcoal lighter fluid. An easy way is to suspend the shoes with wire before lighting, but even resting them on a rock will do.

All that's involved is soaking the pad or shoe and then lighting it. What happens is the heat forces the oil out of the lining and then burns it off. A little over a minute is all you need for this to work. Sometimes just wiping off the pad or shoe with solvent will do, but lots of times you can only get at the surface oil, and more weeps out after you reinstall the shoes or pads and you're right back to no stopping power.

After allowing the shoes and pads to cool, use a little sandpaper to scuff up the lining for better stopping. Keep the dust down, and if there's a breeze, work with the wind to your back because most likely you're working with asbestos.

Usually, this trick works perfectly. However, the brakes may tend to grab a bit, but the result is still worlds better than not being able to stop in a reasonable amount of time.

Burning off contaminants like grease and oil can work in a pinch to make brakes work well.

15 *Frame Up*

OVERVIEW

Many people who were forced to repair a newly painted frame weren't stupid, they just made a basic mistake: not taking all or nearly all the paint off the frame and checking it very carefully. Cracked mounting tabs and bad welds hide easily under multiple coats of paint, bondo, and just plain crud. If you plan to powder coat, all the paint must be removed. For a conventional paint job, get at least 90 percent of the old stuff off, and every bit around the welds and mounting tabs where nasty cracks hide out. The factory manuals are a good source for frame dimensions and swingarm procedures, but they offer little help with a lot of common problems we'll cover here.

Before you can begin to evaluate the condition of a given frame, years of built-up crud will need to be removed. A scraper and wire brush work well to remove crusty accumulations before sandblasting, making the blasting job a lot quicker.

BLAST OFF

Sandblasting is the easiest way to clean up a frame. All that's required for blasting is a compressor and bucket blaster (see photo in Chapter 6). This is most definitely an outside job because the frame is too big for most blast cabinets. Outside blasting, however, will raise a sand storm big enough to gain the respect of most Bedouins. A professional sand blaster has a neat hooded suit; a workable imitation isn't hard to put together. I use an old motorcycle helmet with a bubble shield and drape a towel over my head and neck before putting the helmet on. Long sleeves, pants, and gloves are also a must.

Before blasting, protect the neck bearing races with masking or duct tape. If the swingarm isn't removed, also tape around the seal areas to prevent sand from getting inside. Plug OIF frames at all oil openings and vents.

Whether or not the swingarm comes off depends on its condition and your plans for final finish. Powder coating will create too much heat for rubber seals and will require swingarm removal. With paint, the swingarm can stay resident, so long as it passes your inspection.

This A65 frame is being blasted with a bucket blaster to remove paint, a very important step to locate hidden defects that can range from cracked welds to another set of vehicle identification numbers. Always remove old body filler that can hide problems.

SWINGARMS

If you do find swingarm side play, the swingarm must come off, and you'll have to replace the bushings at least. This involves removing the nuts holding the pivot spindle and then removing the spindle. Some will slide right out; others will test your will and make you wish you had never thought about restoring an old motorcycle. Remember the heat, soak, and time approaches. You might even need to use a hydraulic press.

The manuals show a variety of ways to remove swingarm bushes, ranging from drifting them out (a piece of 1/2-in. pipe works well on many) to using a long bolt or all-thread to pull the bushes out. Usually these methods work fine, but sometimes nothing seems to work. With some BSA swingarms, you actually have to burn the rubber out of the swingarm to remove the bush. Tough bushes can often be freed by using a hacksaw blade to cut a slot into the bush. This relieves the press fit and makes it easier to drive or pull the bush out.

DAMAGE ASSESSMENT AND REPAIR

With swingarm issues decided and after blasting to remove paint, inspect every tab and weld. Correct all problems found. Many earlier frames were assembled with tubing stuck into lugs and then brazed together. Brass and steel welds are incompatible, so unless every bit of brass is removed, brazing must be used for repair. Brazing is a good fix and should not be feared, as it's very strong if done correctly.

With a bare frame, it's much easier to assess collision damage, but damage can be very subtle. The only way to be 100 percent sure is to measure using a layout table with special tools, but even your local pro shop isn't likely to have this equipment. To minimize the possibility of using a bent frame, check for obvious damage and also measure various frame dimensions. Compare the figures you get to what's given in the shop manual frame drawings. If the numbers match up, the odds are very much in your favor the frame is good and straight. Comparing dimensions to a known good frame is another workable alternative.

After removing the nut on the opposite side of this BSA frame, this bolt is removed in order to remove the pivot spindle. Once the swingarm spindle is removed, the swingarm can be knocked off with a soft mallet. The Triumph procedure is similar.

BSA used a number of different swingarms over the years, but the one shown here uses a metalastic bush, a steel bushing encased in rubber. The only way to remove the bushing is to burn out the rubber as shown. Excessive play in these swingarms is often not caused by a worn bush, it's rotten rubber that allows the bush to move. In all its swingarms, BSA neglected to provide grease nipples, so grease them well when assembling; it's the last time you'll be able to do so.

Check the frame for bends and kinks. This simple tool made from a piece of flat bar stock will detect a bent A65 frame neck. This frame is perfect.

This OIF frame has numerous problems, but the Triumph's frame neck and spine were still okay. OIFs are more prone to fracture than bending, and the absence of any cracks or buckles moved the owner to request damage repair of the areas around both passenger and rider foot pegs that were badly bent. Without a layout table and the proper jigs, we really can't be certain the frame is absolutely straight, but measurements taken across the frame in several areas checked out to shop manual standards so we'll try to repair it in an attempt to keep a matching-number bike together. In this photo a bottle jack is being used to straighten the rear support tubing for the passenger pegs. Next we'll heat the tab with an acetylene torch where the peg is attached and place a long pipe over the peg to bend back the tab while the jack holds the tubing in place. You can use these processes to bend any frame, but sometimes you're better off replacing a frame that has extensive damage. Most shops don't have the expertise or tools to precisely straighten critical areas of a frame.

COMMON PROBLEMS

Knowing the weak points of a given frame helps too. Early OIF frames are prone to breaks on the centerstand mounts as they were not sufficiently braced and the stand was too tall to boot. If you have one of these, weld a support gusset to the frame rail on each side. The factory did this on later OIF frames. Additionally, remove the centerstand and shorten it about 3/4 of an inch and then weld it back together. This makes it much easier raise the bike on the centerstand and these two steps eliminate the fracture problem entirely.

Also check OIF frames for cracks at the bottom of the oil tube and also around the frame neck. OIF frames are very stiff and didn't bend in a crash as much as they fractured, so if you find no breaks or cracks, this is very good news. Most OIF frames are also very easy to source and generally inexpensive if you need to replace one.

For both early and later frames, the sidestand mounts are the most frequent problem, so check this very carefully, if you're lucky enough to even have one still on the bike. Many old timers will have nothing left, or just as often, an extremely crude repair. Often this mess was created in an attempt to repair the tab while the engine was still in the frame.

SIDESTAND FIXES

There are several methods that work well to fix a bad sidestand tab for good. Some parts houses market a half lug with the thick tab welded or cast into it, and this can be brazed or welded into the frame. The advantage of a pre-made piece is you can avoid a difficult welding process involving the very thick tab and a relatively thin frame tube, and it's this issue that often created many bad repair jobs.

Budget builders can make their own repair tab, or find a good donor from a junk frame, the quickest way. Cut the frame on both sides of the donor tab and then cut the lug in half. You may need to do some grinding to get the tab to fit snugly against the frame. Also carefully grind the frame to remove old welds and brass so that the new lug/tab fits well.

Before welding or brazing the repair tab to the frame, install the sidestand and check the angle with respect to how the frame will rest on the stand. Once this is determined, hold the repair piece in place with a C-clamp or vise grip until it's tacked in. Weld or braze the tab on both sides and all around the back of the frame tube. If you want this repair to last forever, don't repeat the mistake that most likely broke it in the first place, and that's sitting on the bike when it's only supported by the sidestand. It was never designed to take this stress, and the leverage created by the sidestand in conjunction with Fat Bob sitting on your sled can break even a good repair.

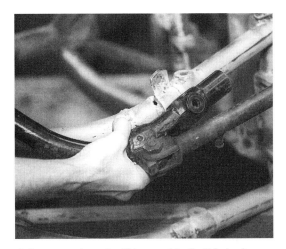

A donor repair part will be used to fix this broken sidestand tab. While this one is identical, taken from one of the worst A65 chopper frames ever created, all sorts of sidestand lugs will work. We'll cut this piece close to both sides of the lug and then cut the lug in half to form a semicircular repair piece. These can be purchased ready-made, but junk frame pieces are abundant and usually much cheaper. Forget about the hacksaw for this sort of work, unless you really want a bunch of exercise. Go for the power grinder and cutoff tools that make this work relatively easy.

Also check all tabs on the frame that hold things like side panels and exhaust pipes and repair as needed. Check all welds/brazed lugs carefully. A magnifying glass can reveal tiny cracks the naked eye often misses.

Once you're satisfied you've checked and repaired everything, it's time for either paint or powder coating. Rattle can gloss black enamel can be used for the budget minded, but try to allow at least several weeks for this paint to cure. Otherwise, it's far too easy to scratch it while building your pride and joy.

Before you can attach a new piece, you have to clean up the mess. Sometimes, you'll have to grind off a lot of bad repair welding too. Beware of leftover brass around some lugs, as brass will prevent a good steel weld. Sometimes, it's best to continue with brass.

A new lug is brazed in place on all sides. This photo was taken 15 years ago and the lug and sidestand are still holding perfectly.

If you don't have a spring tool, use a piece of wire and a vise grip as shown to attach the heavy-duty return spring. Just pull the spring over the post and then cut and remove the wire.

16

Hidden Assets: Seat Restoration

OVERVIEW

Chances are if your budget project even had a seat, it looked like it had been attacked by a pack of wild dogs, and that's a better than average old cycle sitter. The factory manuals usually tell you next to nothing about seats, except for bits on hinges and latches. Fortunately, with the purchase of a new seat cover, just about anyone can restore their own seat to like-new appearance and comfort.

INSPECTION

The first thing to determine is whether or not the seat pan is salvageable. Don't worry about surface rust, and even heavy rust and gaping holes are easily correctable, provided the areas around the hinge, latch, and/or bolt holes aren't rusted out completely. While even a pan this bad can be restored, it is better to get a good used pan or another seat that's easier to restore.

If you have enough pan metal to work with, it's time to evaluate the foam. Sometimes it's in surprisingly good shape, but chances are it's a hardened powdery mess. You can tell bad foam even under the cover by pressing on the seat. If it's hard or crunches like a bag of potato chips, you need new foam. Almost all seats, even well preserved ones, will at least need a new cover.

A seat builder's best friend is fiberglass if the pan has gotten thin from rust and/or has holes right through it. Resin and cloth can be purchased inexpensively at stores catering to auto body supplies and also from boat supply shops.

Just like tank repair, mission one is to treat rust and remove loose particles of it. Use any of the processes previously detailed, but get all loose rust off and neutralize the rest. With a lot of old pans, you'll just need to cover a hole or a thin spot or two with fiberglass.

To cover holes with fiberglass, apply the cloth in precut layers in a cross grain pattern like the wood laminates in plywood, and for the same reason, to increase the pan's strength. Use wax paper held with duct tape on the opposite side of the pan to provide an easily removed base for the fiberglass to rest flat on. The wax paper peels off the fiberglass after it cures. Three or four layers of fiberglass cloth is enough to hold the standing weight of most people and more than strong enough for a cycle seat.

It's best to pre-cut all the pieces you'll need first and lay them out dry as a trial. Once satisfied that you have enough pieces, it's time to mix the resin and hardener and soak the cloth in it. Fiberglass resin, if mixed correctly, cures quickly, so depending on how much work you have, you might want to repair your pan in stages. Either way, simply lay the resin-soaked fiberglass flat and work out any air pockets with a putty knife or similar tool. Lots of people like to wear rubber gloves and work fiberglass by hand. You can also bridge rusted gaps in the raised seat edges by fiberglassing over tape or cardboard placed to provide a shaped surface for the fiberglass to cure on. You can even re-place entire missing lip sections with this process.

After the fiberglass cures, you may have to do some shaping and smoothing with sandpaper; be sure to wear a dust mask and long sleeves or you'll be scratching until next Christmas. Once the glass is cured and shaped, rattle can paint tops the work off for the next step.

SEAT FOAM

You can buy some seat foam pre-shaped, but it's a bunch cheaper and just as good to hit the upholstery store catering to automotive as well as furniture customers to pick up a piece of high-

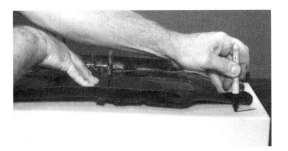

You can get pre-trimmed foam for some seats, but it's much more expensive than buying a block of high-density foam and trimming it yourself. Here a raw block of foam is being traced before the first trim cuts so that it fits this pan.

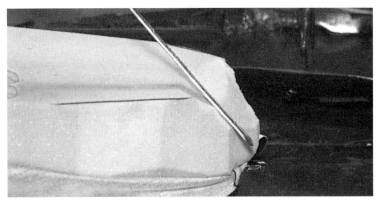

Final trimming is underway, using the best tool for the job: an electric carving knife. Unlike bodywork that has to be perfect, stretching the seat cover over the foam hides crude sculpting, so perfection forming isn't necessary.

density foam. Tell the shop what you want the foam for and they'll give you the right kind. Most foam, by the way, is way too soft for cycle seat applications. Bring along the pan and cover if you have one, as having these available will help the foam seller estimate what you'll need to cover the seat and also aids in determining the thickness required. If you are working on a humped BSA seat, you'll need a thicker piece to fill the hump, so you'll have to cut the front section down or glue a second piece on to fit the seat cover shape.

Believe it or not, sculpting seat foam is simple, providing you have the right tool: an electric carving knife. Unlike bodywork, shaping foam does not require anything even close to perfection, just a roughed out shaping will do as the cover tension evens out imperfections.

SEAT COVERS

Nearly all parts houses can get a seat cover to match your bike, but there's a wide range of quality available. Generally, you get what you pay for. Also, trim pieces are usually unavailable, so grab any used ones you can find as these are pieces worth chroming, since there often isn't any other alternative. Sadly, many covers today come with a cheap imitation of the original trim; it wears out and/or falls off shortly after your first ride.

It's a good idea to test fit the cover by holding it in place before gluing down the foam to check for proper shaping. If all's well, glue the foam to the pan. Spray adhesive works well but most any good glue will serve. Prepare the cover by either

Always try a loose fit of the cover before gluing the foam or making holes in the cover. This late Bonneville seat should fit well. Heat the cover before installing it, to achieve a snug, professional look.

gently heating it with a blow dryer or letting it sit outside in direct sunlight on a hot day. Don't neglect this step because it makes a major difference in the cover's final fit.

Stretch the cover over the seat and begin to secure it to the pan. Many covers come with clips

Many Triumph seats have a latch piece that requires the installer to carefully measure and then cut a hole in the cover to clear it. Leave material to work with on both sides before doing this, but make sure the cover is properly positioned and unwrinkled before cutting the cover. Make the cut very small and pull the cover over the latch for a tight fit and be sure to use glue on the base. Note also the clip to the right, common in lots of seat cover kits. Install them with a soft hammer and crimp them before installing the trim piece that will cover the clips. While neater, these clips do not hold nearly as well as factory original methods or screws.

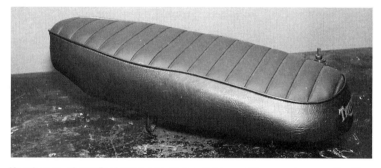

Here's one of our final products. This will be used in a custom application and is slightly smaller than stock. Other than that, it looks factory-new.

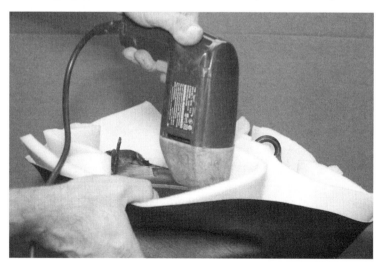

Use an electric drill to make holes in the seat base for attaching screws, but take care not to go too deep. Also, do not try to drill the seat cover at the same time, as the bit will grab and rip it.

that slide over the cover and grip the pan's edges. These clips are frequently marginal at best, so using them in conjunction with glue is imperative. The old pan may also have the original factory prongs, and if so, these can be pried up and used along with glue, but many old pans will be missing prongs in lots of places or they'll be absent entirely.

Even better are special screws and accompanying washers available at upholstery stores. Pop rivets can work too. Both are very good at holding a cover in place far longer than the service life of the material, but the cover must be attached to the base with these methods. With both rivets and screws, you'll need to drill small holes in the pan. Do not attempt to drill through the cover as the bit will grab the material and rip it to shreds. Instead, use an awl or ice pick to pierce the cover and also mark the location on the pan for the drilled hole. After drilling, spray a bit of glue around the hole area, insert the screw through the cover and into the pan, and then tighten the screw.

You'll need to work at opposite points of the cover alternately as you keep the cover aligned and taut. Attach a screw and then pull the cover on the other side of the seat to mark and attach another screw. Sometimes during this process, a wrinkle can develop, and if it does, you'll have to remove a fastener and reposition the cover to remove the wrinkle, very easy to do with upholstery screws, but a lot harder with rivets.

If you have the talent or access to it, crafting a seat cover from scratch is definitely an option. There are myriad choices of material ranging from leather to special seat cover material also available at the upholstery shop. Making your own cover is also generally the most economical, and many builders are capable of very nice final products. Even with custom covers, you may have some trimming to do, but this is easy with some sharp shears.

▶ *BUSTED HINGE MOUNT*

Don't scrap an old seat pan with a busted hinge mount like this (top photo) because the fix is pretty simple. Start by bending the hinge mount back in place (center) and then go to work on it from the back side after cutting off the old seat cover and removing the foam. Once you think you have the hinge in the right place, test it on the frame itself (bottom) to see if the seat swings freely and lines up with catch when closed. Adjust the hinge mounts as necessary. Before attempting repair, remove all the paint, rust and old metal around the hinge and seat pan. With the metal cleaned, spot-weld or braze a small section and again check the fit on the frame. A spot-weld should still allow you to bend the mount a little. You also need to make a small spot-weld that allows adjustment if the hinge mount is broken off completely. When everything lines up, finish welding/brazing the job. Alternately, if working with a bare frame like the one shown, you can do all the welding with the pan right on the frame to guarantee perfect alignment of the hinges. If welding is not your thing, you can even repair a mount like this with several layers of fiberglass on the top part of the pan. Put a bit of grease or Vaseline on the tips of the hinge bolts so the fiberglass does not stick to the bolts. Even if the bolts are frozen, so long as you can remove one of the hinges, you can still remove and install the seat.

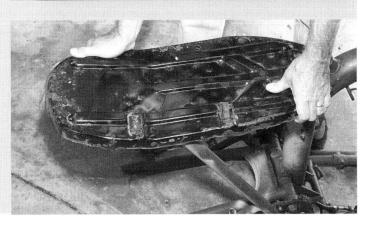

Learning Brit Twin Engine and Transmission Restoration

Many people who do a lot of their own motorcycle restoration work send the engine and transmission out for a professional rebuild. You might be inclined to do the same, and there really isn't anything wrong in doing so, unless your motivation is thinking that you can't do this work yourself. Transmissions, for example, used to frighten me; all those gears and parts shown in the exploded diagrams just seemed so intimidating. Maybe you harbor these fears today and feel the same about engine work. Relax, Brit engines and transmissions don't require graduate work in engineering and are actually fairly simple devices once we know the basic parts and common problems.

You really can do an excellent job yourself, because of something I guess we could call a mechanical equalizer, and this goes back to one of our three Ts: time. It may well take you ten or twenty times longer than a good pro to assemble your first engine and transmission, but unlike automotive/motorcycle painting that really can't be slowed down once started, you can crawl through an engine and transmission build one small, tentative step at a time. This is precisely why it's possible for a careful beginner to do a good job. If you get confused or make a mistake, it's most often easily correctable. Sure, it might cost you a buck or two if you do something like break a piston ring, but I've been very careful at these points of pontential error to make clear explanations and warnings so that you are far less likely to make mistakes that cost money or result in catastrophe.

But no matter how hard I've tried to explain what's important or most often misunderstood and carefully delineated what you need at hand, I am going to be completely candid here, something I wish a lot more tech writers were when they should have been. Simply put, it's very likely that at some point along the way you are going to stop and say, "Wait a minute, I don't get this." When it happens, here's what to do. First of all, re-read what confused you, review relevant photos,

and go over related sections in your shop manual and parts book. If the procedure is still murky to you, work through it with the parts at hand. So long as you don't force things, that giant jigsaw puzzle gets a lot clearer after you just manipulate the parts. This is called kinesthetic learning; you have to touch and manipulate parts sometimes to really understand. Fear not, because it's highly unlikely you'll damage anything in the process. For example, if you flop a gear backwards or install a shift fork wrong, either the parts won't fit together, and you'll instantly know something's wrong, or you won't be able to shift the transmission into gear when you test it. So long as you don't pound the parts, they won't break, so stop, reverse steps, and try again.

Many beginners won't have to do anything more than repeat a procedure a few times or put a part in differently. Some of you, though, may get into a bind that seems impossible. I can't predict what this might be, but a very common one is trying to fit an incorrect part. When you've tried everything and nothing seems to work, stop; take a break. Don't be afraid to ask questions or admit you're stumped. Call in an ally. Might be a friend. May well be the guy you bought the part from, could just be someone with a different perspective. No matter what, there is a solution; give yourself the time to find it. You will, and the thrill of firing up your own engine and banging the gears you held in your own two hands is well worth the time and effort. Be cool, and it'll happen.

One final note. In the instructions of the next few chapters, I've tried not to repeat procedures common to both BSA and Triumph in order to save space for describing particularly important areas for each. Consequently, you will have to refer at times to another chapter, or, as I recommend, read each section carefully. You BSA guys really ought to know Triumphs, and vice versa. BSAs and Triumphs tend to hang out together, so it's good to know the whole tribe inside and out.

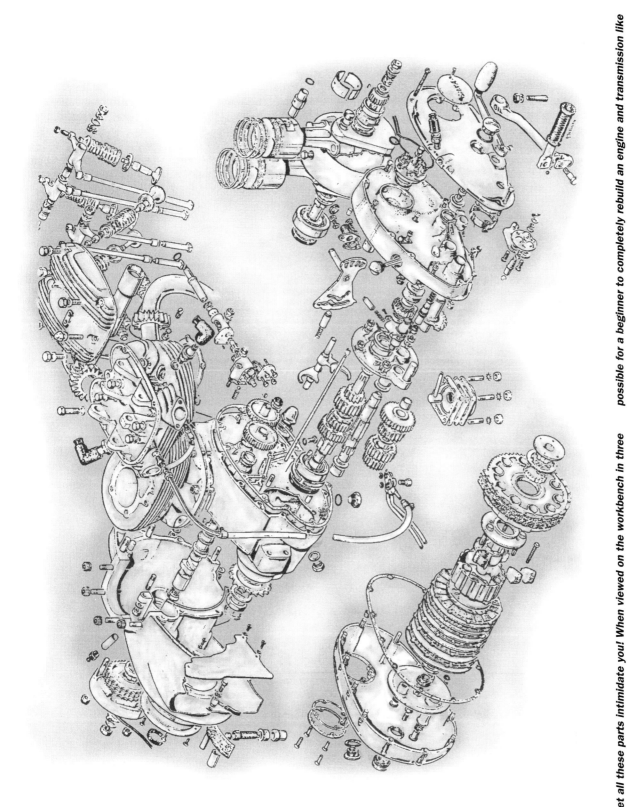

Don't let all these parts intimidate you! When viewed on the workbench in three dimensions it's much easier to see how things fit together and also very possible for a beginner to completely rebuild an engine and transmission like this 1971 BSA A65 shown. (Image is used courtesy of BSA Company, Ltd.)

► *NICHOLSON'S SPECIFICATIONS*

Perhaps the most perplexing question facing novice builders is whether or not to re-use a given part. The myriad issues range from parts budget to service wear imperceptible to the naked eye. Unfortunately, some unscrupulous people take advantage of beginning motorcycle restorers trying to carefully and intelligently weigh part replacement decisions. One who didn't abuse his customers was Bernie Nicholson who developed and published an excellent set of wear specifications applicable to most Brit twins and many other motorcycles. Those who did business with Nicholson said he wouldn't sell you a part unless he thought you really

needed it, and fortunately there are still folks like him around today to carry on his noble mission. (See Resources list at the end this of book for specific recommendations.) Although Nicholson's numbers often allow more wear than factory specs, given his reputation and deep experience, the following figures are worthy of serious consideration, especially if economy is a major consideration. Nicholson's wear specs should be used in conjunction with those given in the measurement chapter and your shop manual. Together these resources make an informed parts/service decision possible for even first-time builders.

Valve guides
New clearance: 002–003 intake .003–005 exhaust
Replace when .002 over original

Cam bushings
Replace when clearance reaches .003

Piston pin bushings
Replace when clearance is more than .0025

Valve stems
Replace valve if stem shows .003 wear

Camshafts
Replace if wear measured at highest part of cam lobe is more than .020 or severe flat spot is found

Cam followers
Replace at .010 wear

Crankshaft
Regrind rod throws at .003 wear

Connecting rod bearings
Replace at .004 clearance or greater

BSA timing side bush
Replace if wear is more than .003

Cylinder bore
Rebore cylinders if wear is more than .008 (.004 if new pistons must be fitted)

Piston skirt to cylinder skirt clearance
Replace piston when clearance is more than .002–.003 over original

Piston ring grooves
Replace piston if more than .007 clearance is found between ring and groove

Piston rings
Replace if ring gap is more than .030 when measured at bottom (unworn) part of cylinder

Valve springs
Replace if 1/8-inch less than original length

Main engine and transmission bearings
Replace if perceptible movement is found when lifting shaft or crank or if roughness is detected in rotation

Of course, wear isn't the only factor to consider when examining a used part, as damage also must be assessed. This piston seized in the cylinder at some time and must be replaced. Occasionally, very light seize marks can be removed with fine sandpaper but damage such as that shown here means the piston is junk.

Many wear measurements are easy to make and require only simple tools. In this case a feeler gauge is used to measure the clearance between the piston ring groove and the ring. Since the biggest gauge that fits is .004, this means wear is within the acceptable limit of .007. Use can also be made of the old ring and feeler gauges to measure bore wear. To do so, just place the ring close to the top of the bore just slightly below where the top ring stops in operation. Measure the gap with a feeler gauge and then move the ring to the very bottom, unworn part of the bore and again measure the gap. Subtract the bottom gap figure from the top gap figure. The result is approximately three times the bore wear. For example, if the difference found was .030, the bore has worn .010 and must be machined to reuse. See, you can do this!

17 Crank Strip and Rebuild

OVERVIEW

"It is not usually necessary to disturb the crankshaft assembly unless the lubrication system has become contaminated, in which case it may be advisable to clean out the central oil tube." – Very bad advice from a widely distributed aftermarket BSA shop manual.

Not cleaning out the crankshaft sludge trap during a Brit engine rebuild is like performing open-heart surgery with a dirty pocketknife. That trap *must* come out. It can be a real stinker and the manuals aren't much help. Also, you should always remove the sludge trap before taking the crank to the machine shop, something the manuals don't mention but important for a number of reasons we'll discuss. Since the processes are identical, or nearly so, for BSA/Triumph crankshaft rebuilding, we'll tackle this project collectively. We'll start by attacking the plug problem strategically and then we'll rebuild the entire crank assembly.

INITIAL STEPS

First of all, except for early ball-bearing drive-side engines, we have to remove the inner roller bearing on the crank's primary side. It may need to be moved out a bit to fit some pullers, and this can be accomplished by placing a chisel behind it and gently tapping it with a hammer. Once it moves a bit, you can get a puller behind the bearing and take it off. Check the threads on both sides of the crank. If they're damaged, it may be cheaper to get a good used crank than to repair the old one.

You should have already removed the rods during the measurement checks so now we're looking at a bare crank. Place it in a vise, holding it firmly on the flywheel with the slotted plug facing you. Say something nice to the plug; it might help.

Unless you're extremely fortunate and have a crank with an aftermarket Allen-head plug, you'll be facing one tough screw. Before going to work on it, it's very wise to wrap the end of the crank below the plug and at least the closest rod

A gear- or bearing-puller will be required to remove the roller bearing from BSA and Triumph cranks. The BSA crank shown may also have to be removed and installed a time or two to test shim thickness and to measure crankshaft end play.

journal with several soft rags taped tightly in place. This is to protect the crank surface from accidental damage as you do battle, another reason you want to take the plug out before going to the machine shop.

The factory manuals say to use a hand impact wrench to remove the plug. Those guys sure did have a sense of humor. Try it if you'd like, but this hardly ever works. There are, however, various effective methods to loosen the plug. First we have to drill out the punch mark or marks used to dent the threads to prevent the plug from loosening in operation. Use a one-eighth

inch drill bit and drill just far enough to remove the punch mark. Pull the drill a bit toward the center of the plug while working to "worry" it and you won't have to drill as deeply.

Now the fun starts. My preferred method is using an air-powered impact wrench with a screwdriver tip. The impact wrench works well for me in the majority of cases, although some people fear damage to the threads. In any case, once the plug just begins to turn, stop the impact wrench and then use a regular screwdriver or the tool shown in the photos to finish the job.

► HARD CASES

The plug still won't budge and you've begun to chew up the slot? Don't fret; we'll bring in the big guns. The ultimate weapon against bad acting plugs is to drill several holes close together along the slot. Drill size depends on the tool tip you plan to use next. What you want to do is create a ragged slot through the plug to permit driving a large screwdriver tip deeply into the plug (see photo). You can buy large screwdriver tips already on socket drives or make the tool shown. With the tool driven into the slot you just made, heat the crank area around the plug with a propane torch. When it's good and hot, attach the impact wrench and let it go to work. This method has yet to fail me and has removed plugs others gave up on in frustration.

You can make a crankshaft-plug removal tool like this easily out of the end of an old tire iron, a deep half-inch-drive socket, and a large nut. Most screwdriver/impact tips aren't wide enough to fully cover the plug slot; this tool applies greater force across the slot.

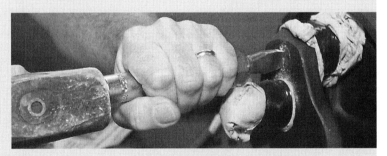

A tool is driven deeply into the slot you created by drilling, to provide a very secure grip. Next we'll heat the plug and use an impact wrench on the end of the tool.

This Triumph plug was one of the tougher ones I've encountered. For these tough situations, drill several holes into the plug as shown. The drill size will depend on the tool you use in the next step.

Got it! The plug can now be turned out using a large wrench on the nut as shown.

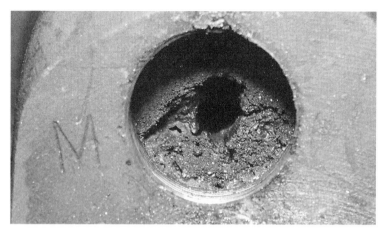

Here's the best case I can make for cleaning out the sludge trap. This trap was almost completely filled with crud!

Use a small brush to clean out oil galleys.

Our Triumph crank is about to get a new Allen head sludge trap plug. It's far superior to the slotted plug, easer to install, and much easier to remove. Also shown is the large easy-out used to remove the sludge trap, and the trap itself partially inside the crank.

TRAP REMOVAL

To get the trap itself out, first remove the bolt in the flywheel that holds it. Next avoid a dumb but widely published method of driving a hardwood stake into the trap. Save the stake for vampires. Good methods include using a large tap, drill bit or easy-out to grab the trap and twist it out. It is also much easier to remove the trap after it's soaked in a mixture of WD 40 and kerosene overnight; it helps with cleaning too.

Okay, it's all downhill from here. Use an old hacksaw blade to scrape out the crud accumulated inside the crank and then clean the entire crank with clean solvent. You don't have to be meticulous now. That part comes after the machine shop work. Let fast-forward to this now.

AFTER MACHINE SHOP WORK

With a freshly machined crank, tiny bits of metal will be all over and inside the oil holes. We must remove it all along with any remaining crud. Even if you will be using the crank without having it turned, it must be carefully cleaned. Soak the entire crank in solvent in a clean plastic bucket to prevent damage to newly machined or polished surfaces; be sure to cover the crank completely with solvent. The longer the soak, the better. After soaking, use small brushes to get into each oil passage (see photo) and a larger brush to scrub out the trap hole. Think it's perfect? Don't bet on it; give it another dunk and then blow out the oil passages with compressed air.

Next, wrap a clean rag around a screwdriver, dip it in clean solvent, and go to work again in the trap hole. Finally, when you think it's absolutely clean, pour the used solvent into another container for general cleaning, clean the bucket carefully, and pour in fresh solvent. Yep, the crank goes back in. You'll see why. Let it soak for a good bit and then dunk it in and out of the solution. Got dirty, didn't it? Keep at it until the solvent remains perfectly clear. Once again, blow out all oil passages with compressed air.

Now take your pristine crank, and insert the equally clean sludge trap. Be careful to align the hole in the sludge trap with the hole in the flywheel. Insert a small Philips screwdriver into the flywheel hole and wiggle it around to align the trap to the crank hole. Insert the bolt now after coating it with a little threadlock and torque it to 33 foot-pounds.

If the plug you removed is in decent shape it can be reused, but it's much better to go with an Allen-head plug. Stake the threads once on each side when it's tight and you're finished. The plug should be flush with the crank surface. If you choose, you can threadlock the plug too.

SMALL-END BUSHES

Be sure you've serviced your rods prior to installation on the crank. If you need to replace the small-end bush, this is easy to do by using a vise to push in the new bush as it pushes out the old one. Position a piece of pipe or socket on one side of the rod to allow the old bush to slide out and put the new bush into the rod on the opposite end. Gently tighten the vice first to be sure everything's aligned perfectly. It helps to have a second pair of hands to line things up. Be sure, too, that the little oil hole on top of the rod is aligned with the new bush hole. Use pre-fitted bushes; some early ones require reaming to size. Either way, check the fit of the bush and wrist pin before continuing.

Triumph small-end rod bushes are often sold today without the predrilled oil hole, the concept being that it's easier to install the bush first and drill the hole afterwards than getting the hole perfectly lined up with the rod hole during installation. Installing and drilling the bush is lots easier to do before building the crank as just explained, although possible with the rods in the case too. It's not at all hard to drill the hole in the Triumph bush as the rod hole provides a simple alignment guide. Use a drill bit just slightly smaller than the rod hole and take care to keep the drill straight. Put a large bolt inside the bush before drilling to prevent accidentally damaging the bush with the drill bit. If this isn't

The connecting rod is first installed just a bit more than hand-tight on each side and then gradually tightened on each end. Once the nuts are tightened lightly with a short ratchet like the one shown, move to a torque wrench for final tightening. Don't forget to use threadlock and new locking nuts.

your cup of tea, let your machinist take care of rod bushes. It's an inexpensive job.

To change bushes with rods installed, you'll need to pull the new bush through the rod while simultaneously removing the old bush by using a long bolt or section of all-thread and a thick washer. Position the new bush on one side of the rod and a sleeve or deep socket on the other side to allow the old bush to push through as you tighten the bolt and pull in the new one.

BSA guys must remember to check that the rod's big end isn't worn out-of-round; have it machined if it needs correction. *Failing to check for and remedy this problem has resulted in many poor BSA rebuilds.*

ASSEMBLING RODS AND BEARINGS

Okay, now take the clean crank and hold it on the flywheel in a vise. To install the new inside roller bearing easily, place it in a clean pan and cover it with fresh oil. Heat the pan on a small electric burner until the oil starts to smoke a bit. Pick the bearing up gently by hooking it with a screwdriver or pliers through the center and bring it to the crank. Wear thick clean gloves for this unless you like second-degree burns. Use your gloved hands now to guide the bearing on the crank. Since it's both lubricated and very warm, it will slide on easily. Alternatively, you can just drift it on with a piece of pipe, but I hate pounding on a new bearing.

Now take your first rod and carefully insert the new big-end rod bearings. Position each bearing so that it's even on each side of the cap and rod and be sure to check to see that the rod is the right one for the crank throw. Also check that either the dots, for Triumph, or numbers,

for BSA, go together on the rod and cap. It's very wise to test-assemble and check the clearance with Plastigauge. Use the old rod nuts for the test assembly.

FINAL ASSEMBLY

If the Plastigauge reading indicates proper clearance, it's finally time for assembly. Gently push the lubricated rod and cap together around the also-lubricated crank. Sometimes the cap hangs a bit on the rod bolts. You can use a small plastic hammer to tap it on, but be very gentle doing so, you don't want to damage either the bearing or journal. Use the new rod nuts and apply high-strength threadlock to the rod bolt threads. Many recommend using new bolts, and if you can afford it, do so, but no matter how poor you are, use new rod nuts. Tighten the nuts gradually on each side in increments of about 5 foot-pounds each. Finally, use a torque wrench and tighten to manual specs for your engine. When fully tightened, check to see that each rod feels absolutely smooth in full revolutions around the crank.

We're on the final step. Take your oilcan and gently insert the tip into the end of the Triumph crank or the oil hole in the crank slot on the BSA's timing end. Pump the oilcan until oil runs out around the rods. This way you know the oil galleys are clear and you've filled the sludge trap with fresh oil to help avoid a dry first start of the engine.

That's it, mate. You have a completely rebuilt crankshaft.

▶ *TOO LOOSE?*

Okay, so I've failed at this point to convince you to do a complete teardown of your project. The issue now is whether or not you have any choice in the matter. For this assessment we'll resort to an old timer's test to determine suitability of doing a top-end-only job. The critical question is the condition and state of wear in the crank main and rod bearings. According to Nicholson and many others, if you cannot detect appreciable movement in the main bearings by lifting both ends of the crank at the timing and drive side, the main bearings are serviceable, provided no roughness can be felt in rotation of the bearings. The test is similar for rod bearings. If you can't detect movement by pushing and pulling directly up and down on the rod, the rod bearing clearance isn't excessive. Some mechanics refer to this condition as "tight" as opposed to "loose" meaning too much clearance caused by wear. Be careful to test the rods by pulling straight up and down, because tugging on an angle will result in movement that's perfectly OK and due to the relatively narrow bearing used. Readers should note the engine being tested is probably the best candidate, if there really is one, for a top-end-only job, and that's a late 500 Triumph motor that many rightfully consider almost bulletproof. The opposite end of this spectrum is the A65 engine. Always use a dial indicator to test the bush-to-crank clearance in A50/65 engines as shown in the measurement chapter. At .003 the clearance is very marginal and .004 calls for a full teardown. Sorry, mate.

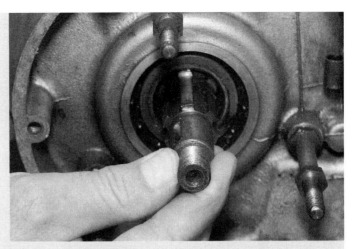

If you can feel anything but the tiniest bit of movement when you try to lift on either end of the crankshaft, the main bearing(s) need replacement and you must split the cases.

Be careful to push and pull the rod directly up and down to check for bearing play. If you feel the rods move, it's time to pull the engine apart for full rebuild.

18 Building the A50/65 Lower End

"You have no idea how controversial this is."
– Anonymous BSA source commenting on BSA A-series lower-end rebuilding.

OVERVIEW

Having rebuilt the crank, you can now reassemble the cases. Both case sections need to be checked carefully and serviced before this happens. No one disputes the need to check cases carefully, but many differ almost violently over the cause and effect of various BSA lower-end issues we're about to cover.

I'll assume the case has been meticulously cleaned and checked for cracks and damage, most common on chain runs near the primary and at the nose where the front motor mount bolt goes. A good alloy welder can fix most problems.

On cases before 1970, loose cylinder base studs are very common. Even if they're tight, remove each stud and use a small rotary file with a 60-degree angle to dress off each hole slightly. This removes the slight lip formed by the stud being pulled up by operating force. If this isn't done, an area around the base will almost invariably leak at some point, if not immediately. All screw holes in alloy can benefit from this treatment, but the cylinder base holes are the most in need. Many top-notch builders, Ed Valiket of E&V Engineering for example, also deck the case surface where the cylinder base fits, to assure a leak-free assembly.

Use a rotary file as shown for cylinder case stud holes, and appropriately smaller rotary files for other case stud holes to remove raised metal caused by operating stress. It will prevent later oil leaks. Check all threads in the case. Many pros run a tap through each threaded hole and repair any damaged threads with an insert kit like Helicoil. This takes time but the benefits are worth it.

Always check carefully for case damage. This one has been repaired by welding but can be reused. The fix was almost invisible from the outside, a pretty good job. However, an obvious weld can detract from the value of the cycle, so factor this into your decision making process when considering whether to fix or replace parts. Good used cases are fairly inexpensive, often under $50.

Also make sure the cam bearings have been checked and/or replaced and that all studs and threaded holes have good threads. (See the Triumph Lower End chapter for cam bearing removal/installation.) The cam itself should get a close inspection for wear and damage. So far, we're still within universally accepted practice, but now it's on to the raging controversy. The factory manual says very little about the most controversial aspects of BSA lower-end assembly. Perhaps if BSA had studied these issues more thoroughly and engineered solutions to them that we could now employ, it might have avoided bankruptcy.

YOUR CHOICE

There are a number of distinctly different ways to prepare an A50/A65 lower end and probably thousands of different, often vitriolic, opinions on the merits of each. Let's begin with one approach that's unquestionably the best, but beyond most budget builders. Still, if you can afford it, a needle roller conversion of the timing side bush is the way to go, as it creates a bulletproof lower end (except for the con rods, that is; but even there we have alternatives).

The needle roller conversion eliminates the wear-prone bush and firmly fixes the crank. The case, crank, oil pump, inner and outer timing covers, idler pinion gear, crankshaft pinion gear, and oil pressure release valve must be sent out for this service. E&V Engineering does this work in the states; SRM does it in England. The conversion also reroutes the oil flow. SRM claims a 40 percent increase in oil pressure over stock, a service of life of 80,000 miles for the con rod bearings, and 100,000 for the mains. For most people, this is a lifetime motor but the expense of shipping the engine parts and the service itself is considerable.

Ditching the stock rods in favor of steel Carrillo rods eliminates the second big issue: the wear-prone stock alloy rods. E&V Engineering stocks these rods. Many advocate this change alone for significantly increasing engine durability, but used in combination with a bearing conversion, the end product is unbeatable. Since our emphasis is home building on a budget, we won't go further into these options. Those with

the resources can get all pertinent details from SRM or E&V Engineering. I recommend both concerns highly.

The real question facing the A50/65 engine builder contemplating alternatives is planned service use vs. longevity. If your intention is maximum horsepower through any combination of larger displacement, hotter cam profiles, or increased compression, you must either use the needle roller conversion or expect a decrease in engine life.

BALL BEARING CONVERSION

While the evidence is only anecdotal, an excellent case has been made by a good number of BSA experts for reverting to the early-style ball bearing to replace the later use of a roller bearing on the drive side. These experts report that ball bearing A65s made from 1962–1965 were less prone to rod failure and more robust in general. From an engineering perspective, controlling the crank's axial loads makes sense. On the other side of the coin, a ball bearing is weaker than a roller at handling radial loads, something it also must do well.

BSA also shimmed their ball bearing motor and called for the same endplay of .001 to .003 as it did on its roller motors, and yes, there is some axial play in a good ball bearing. I measured over .004 on the new one I just installed, a quality RHP unit. Although a number of builders I respect say that endplay isn't a major issue with a ball bearing motor because the bearing now controls axial loads, my paranoid sensibilities move me to put a ball bearing motor together with the specs given for the engines in the 1962–65 factory manual. This means measuring end float when the ball bearing is locked to the crank. The manuals—both factory and aftermarket—are mute in this regard except to say that it's okay to use the same shims so long as the crank hasn't been changed. That turns out to be very bad advice that I took 20 years ago and lived to regret deeply. Always, and I do mean *always*, measure BSA endplay carefully with a roller bearing motor, and I'll always do it on a ball bearing motor, too.

For the photos in this book, I installed a ball bearing into a '69 case, and this goes in without

A ball bearing is driven into a pre-heated case using the old roller race as a driver. The old race has been ground down to fit easily inside the case. This trick can be employed with any old bearing for use as an installation tool.

The case must be heated as shown before removing or installing bearings.

need for any modification. To install it, simply heat the case as you would for the installation of the roller race, and then drive in the cold bearing until it bottoms out in the case.

Removing and installing case bearings is simple, except for the occasional roller race that refuses to budge. Forget the hype in the manual about needing a special tool; you don't, because most times if you just heat the case and then flip it over and give the case a sharp rap on a wood workbench, the race will fall right out. If you hit a stinker, take a die grinder or electric drill with a small cutting wheel and cut a notch in the race. With this cut recess you can fit a small chisel and knock out any stubborn race without a special puller.

Once the ball bearing is home, insert the crank into it. This requires blocking up the case half with either kind of bearing to allow for the crank's protrusion or using a workbench with a hole cut through it for this purpose. You can use almost anything for a shim between the crank and bearing for a test build; just be sure to measure its thickness with a micrometer. I found that without any shims between the crank and ball bearing, the crank web slightly scraped the case half; that's why you need a shim to begin

with. If you have the original shims, at least use the thickest one after measuring it or try the whole shim stack with the shim case; you might get lucky.

Either way, lubricate the ball bearing and insert the crank through the shim(s) and into the bearing. Use a soft hammer on the thick crankshaft web to seat the crank into the bearing. Next, use a spacer to go over the crank (see photo on page 128) and torque the rotor nut to its factory spec of 60 foot-pounds.

You have several options for use on the bush side. Earlier ball bearing motors used a steel encased bush with an insert inside the casing that was pinned to hold it in place. The steel face of the bush is also thicker than the face of the bush used for roller bearing motors. Finding one of these today is next to impossible. The ones you can find today either aren't pinned or are a solid piece of metal. If you do use one of the repop bearings with an insert, it's advisable to have it pinned in place by a machinist. The solid ones are easily obtainable and don't require this work, so I used this along with the thrust bearing on top of the bush as used originally for the roller bearing motor, so that the crank is positioned as it was before. With any kind of bush, it is imperative that the bush is reamed after installing it in the case to give perfect alignment with the crank and a clearance between the crank and bush of

The timing-side bush must be perfect. Make sure it's flush against the case before align boring to size and always check for clearance to the crank as explained in the text.

With a roller bearing, the crank will just drop into the case if you carefully guide it. A ball bearing may require use of a soft hammer on the crank webs and flywheel to tap it home. For roller-bearing motors, the inner part of the bearing that contains the rollers is first installed on the crank. The outer race is installed separately into the case after the case is heated to permit easy installation of the race. The cam does not have to be installed during a test build to determine end float of the crank assembly. When correct endplay is determined, the final assembly will include the cam breather disk, spring, and the cam itself.

.001 to a maximum of .002. This is not horse-shoes; close enough won't cut it. Unless you are a professional machinist, this is a job for a pro shop. Bring your case, crank, and bush to the shop for this service.

For a ball bearing conversion, measure the maximum float in the bearing first and also when it's tightened on the crank (see photo). Experiment with shims until the endplay is between .001 to .003. You know the crank is being limited by the shim when the endplay is less that that found in the ball bearing itself. As I stated previously, with a ball bearing you may not have to be this careful, but I'll still take the extra time to test assemble and measure just to sleep better.

SHIM STOCK

It's still easy to get BSA crank shims but it's often impossible to get the little cup that is supposed to hold them together. I say supposed to, as it is all too common for one of the paper-thin shims to rip and fall off in service. This allows extreme endplay that permits the crank to slam repeatedly against the bush. Then, the bush turns in the case and cuts off the oil flow to the rods. Bad news, and one of the main reasons A-series twins have a bad reputation in some circles.

While it shouldn't be necessary to use a solid shim in a ball bearing motor, it's a very good idea to use a solid one made by a machinist after determining the exact thickness you need using the stock shims and shim case for your test

build. The last one I had made was .032 thick and was cut from heat treated 4140 steel tubing. The bill was $30 for this piece and I think worth every cent. Also you don't need a shim cup with this setup.

ROLLER BEARING

Without question, setting endplay with the roller bearing is extremely critical. We want to get this as close to .001 as possible, and some go even less than that to an almost imperceptible float when measured cold to allow for expansion of the cases when warm. Just be darn sure the crank turns easily and smoothly. If endplay is off by any appreciable margin either way, big trouble is around the corner.

With a roller bearing, install the shims and holding cup and then the inner part of the roller bearing so that the inner bearing is flush against the shims. Next, insert the crank into the case that already contains the outer race of the roller

The only way to correctly check endplay is with the rotor nut and case hardware fully tightened. A spacer made from an old fork tube and thick washer is used in place of the crank gear and rotor.

With crank endplay checked and everything tight, check to see that the crank turns smoothly and easily by moving the rods as they would in operation. Once you are certain that all's well, you can install the main oil seals. Note the new needle bearing deep in the transmission cavity.

bearing. Some people like to drift the inner part of the bearing onto the crank; I like to heat it up in oil on a hot plate so it just slides on the crank.

Start with a test assembly, using the existing shims, and measure the float with a dial indicator (see photo). Use simple math to determine the shim combination you need. Stock BSA shims come in .003, .005, and .010 thicknesses and are encased in a cup. Keep at it until you have both the proper end float and a smoothly turning crank assembly. Be sure to tighten the crank nut with the spacer before measuring endplay or you won't get an accurate reading. Once you arrive at the right shim combination, you can use what you have or measure the shims and cup and go for a solid piece as just explained. You can also test build with the largest shim by itself, measure the end play, and have a solid shim made by calculating the thickness you need to achieve .001 end float.

FINAL ASSEMBLY

Once the endplay is set with either bearing type, we can proceed to final case assembly. Now we need to insert the camshaft rotary breather valve and spring into its hole in the case and then the camshaft itself, being sure it properly engages the breather valve. With both the cam and crank in the primary side of the case, use a good sealant on the case seam; Hondabond #4 works great. Install the bush (timing side) case-half gently over the crank and cam. Don't forget the thrust washer that goes between the crank and bush as is used on roller bearing motors. It can be used on ball bearing motors if the bushing for the roller engine is used. Hold it in place with grease so it does not slip off during assembly. The slots in the thrust bearing face the crank.

Once both halves of the case are together, flip the case upright and begin installing the case hardware. I start by putting the washers and nuts on the three studs in the center of the primary case, tighten these a bit, and then go to the outside hardware, and then back and forth inside and outside for final tightening.

With the case halves bolted together and the rotor nut tight, we want to check our machinist's work. Remember, the bush fit is very critical and it must also be properly aligned. Use the dial indicator as previously shown in the measurement section to determine the clearance between the crank and bush. It bears repeating that you want something between .001 and .002. If the clearance isn't right, it's time for a polite chat with the person who did the work. If the crank binds, it's quite possible that the bush reaming wasn't properly aligned; this will cause rapid wear and overheating. The crank may also bind because of insufficient endplay. Again, we must have

Always check the pump for warping and disassemble beforehand to check gears and body for wear. Also, if you have not checked your pump during the initial teardown, it is imperative with alloy pumps made prior to 1971 to use a straightedge across the pump body to be absolutely sure it isn't warped. With all pumps, the internal gears require inspection for wear, damage, and the ability to turn freely with no binding when the pump is assembled.

You can install the oil pump as shown by turning the worm gear and moving the pump as you do, or remove the studs and install the pump after the worm gear is in place.

several things exactly right: correct endplay, proper clearance in the bush, and a very smooth crank rotation when everything's been fully tightened.

If all is well, it's time to reinstall the pinion gear by driving it on with something like a deep socket. At this point we can install the intermediate gear that turns the camshaft. The gear has two timing marks on opposite sides. Be sure to line up the marks so that one mark lines up with the timing mark on the cam gear while the other lines up with the timing mark on the pinion gear. Now lets check and install the oil pump.

OIL PUMPS

Before we install the oil pump, let's explore some options. BSA made numerous changes to the pump during the life of the A65, with the last change being a cast iron body instead of cast aluminum. The change was made to eliminate a

warping problem, and if you can get a pump from a '71–'72 motor, this is the best. The earlier alloy pump bodies will work if they aren't shot—early pumps usually *are* shot—but any pump should be taken apart to check the gears for wear and damage. Carefully check the alloy pumps for warping by using a straightedge. SRM markets a high performance pump as well. E&V Engineering markets a steel oil pump replacement body that uses the stock gears from your old pump and eliminates oil pump warping.

Aside from warping, stock pumps have been known to get loose and leak, causing low oil pressure. Always use self-locking nuts, washers, and medium grade threadlock for assembly. The oil pump studs are quite small, however, so don't over-torque them. It's very easy to strip the stud threads in the case, another way these things work loose.

Once you have checked the pump, install the

Install the kickstart gear and shaft and the shifter mechanism, as shown, after the transmission is in place. Both just slide into their respective bushings; check them for wear. Carefully check the kicker gear, especially the tooth adjacent to the truncated tooth, as it is often worn badly and can then break easily or be too worn to engage the ratchet gear. Also check the shifter engaging plungers and springs.

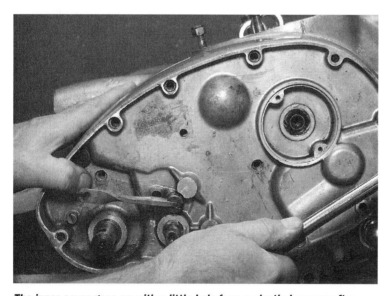

The inner cover goes on with a little help from a plastic hammer after making sure the timing marks on the intermediate gear, cam, and pinion all line up as they should. Be careful with the points seal as there are different ones for different years. All should be a good tight fit. BSA machined the opening of some points holes a bit too large in 1969; there's a seal that will fit this oddball too.

gasket with a thin smear of grease and then insert the tiny spring into the case hole that's supposed to hold an equally tiny ball against the pump when the engine isn't running. Even when new, this arrangement can cause problems; some folks fit anti-sump valves into the oil intake line to prevent wet-sumping, a very common BSA problem. Anti-sumping valves are also very controversial. Personally, I lean toward tolerating a little smoke at startup rather than risk the possibility of a faulty valve cutting off the oil supply. When installing the pump, carefully check the gasket holes for size and placement, as many aren't perfect and interfere with the check ball. A lot of wet-sumpers have been cured simply by enlarging the gasket hole to remove the interference.

You can install the pump with the studs in the case by installing the worm gear with the pump and turning it and the pump drive together. Or, go with the book method of installing the worm gear first and then inserting the studs once the pump's in position. In either case, make sure you have the check ball stuck in place with a little grease in the pump's recess (see photo on page 129) or you'll really have a wet-sumping mess. Finally, lock the engine by placing a long socket extension through the rods. Now you can torque the crank nut to 60 foot-pounds after installing a new lock tab washer. Don't forget that the nut is left-handed. Also install a new lock tab washer on the cam and tighten its nut. Finish by folding over the lock tabs on the cam and crank nuts.

INNER TIMING COVER

The transmission and shifter shaft (see transmission chapter) must be installed before installing the inner timing cover. Once in place, use a light coat of gasket cement on the gasket surface of the engine and install the gasket. The points seal must also be installed in the inner cover. There are different seals, early and late, so check the fit. It should be very tight. Also, BSA made the '69 timing cover hole too large on some engines; there's a special seal to correct this error. Now you can install the cover and the screws that hold it.

Note the new later-model oil pressure relief valve at the lower right and new lock nuts on the oil pump, both highly recommended. The inner cover gasket is being installed now.

PRESSURE RELIEF VALVE

We have one final, very important detail, and that's converting earlier engines with the flat oil pressure release valve to the later Triumph domed style valve (see photo). Many, many low-pressure problems have been traced to faulty stock BSA pressure relief valves. SRM reports that even the later model stock pressure relief valves were machined wrong and often leaked around the threads, so they commissioned their own. Also, the bypass hole location in the case can vary in location, and if the valve and hole aren't properly positioned, oil pressure can be affected greatly. If you encounter pressure problems after a rebuild with a late style valve, try swapping the stock washer for a Vinton O-ring as a dramatic difference can be made with this simple change if positioning is the problem.

Well, this describes what amounts to BSA open-heart surgery. If you've been careful with the crank and case so far, no matter which way you went, you can expect many miles before you'll see the insides of this engine again. You won't get the 80,000 miles that are possible with a needle bearing conversion, but many experts report that 40,000 to 50,000 miles are quite possible on a well-maintained stock lower end. For the limited road use many of these engines see today, you may well have a BSA lower end that lasts longer than you do.

While these A65 rods look identical, they really aren't. Up to 1965 A65 rods were interchangeable but from 1966 on, the primary drive side rod featured a tiny oil hole. This was added to increase the lubrication in the left cylinder. The right one gets more lubrication because of its closer proximity to the timing side bush's oil spray. Be sure to check for the hole before assembly. Some rods have an outlet hole on only one side of the rod, and if this is the case, point the hole toward the flywheel. Also be careful to measure both rods for big-end diameter. If they are out-of-round, BSA rods can be machined to correct this wear so long as the rod isn't more than .005 out-of-round. If over .005, replace the rod.

19 *Triumph Lower End*

OVERVIEW

Triumph lower ends are legendary for durability. Many builders who put a Triumph twin together carefully and maintain it properly can reasonably expect to never see their bottom end again, unless they look over their shoulders at a mirror (sorry, couldn't resist that one). There are also numerous performance enhancements available, ranging from hotter cams to high-output oil pumps, but we'll stick to stock components for our budget build. And even stone stock, the unit Triumph is a great performer.

The cam bush is installed with a junk camshaft. If you don't have one, ask for one where you get your parts. Many times, a parts supplier will throw in a junk cam for free if you're a customer. Junk cams are also widely available in prime rusty condition for peanuts at swap meets. See the text for more cam bush removal/installation details.

MAIN AND CAM BEARINGS

The crank ball and roller bearings are tough, long-wearing parts; reusing them should not be feared if they pass muster. Installation and removal of roller/ball main bearings are covered in the previous chapter on the BSA lower end and crank.

If the cam and its bearings are okay, they do not need to be removed during teardown and the gears can remain on the cams. Some model years require special pullers to remove gears, but many have two threaded holes to allow use of just about any puller.

If you do need to replace cam bearings, presized bushes are available, but check them for fit. Raw cam bushes will have to be align bored to size; a special tool exists for this purpose. Many machine shops can jig something up to align bore the bushes.

The timing-side cam bushings can be driven out using a drift of suitable size or a socket and extension to serve as one. Be sure to heat the case prior to driving out and installing new bushings.

Install the transmission oil seal as shown here with the case split. Top gear and then the drive sprocket, nut, and washer go next. Finally, hold the sprocket in a vise and tighten the nut. This can all be done with the cases joined, but it's a lot easier to do beforehand.

Insert the crank into the case-half gently to avoid damaging the roller bearing.

The timing side of the case can be joined over the crank to the primary side with the cams and gears installed as shown if there was no reason to remove the cams during rebuild—a fairly common situation.

The cams can also be installed in the primary side first if the gears were removed. Always use a good sealant on the case seam, as shown, before joining the case halves.

A soft hammer may be used as shown to help join the case in which the ball bearing is a very tight fit on the crank, but be sure the problem isn't a misaligned breather disk on the intake cam or some other obstruction.

The blind bushes are a bit trickier. If you have a large enough tap, you can thread the bush and then insert a matching bolt through a deep sleeve and screw it into the bush. A short piece of 3/4-inch water pipe and thick washer make a perfect pulling tool. Tighten the bolt and the bush will be drawn out into the sleeve. If you can't get a big enough tap, ask your machinist how much he would charge to pull the bush, as what he charges may be a lot less than the tap itself.

Bush installation is easy if you have the right tool: a junk camshaft. Just heat the case and drive the bushes home. This can also be done with a socket on an extension, but it's more difficult to accomplish, and it's much easier to accidentally damage the bush.

Like the BSA, early unit-construction Triumph engines have a breather disk and spring that require care to align with the intake cam while joining the cases. Alignment is done by rotating the cam as the cases go together until proper engagement is achieved. Some builders prefer to place the cams in the primary side of the case with the intake cam already set properly, and then install the other case half over the cams and crank. The gears, of course, must be removed first to do so.

After the case is joined, install center hardware before turning the case over.

If your case has three small holes in the primary side like these, you do not fit a breather disk on the cam or a crank oil seal.

Timing gear marks and placements vary on Triumph twins so you have to be sure to set the gears according to the shop manual diagram for your specific year and model. All Triumphs, however, have the same gear arrangement as shown. White paint on the gears of this late model Triumph 500 mark the three areas that must be matched and properly aligned.

Later engines breathe through the primary and eliminate the cam alignment step entirely because there's no breather disk and spring to fiddle with. You can easily recognize the later case by looking for the three small holes drilled inside the primary case (see photo) to allow oil to return to the sump. These engines also don't need a crank oil seal as this is how the engine breathes and keeps the primary oiled.

To join the cases, coat the seams with a good sealant and install the crank roller bearing end first into its raised and supported case half and then the lower the ball bearing (timing-side) down. Also, make sure the cams are aligned with their respective holes. A soft hammer may be used on the case that can be a bit resistant to close completely, especially with a new ball bearing in the timing side.

Once the cases are in place, install the nuts and bolts holding it together, and check to be sure the crank and cams rotate smoothly after everything's tight.

CAM GEAR TIMING

The pinion can be driven on with a thick socket, but don't install the crank nut yet because doing so hides the cam timing marks on the pinion. Triumph used different marks over the years to reference the timing of the intake, exhaust and intermediate gears, and it's imperative to know what's right in order to position the marks correctly to set cam timing. Because of year-to-year variations, some aftermarket books have referenced timing marks incorrectly, so always be sure to use the factory manual only for the correct marks and positioning for your specific engine year and model. If you took the gears off of your cams, line the timing mark up with the cam's keyway when installing the gears. The intermediate gear will just slide on its shaft to engage the other gears, but be careful it does not fall off and change position after aligning the timing marks, or you'll have to start all over again. The photo in this chapter of a late model Triumph 500 shows the proper arrangement and layout that is correct for all engines with respect to the three points that must be checked (highlighted with a spot of white paint for easy reference) but, I say again, the specific gear

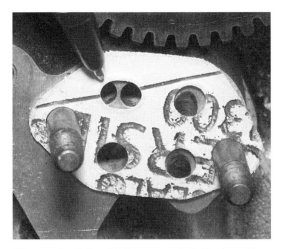

Always check the fit of every gasket. Far too often they're very poorly made, as is this Triumph oil pump gasket. The pointer shows a hole that is badly obstructed, and the others need some trimming too. This is also very common on BSA pump gaskets, where obstructions frequently cause severe wet sumping. Correction is simple. Mark the gasket with a felt pen indicating the area(s) to be cut, and then remove the gasket for cutting on a flat surface with a razor or similar sharp tool. Install the gasket with a smear of grease after trimming.

marks differ from engine to engine. Once you're sure the cam timing is correct, install and tighten the cam nuts (they have left-hand threads) and then the pinion nut. You will have to lock the engine with a socket extension through the rods before tightening the nuts. Now we can install the oil pump.

Carefully inspect the oil pump for damage, especially the plungers. A simple check is to hold a finger or two over the pump holes while pulling on the plungers. You should feel a strong, pulling vacuum. Plugs at the pump base will be removed next to clean and inspect the check balls. Often, the soft alloy piece that attaches to the cam is pretty banged up. Replace the alloy piece if it is badly worn. The one pictured here is in great shape.

OIL PUMP

High-performance oil pumps are available in several forms, but the stock one performs well as long as it's undamaged. Make sure to check the pump carefully (see photo). The later pump has special domed nuts that fit the recess of the pump and are used in conjunction with special washers that should be new. Position the intake cam to accept the pump drive block as the pump is installed.

All in all, the time involved taking apart and assembling the Triumph lower end isn't excessive or unduly complicated, and the peace of mind you now have, knowing everything about your engine, is well worth the effort.

20 *Shifty Business*

OVERVIEW

Once again we lack precise wear specifications from the factory that will tell us with certainty whether or not a given transmission part is good enough for service. It would be wonderful too if we could bench test our gearboxes, but that just isn't feasible. Mainly because of the inability to thoroughly assess the condition of transmissions on the workbench I like to run a rat project before teardown. That way, I can give the gearbox a workout and pinpoint its problems while answering other questions.

The closest you can get to a transmission bench test is to install the engine and transmission in the bike and operate the transmission while a friend spins the back wheel. It works best to do this before installing the primary chain so that you don't have the force of the engine working against you. While BSA and Triumph 500s do not have this issue, it is very common to have indexing problems after a rebuild of the Triumph 650/750 unit; a bench test will reveal problems.

The real stinker of the bunch is the Triumph leaf spring transmission that can't be securely positioned in a gear upon installation and will frequently change camplate position because

the leaf spring moves it on installation. Triumph only used this miserable arrangement for a few years and then regained its sanity and went back to the good old reliable plunger. Anyway, it is highly advisable to test these units carefully and be prepared for some aggravation. You can recognize a leaf spring transmission by the lack of a large threaded hole on the bottom of the transmission case for the plunger and the addition of a leaf spring on the inner transmission cover.

This brings us to another issue I've grown to accept with budget transmission building, and that's the possibility of having to go back into a transmission a second time to replace something that didn't live up to my expectations. Fortunately, going into the box for round two isn't as hard as it sounds, because all transmissions covered here can be rebuilt completely with the engine still in the bike. Also, the only 100 percent guaranteed way to avoid problems is to replace every part with even moderate wear, a highly expensive proposition. As they say, the choice is yours. We can, though, cut down on second repair trips enormously, and generally eliminate them, by recognizing common trouble spots and correcting the problems we find.

INSPECTION

A good way to begin inspection and learn assembly is to lay the parts out carefully on a workbench piece by piece, in order, using the shop manual and parts book as a guide. Don't worry about the press-on gears, just pull apart the pieces you can. Make reference notes if you need to. After a short time, you'll find it easy to take apart and assemble the layshaft and mainshaft correctly.

BSA and Triumph 500 transmissions come out complete with the camplate and forks attached. To disassemble these units you first have to pull out the pin the camplate rotates on in the

A late model Triumph 4-speed transmission is shown complete with forks in their proper position. Note the camplate at left that's in perfect condition. This unit has very low mileage.

Perhaps the most common troublemaker for Brit box builders is shown: a gear with badly worn driving dogs. Note wear on the edges and corners of the dogs, evidence of gear jumping. This is a 5-speed Triumph top gear pulled for just this problem.

Pressed-on gears can be removed with a puller as shown, as well as with a hydraulic press.

cover and also the shaft the forks ride on. After that, pull apart the layshaft and knock out the mainshaft from the cover with a soft hammer if it doesn't just pull out after you've taken off the nut and kickstart assembly. You should have loosened the kickstart rachet nut during teardown. If you didn't, put the shaft in a soft vise and remove the high-torque nut.

TROUBLEMAKERS

Almost any time you see a used transmission for sale, "no broken or chipped gears" will pop up in the seller's description. That's cool, but broken and/or cracked gear teeth, while hardly unknown, aren't the most common troublemakers.

Far more troublesome are worn driving dogs (see photo) that frequently go bad long before the outer gear does. It takes very little wear on driving dogs to cause problems, generally evidenced by the trransmission popping out of gear. Worn dogs often require replacing both gears that engage with each other because if one gear's dogs are badly worn, the mating parts on the gear it engages have worn too. Some people and manuals say that one should also replace any gear that runs on the opposite shaft of a troublemaker, meaning that if you replace third gear on the layshaft, you have to replace third gear on the mainshaft. While this ideal is noble, considering matching wear patterns, I've built

more than a few boxes out of completely miscellaneous parts that worked very well, so I'm now of the "If it ain't really broke, don't fix it" school of transmission repair.

Also high on the list of problem causes are worn or bent shift forks and the camplate that moves them around. Check each fork for excessive wear and scoring. If you find a lot of wear, take a close look at the gear slot it rides on. If you find burs, bluing, marked grooves, or any obvious sign of damage and/or distortion, get another fork and/or gear. Also carefully check the round fork part that rides in the camplate. Many Triumphs have hardened steel rings that ride on the fork and in the camplate. These rings should be a close fit on the fork and in the camplate, and are permanently fixed on later units. Five-speed Triumph forks don't have this ring, just a bigger rounded piece on the fork that rides directly in the camplate. BSA forks have rings on the forks that are pinned in place. All of these parts suffer from wear and damage in operation and need close scrutiny.

Bad camplates are very common and are damaged in two main ways besides general wear: by riders who use their gearshift levers

An extremely worn and damaged camplate is shown at left. The good camplate at right has just a slight bit of surface rust that can be removed easily. Note too the lack of an indexing mark at the bottom of the right plate. This is a leaf spring camplate. You don't even need the notch with the installation method described in this chapter, but if you are using this camplate with the original leaf spring you may need to re-index this quadrant because the camplate can move on installation.

Old- and new-style Triumph top gears are shown. Notice that the bushing at left is worn to make a ring around the bush. It must be replaced. Later gears have a projection to protect the bush as shown at right. These gears can be interchanged but also require a different clutch door and seal to match the gear.

with kickstart-like force, and worn main transmission bearings that allow the shaft to slop back and forth. Consequently, a bad camplate usually indicates bad bearings and/or a lot of general abuse.

Damaged camplates are fairly easy to spot (see photo). Look for bumpy running tracks and dents where the forks ride. Wear, however, is more subtle but still spells trouble. To detect wear, place the fork in its running track on the camplate. The fork should fit in the camplate without a lot of free play in the tracks. A lot of room means it's well worn and should be replaced. Also check the camplate gear teeth on Triumph 650/750s and both sides of the engaging quadrant. The shifter plungers that engage the camplate or quadrant also should be inspected for wear and collapsed springs. Also inspect the notches and tracks on the outside of all camplates used by the plunger (or leaf spring) in the case to index each gearshift. Finally, check the condition of the plunger/leaf spring itself and the plunger spring.

High gear runs through the case and connects to the secondary chain sprocket; it can suffer a

lot of wear. In 4-speed transmissions there's a bush that can get pretty worn in several areas. On BSAs and early Triumphs, the bush sticks out and gets worn by the clutch door oil seal too. This can cause severe leakage (see photo). High gear also wears a lot inside the bush where it rides on the mainshaft. If excessive wear/play is found, you'll have to replace the bush by pressing the old one out and a new one in. Check all gear bushes and teeth and also measure the mainshaft and layshaft they ride on and compare to manual specs for diameter. Check the shafts for scoring and other damage, especially to the threaded ends.

On 5-speeds, instead of a bush there are two needle bearings inside top gear which also suffer a lot and are wise to replace on any rebuild. The same goes with layshaft needle bearings on all of these transmissions. While one can usually get by reusing the big ball bearings, I always replace needle bearings. All of these bearings can generally be sourced generically at much lower cost than a factory-numbered part. Bring the old ones to the bearing shop and they'll match up new ones.

You can make a drift to replace needle bearings as detailed in the shop manual and shown

A set of circlip pliers like the one shown is needed to remove transmission main bearings in the case and cover. The case will be heated next and the bearing driven out.

This Triumph 500 transmission is broken down for inspection. There are lots of miles on this one, so it will be inspected closely.

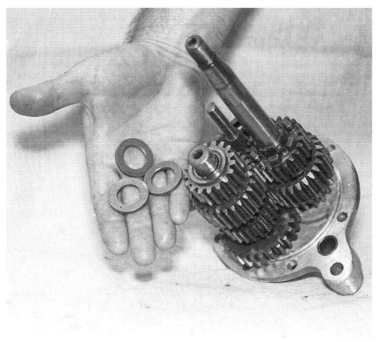

This BSA transmission is ready for installation. The mainshaft top gear is already in the case. BSA uses different thickness spacers on the layshaft to set the correct amount of endplay. Use of a transmission from another engine can require a change in spacer, but always check endplay even if you are using the same transmission you took out.

in the teardown chapter. However, it is possible to install needle bearings with the layshaft itself used as a drift, so long as you're careful and use only a soft-faced hammer. Old bearings can be drifted out with a small socket or any drift of appropriate size. Always heat the case or cover before replacing bearings. After installation, be sure to put a glob of silicone sealant over the needle bearing cover in the outer case after it is replaced to prevent leaks around the case hole.

All of our Brit twin mainshafts run on two ball bearings, one in the case and the other in the cover. These are pretty tough bearings and last for many miles but they do go bad. The bearings should turn smoothly and have very little play in the races. If they're rough, pitted, loose, and/or show signs of bluing from heat, they've got to go. Remove the seal and/or the holding circlip with circlip pliers and then heat the case/cover before drifting them out. New ones should be installed with the case/cover still hot.

After you've inspected parts and replaced those that are worn, it's time to reinstall the transmission. The BSA and Triumph 500 are as-

sembled on the bench and then inserted as a complete unit back into the case, except for the mainshaft high gear. This gear is installed through the case bearing separately and then the mainshaft is inserted into it. Don't forget the spacers on the BSA layshaft nor the brass washer over the layshaft needle bearings. Also make sure you've checked and installed the plunger and spring. Generously oil all parts and then guide the transmission into the case.

Forget the manual's instructions for installation of the 4-speed Triumph transmission. Hughie Hancox has a much better method. Begin by installing top gear and the camplate in the first-gear position as shown. This is harder to do with the leaf spring model shown, as the camplate can rotate easily. This photo show the camplate in first-gear position, correct for plunger models. For a leaf spring unit, position the camplate in fourth-gear position and the quadrant to the top. Still, camplate movement caused by inserting the cover with its leaf spring can create problems. See text for more details.

HUGHIE'S WAY

Ignore the manual's instructions for installing Triumph 4-speed transmissions as a unit; there's a much easier way discovered by Triumph factory mechanics and publicized by Hughie Hancox. Proceed as follows:

1. Insert top mainshaft gear running through case.

2. Assemble the cover after installing bearings. Insert mainshaft with attached first gear and assemble kickstart ratchet parts, tab washer, and nut. Hold assembly in soft-jawed vise and tighten nut. Leave the tab washer unbent until the very end, just in case something's wrong and you have to remove the nut. Fold over the tab after testing.

3. Insert the camplate, plunger, and spring, positioning the camplate so that it is in the first gear position (see photo).

4. Install third and then second gears on the layshaft and insert this assembly into the case being sure that the thrust washer is in place with the grooved side facing the gears.

The layshaft with second and third gears is inserted next and then the fork positioned as shown.

Insert the mainshaft fork next and then the rod as shown.

5. Insert layshaft fork on second and third gear and position the fork with a greased roller to hold it on the camplate running track.

6. Insert mainshaft selector fork into camplate track behind the layshaft fork and then insert the rod through both shift forks into the case. If the rod won't go though, you probably have the forks wrong. Reposition until the holes align to let the rod slide in easily (see photo).

7. Insert the mainshaft third gear into its fork groove and then the second gear, also locating it in the groove in the fork. Check now to make sure the gear holes are lined up to allow the mainshaft to slip in easily.

8. Insert layshaft low gear.

9. Fit layshaft thrust washer with grease to hold it on the transmission cover. Be sure slot faces gears.

Mainshaft third gear is installed next in its fork as shown.

Mainshaft second gear is installed in the same fork as shown. All that's left now is to place the layshaft first gear on its shaft and then insert the cover, complete with first gear and layshaft washer held on the cover with grease. This method is super easy compared to the procedure described in the factory manual.

10. Apply gasket cement to cover and insert lubricated mainshaft into the case. Since this method indexes the shift quadrant differently from the manual, you won't have to fiddle with its position. When the quadrant is all the way down, that's first gear position. However, after installation, it's wise to use a screwdriver to move the quadrant to be sure it's located properly and moves properly. This means that one click up is neutral, and then second, third, and fourth gear.

When you're finally sure all is well, it's best to use both the tab washer and threadlock to secure the high-torque transmission nut. If it comes loose in operation, this can allow the mainshaft to move so excessively that it's possible for two gears to engage simultaneously, locking up the gearbox and quite possibly throwing the rider down hard in the process. Also be sure after final tightening that there's just a bit of end float in the layshaft.

LEFT/RIGHT CONVERSION

Many owners have been faced with the need to use a later-model left-shift Triumph 750 engine in an older frame designed for right-shift. Left-shift to right-shift is an easy conversion. Right to left, however, requires special homemade linkages, but it has been done. All that's required to convert left-shift to right are the outer primary and transmission covers from a right-shift engine and the parts that go into the outer shift cover.

You'll need to strip the primary and remove the shift rod that runs through the case. Block the remaining shaft hole; a rubber expanding automotive freeze plug works well. Also make sure that the shift quadrant is correct for the transmission; 4- and 5-speeds are different, as are the shift quadrants behind the plate in the shifter cover. Everything else fits perfectly now and you can use the same mounting hardware. Also, plug the shaft hole on the gear side.

4-SPEED TO 5-SPEED CONVERSIONS

While more involved than switching from left- to right-shift, 5-speed conversion is relatively simple, provided you can find a 5-speed transmission. These are now commanding premium prices. Actually, because of cost and also because the 4-speed box is frequently less troublesome and more durable, I've also converted bad 5-speed bikes into 4-speeds.

You need to swap the following parts from 4- to 5-speed or vice versa, going from the primary side back: clutch door and seal, drive sprocket and nut, gearbox seal, main bearing in the case, camplate and plunger, shift quadrant in the inner cover, and the shift quadrant in the outer transmission cover. For '72 and later engines, this is usually just a direct swap, but earlier cases will require a bit more work. Earlier cases require enlarging the mainshaft hole where top gear runs through the case to a diameter just a little larger than 1-11/16 inch and the mainshaft inner cover hole should be 1-1/8 inch. It's easier just to use the inner cover from the 5-speed unit.

With earlier cases, you may need to clearance the inside of the case to prevent contact with top gear. Some modification of the layshaft gears and/or outer cover may also be required to keep the proper clearance of .015 between fourth and fifth gears and to maintain slight end float of the layshaft.

Here's what you need to convert to a 5-speed transmission, except for the missing cruciform-shaped piece at the end of the layshaft.

The 5-speed transmission is installed much like the 4-speed but the instructions given in the shop manual are good for the 5-speed. Take special note of the small cruciform-shaped piece at the end of the layshaft. This indicates an early 5-speed that has a rotten reputation, especially for breaking off this cruciform, which was way too thin to handle the loads it was given. Later 5-speeds have a much larger cruciform. Note also the plugged shift shaft hole. This is a left-shift 750 case that was converted to right-shift for use in this chopper. Details are given in the text.

TESTING

As I explained previously, if there's any doubt about correct indexing, test the transmission before building the primary side. Just because you lined the quadrant teeth up like it shows in the factory manual does not mean the box will shift properly. Trust me on this one. Be sure to torque the sprocket nut and mainshaft nuts fully before testing, because performing this test with loose nuts will not provide accurate results.

Install the drive chain and then get a helper to spin the back wheel of the bike to imitate, in a very limited way, how the transmission will behave in operation. While a partner spins the wheel, shift the bike up and down the gears. The shifts should be clean and precise in both directions. False neutrals, difficult shifts, and hanging in gear means something's wrong. Commonly, it's an indexing problem and means you have to move the gear quadrant up or down a notch.

Everything's okay? Great, assemble the primary, which is really also a part of the transmission. In fact, many so-called transmission problems are actually bad clutch issues. We must make sure this isn't a problem.

CLUTCH HITTER

Inspect the clutch bearings for wear and replace the primary chain on any major rebuild. Make sure that each bonded plate is checked for thickness and surface problems like missing material. If they're badly glazed, also replace the bonded plates. Each plain steel plate must also be inspected for damage. After these checks, inspect the tangs on the plates for wear (see photo) and replace them if they are worn. If the tangs look good, check each plate for warps by placing it on a piece of thick, flat glass.

If you find a lot of bad clutch plates, or if your budget allows, go for a 7-plate conversion. You'll get seven new bonded plates and one new steel one. This conversion does wonders for stuff like finding neutral at standstill, improves shifting, and also allows using less clutch spring pressure for easier operation.

Inspect the clutch basket and hub slots for wear. If moderate notching is found, this can be removed with a file before installation, but bad notching (see photo) means replacement.

I cheat a bit sometimes on the hub holding the clutch rubbers and inspect it only by using the tool (see photo) to check for play and rebounding. If it feels firm and has no free play and adequate rebound, I leave it alone. If you detect problems, remove the screws or bolts, take off the cover, and then use the tool shown to hold the hub to push and pull it to allow replacing the rubber pieces inside. Later hubs have straight-through bolts instead of screws on each side.

With everything in order, install the clutch door with a new seal and then the inner clutch hub making sure the keyway is engaged. It's a good idea to replace the thrust washer between the basket and hub, as a worn one can cause the basket to wobble a lot; a worn basket can do the same even with a new washer. Now place the primary chain on the front drive sprocket and clutch basket and bring both over their respective shafts.

We now need to install the 20 roller bearings inside the clutch basket. Use grease to hold them in place. Once you get a few bearings in, a needle nose pliers works well to install each one, turn the clutch hub by hand and this will run the rollers around the inside of the basket to facilitate installing more bearings.

Install the inner hub and then the thick washer and clutch locknut. If you're reusing the nut, use high-strength threadlock on the threads and then use the clutch-locking tool to hold parts in place while you torque this nut. Either lock the engine with a bar through the rods or put the transmission in high gear and use the back brake on the bike to hold things still.

Install the lubricated clutch plates, greased clutch rod, and cover now, followed by the cups, springs, and their holding nuts. Check the clutch operation to be sure the cover moves out evenly around the plates. Aftermarket alloy covers improve performance. Adjust the spring nuts to correct until the cover lifts evenly all around the clutch. Use feeler gauges to check for even lift of the cover.

Beware of cheap aftermarket clutch nuts and springs. Get the steel nuts if you need replacements, not brass ones, because the cheapo nuts

Both the clutch basket and inner hub must be inspected for notching. If notching is moderate, it can be removed by filing, but notching such as that on the hub at right means you must replace the hub or basket. The left hub is very usable.

The clutch rebound rubber is removed by holding the hub with the homemade tool as shown, and prying out the rubber pieces. The tool is made from a steel bar welded to a junk plain clutch plate. A junk inner hub on an old transmission shaft is also in use and held in the vise. You can use your good shaft if it's held with soft-jaws. Putting a shot of spray carburetor cleaner on each new rubber piece makes the new rubber much easier to slip in.

A badly worn clutch plate is shown at right opposite a new plate from a 7-plate conversion kit. Note extreme wear on the tab and missing bonded material; either defect is cause for rejection, as is any evidence of warping.

like to lock on and hold the clutch springs and then make it impossible to adjust or remove the nuts later. Quality clutch plates also make a big difference in operation and can often cure what seemed to be a transmission problem.

Install the alternator and rotor and use a new tab washer on the rotor nut. I use threadlock in this assembly as well. To make sure you have proper clearance between the rotor and stator, slide a dollar bill between them and move it completely around the circumference. If nothing hangs up, it's okay. If the bill sticks somewhere, you most likely have the stator on crooked and you need to remedy that.

Finally, adjust the primary chain. You want about 1/8 inch movement in the upper chain. An inexpensive tool exists to adjust the 650/750 Triumph primary chain that is far easier to use than a short screwdriver. With the Triumph 500, you have to adjust the primary after the cover is in place, since the adjuster is built into the cover. The BSA has an adjustment bolt at the bottom of the primary case.

All we have to do now is make sure the joint faces of the primary cover and engine are perfectly clean. If the slightest bit of old gasket remains, it's likely to leak, as and many did straight out of the factory. Always use a new gasket with cement, even if the old gasket looks perfect because, as sure as the sun rises tomorrow, you'll have a spot of oil under the engine if you try to slide on this. Please don't ask me how long it took for this last lesson to sink in, but I'm told there's a statue of me somewhere in Kuwait in appreciation of excessive oil consumption.

Check for play in the clutch basket assembly by rocking as shown before loosening the clutch nut. If excessive play is found, replace the thrust washer behind the basket and closely inspect the basket, bearings, and inner hub, since wear on these parts also causes excess play.

A relatively recent innovation is the 7-plate clutch conversion shown at right next to stock bonded plates. This clutch is installed exactly the same way and just adds an additional bonded plate and steel plate. I highly recommend this conversion, as it can greatly improve shifting and overall clutch performance.

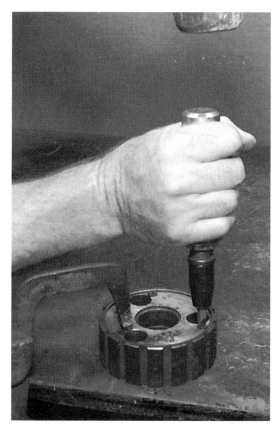

To get the screws or bolts out of the clutch hub, first firmly secure the hub and use a heavy hammer and impact wrench to loosen them.

▶ KICKSTART ASSEMBLY

The kickstart assembly of most Brit twins seldom causes problems unless severely worn from long use or abuse. The same cannot be said for the 500 Triumph assembly. Its kicker is fragile for a number of reasons so it pays to inspect the components carefully. Unlike our other twins, the 500 uses a splined shaft to mate with the kicker lever and this often gets chewed up when it gets loosened in operation. If yours is worn or damaged to any great degree, replace it, and replace the kicker itself if its splines are worn. The splines shown here are in great shape. Also scrutinize the inside of the kicker assembly carefully. Early ones have a bush; later ones a needle bearing. Replace either if worn or damaged. The real culprit, though, is the little engaging pawl shown installed on the assembly and also separately next to a new replacement. Note the slight difference between the two. In operation the worn one at right caused the kicker to fail to engage. When replacing the pawl, also check the spring and plunger under it and the gear teeth it engages. If you replace the pawl, it's a good idea to also replace the spring.

21 *Heads, You Win*

OVERVIEW

A lot of unnecessary damage is inflicted on old Brit motorcycle heads by so-called professionals and backyard builders. The repair manuals contribute to these atrocities by recommending hot water immersion to heat the head prior to removal/installation of the valve guides. Since water boils at 212 degrees Fahrenheit (even less at high altitudes), it can't get the head hot enough to help much; this often results in excessive force being employed to do the job. You also aren't likely to have valve seat cutters nor the skill a good machinist does to do this job well. Skipping steps and/or cutting corners when rebuilding a motorcycle head also ranks as a major cause for poor performance and oil burning. Let's do this right because it isn't that hard or expensive to do so.

FIRST STEPS

Once the rocker arms (BSA) or rocker boxes (Triumph) are off, there's virtually no difference between BSA or Triumph head rebuilding, so we'll cover this as a single topic. Our first mission is to strip the head for media blasting. The only valve removal tools you need are a hammer and an old spark plug socket. Simply place the socket over the valve spring and give it a shot or two with the hammer and the keepers pop right off. You can also use a valve spring compressor; it just takes a lot longer. You will need the compressor for spring installation, however. A spring compressor designed for Brit heads works a lot easier (see photo on page 150) than the generic C-type, and some compressors are too big to work at all.

With the springs and keepers off, remove the valves by pulling each out. If a valve resists, it's usually because a slight ridge has formed on the

A super quick way to remove valve springs involves use of a deep socket and hammer as shown. One or two moderate shots will free the keepers and allow for removal of the springs and valve.

Always inspect all parts, like the valve spring retainer and keepers shown here. These are usually in good condition and are reusable, but the springs are often shot.

Old inner and outer valve springs are shown beside their replacements. Note the significant collapse of the old springs; that's why these needed to be replaced. New valves in background will also be used, as the old ones were also too worn to reuse.

After cleaning, carefully inspect the head before doing any more work. There's a lot of metal left on the valve seat pictured here (not true with all heads), but we have a crack running from the spark plug hole to the valve seat. While this BSA head can be repaired, a good used head is usually a lot cheaper than repairing one with a serious defect. Consequently, this head will be rejected but not discarded, as a time may come when fixing it is the cheaper alternative.

valve where the keepers ride. In a way, this is good news, because you would never notice the raised lip if the guide is totally shot. To remove the valve lip, use a piece of fine emery paper around the ridge until the valve will slip out of and then into the guide without interference. If you force the valve out of or into a good guide without removing the ridge, you can damage the guide.

Refer to the measurement chapter for guide and valve checks. Also check the valve tips carefully for wear. Lash caps (steel caps that fit on top of the valve stems) can be used to repair otherwise good valves, but new valves aren't all that expensive and are a better option. Shims are also available to raise slightly worn springs back to stock specs, but not as good as new springs.

GUIDE REMOVAL AND INSTALLATION

We'll use two special drifts for guide replacement, but one will do if you're careful. The stepped drift you need is available from most parts suppliers and frequently sold on eBay. To avoid damage to the new guides I install them with an aluminum drift, but I use a steel drift to remove the old ones.

Some controversy exists as to whether one can replace an old guide with another standard OD guide or whether you must use an oversize guide

as a replacement. I suspect much of this has to do with previous butchery, but if the removal and installation are done correctly, and the guides weren't loose in the head to begin with or the hole broached, a standard OD guide should work well. It's also very possible that the existing guide is oversized already, so be sure to measure before ordering new ones. Loose fits are corrected with oversized valve guides. When in doubt, it's another good time for a consultation with your machinist.

Actually, if this is your first valve job, it's a very good idea to bring the cleaned head down to the machinist before doing any other work as he can tell you if there's enough metal left to cut the valve seats—a must with the installation of new guides—and also cast an expert eye on the entire head. If you have to replace valve seats, make sure to use the hardened ones for unleaded gas, but stock seats seem to hold up pretty well as long as they aren't worn out. It's often much cheaper to buy a good used head than to replace valve seats in a head that needs them.

Also check all studs and threads. It's fairly easy

An old valve guide is driven out and the new one will be driven in next, using the aluminum drift shown in foreground. Note the rag to protect the mechanic's hand. This head is hot, as it needs to be for this work, to prevent damage.

Nothing like mom's home cooking! Actually, the oven here is an excellent way to control the temperature accurately and to distribute heat evenly. The thermometer will let us know when we reach a temperature between 250 and 275 degrees F. That temperature range makes removing and installing guides much easier and consequently less likely to damage the head.

to install a Helicoil now, more involved and easier to foul up once the head's on the bike. On Triumphs, pay close attention to the holes for the smaller rocker box bolts as many will have bad threads. Both makes commonly suffer from stripped and/or cracked spark plug threads. Stripped spark plug threads are easy to repair with one of a number of commercial tools that supply a guided thread cutter and new inserts to match it. Cracks are common on all heads so careful inspection is required.

KITCHEN MAGICIAN

For the next steps, send your significant other out shopping, because we have to use the kitchen oven. No kidding, this is a superior way to heat the head uniformly instead of using a torch. Uneven and unmeasured application of heat with a torch can result in the new guide position changing significantly from its original angle in the head. That would require a great deal more machine work on the seats, with subsequent loss of service life, to restore concentric position.

With the oven thermostat and a thermometer, precisely control temperature and evenly heat the head, in this case to 250–275 degrees F. Be darn sure this is done with a very clean head, or you'll set off all the smoke alarms and the next meatloaf you cook is liable to taste like a dirty shop rag. (Don't ask me how I learned this.) Of course, a small electric oven for your shop is a much better idea and is also useful for powder coating. Prior to heating the head, place the new guides in the freezer.

Once the head is hot, move it to the workbench. Might as well grab the oven mitts for the job, or at least use rags, because the head's hot enough to cause severe burns. Have your workstation already set up (see photo) and just drive the old guides out and the new very cold ones in. If you work slowly, you might want to two-step this and reheat the head, and then install new guides. Either way, you now have brand new guides. You may need to ream the guides for proper clearance between the valve and guide.

Never assume that the head surface is flat and will make a good seal. Many heads—maybe most of them—are a bit warped and need to be lightly skimmed as shown. This is the same glass plate and fine sandpaper we used to flatten warped carburetor flanges. Move the head back and forth and also in semicircular motions until all gasket surface parts are lightly cut. Sometimes the head is so badly warped it's best to let the machine shop skim it. Beware, the more you cut, the higher the compression becomes; with gas today it's easy to raise compression too much and cause detonation problems.

MACHINE SHOP WORK

Now take valves and the head down to the machine shop. Even if you have new valves, the machinist will want to see how they sit after cutting the seat. Get his opinion on the guide clearance too. He may also recommend removing some metal from around the seat to correct pocketing.

LAPPING VALVES

If you have the marvelous good fortune to have usable guides and unpitted valves—one in a hundred today—you can get by with just lapping the valves into their seats, but far too many builders try this when machine work and guide/valve replacement are really essential. Conversely, if you are using new or refaced valves on fresh-cut seats, you shouldn't need to lap the assembly and can install the valves as-is. Be prepared, though, with fresh-cut valves and seats, as it can take several valve adjustments before the valves stop recessing slightly and causing tight valve clearance.

Fill both head chambers with kerosene to check for leaking valves. It should hold fluid for at least 10 seconds before any seeping can be detected.

If you do lap the valves, make sure that you use a back and forth motion on the valve grinder, an annoying suction cup device that slips off every ten seconds or so; pick up the valve and rotate it 180 degrees occasionally to evenly cut the seat and valve.

Check your springs as I described in the measurement chapter, or better yet, replace them. Also, carefully check the keepers.

SPRING INSTALLATION AND TESTING

To install the valves and springs, lubricate the guide, insert the valve and bottom cup, and then hold it in place while replacing the top cup and springs. Now use the spring compressor to compress the springs far enough to drop in the keepers and then slowly release the compressor. Putting a bit of grease on the keepers helps them stay in place. Do this work with safety glasses, as it's very easy to have something slip out and go flying at speed.

Getting the valves, springs, and cups all lined up and then putting the valve spring compressor in place requires a bit of dexterity; the job is easier when the head is held in some manner. This vise has aluminum soft jaws and a rag to protect the head that is only lightly clamped.

Once the springs are compressed, the keepers can be dropped in. Put a little grease on the inside of each to help hold them in place and then slowly decompress the spring.

With everything together, install a set of old plugs and then flip the head upside down. Pour kerosene into each combustion chamber and let it sit a spell. If the valves hold the fluid without leaking for at least 10 seconds, you're done. Check for leaks in and around the intake and exhaust ports. If a valve does leak, find out why and correct the problem.

ROCKER ARM INSTALLATION AND INSPECTION

Rocker arms on both Triumph and BSA are similar and removed the same way: by removing the holding nut and drifting out the shaft. Inspect the washers and springs for wear and also the adjustment nuts and rocker tips that can get pretty chewed up and may need replacement. With the BSA, the rockers must be removed to do a valve job, but not so with the Triumph that has detachable rocker boxes—and its own set of problems.

Triumph oil leaks in and around these boxes are legendary. New gaskets take care of many problems, but the rocker arm oil seal around the shaft presents special headaches. Some guys approach this with a tiny screwdriver to work the seal into place, and there's also a special shop tool (see photo) that helps.

Heating the rocker box seal area with a torch to expand the opening helps get the job done. Before heating, make sure you have the arms, springs, and washers aligned correctly so that the shaft fits through the box; lining these up can take some fiddling. Once in place, though—as long as you don't move the rocker arms—the alignment generally stays put. If it doesn't, the rockers are often too loose, and you may need new springs or else you're missing a part somewhere.

Triumph rocker boxes are installed after the head is in place, and you can do the same with the BSA rocker arms or install the intake rockers on the bench. The exhaust rockers must wait until the head is on the bike so you can get to the head bolts under it.

Okay, now move up to the head of the class!

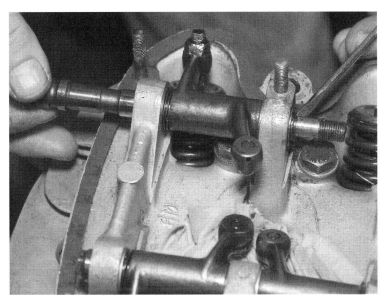

BSA rocker arms are installed by driving the rocker shaft into the arms. Keep the springs and washers in place by adding a bit of grease, but expect to fiddle some until you get everything aligned. Never use undue force drifting the shaft. If it won't go in, you have something misaligned.

Triumph rocker boxes will require a new seal. The factory tool is shown here, and is supposed to compress the O-ring enough to slip in, but often the tool just wrecks the O-ring. Some builders work the seal in with a tiny screwdriver. In this case, we've heated the box around the seal area before installing the shaft, as this often works too. A vise can also be used as a press.

22 *Top It Off*

OVERVIEW

With the lower end and transmission together, we can now install the top end and outer covers. Since so much of this process is similar for BSA and Triumph, we'll cover all of our engines together, emphasizing what's often misunderstood or underexplained in the manuals.

If you haven't already done so, be sure to measure ring gaps and piston clearance. A mistake with either is serious trouble, ranging from no compression to quick piston seizure. I will also assume you measured the bore as I described in the measurement chapter. If you're reusing pistons for a ring job only, be sure the pistons go back into the same cylinder and face the same way as when they came out. Also make sure you've left absolutely no carbon or other deposits on the pistons, especially in the ring grooves. You can clean the ring grooves with a broken piston ring. Tape the ring end you hold to avoid cutting yourself.

Before installing rings make sure you check the end gaps first. See text for more details. All piston photos in this chapter are from a late-model Triumph 500.

RING INSTALLATION

While I mentioned this earlier, it bears repeating here: *do not use low-buck Taiwanese rings.* Not only do they often fail to perform adequately, the three-piece oil ring can be a real challenge to install, especially in bored cylinders where the chamfer that helps guide the rings into the cylinder has been almost eliminated by an oversize bore. El Cheapo pistons, however, perform well as long as they're mated to a good ring set.

Install piston rings very carefully onto the pistons. There's a special tool, but your fingers will work fine; just be careful not to cut yourself or break a ring when installing, both of which are very easy to do. Just pull the ring open gently and slide it over the piston and into its correct groove.

There are many different kinds of rings marketed for Brit twins, and each will have instructions for ring position. If there's any question, contact the parts house where you bought them. In some cases, it makes no difference which ring side is up or down, but in others, incorrect placement can make your motor smoke like a fire at the oily rag factory. If your fresh rebuild smokes, it's 99 percent certain that you've installed a ring upside-down.

PISTON CLIPS

Once the rings are installed, use a small needle nose pliers or tiny screwdriver to install the wrist pin clips on the inside of each piston, meaning the clips will face each other in the center of the motor. Now position the piston over the connecting rod and slide the wrist pin through the rod bush and into the other side of the piston so that the pin contacts the clip. If you haven't already done so, pad out the case to prevent accidentally dropping the outer clips into the motor. Now install the outer clips.

With the clips and pistons on, check each clip

Wrist pins are generally an easy push-in fit with fingers. Always pad out the case opening before installing wrist pin clips to prevent losing them inside the case.

Pistons are ready for the cylinder block to be placed on top so the pistons can slide inside. Pieces of wood support the pistons to make this a lot easier.

by using a small screwdriver to push the clip so that it rotates slightly in its groove. If it doesn't rotate or if it pops out, it wasn't installed correctly.

PISTON INSTALLATION

You can buy piston ring compressors, but large hose clamps work very well and are much cheaper. Make sure the ring openings are positioned so that each opening is in a different part of the piston circumference; they should never be lined up together.

The next steps are critical for an easy assembly. We also have some controversy between advocates of wet vs. dry assembly, meaning the use of oil on the rings and/or in the cylinder. Dry assembly, many say, allows the rings to seat better, and this is certainly true. Oil, however, eases the process of slipping the rings inside the cylinder and off the ring compressor and makes breaking one less likely. My two cents? I use 30-weight non-detergent oil in moderation on the rings and keep the bore dry; I have had no problems with rings seating properly. More on oil in the next chapter.

You can compress rings too much or too little. If you clamp down too hard, the tool won't slip off the rings easily and you can also break the ring. If the tool is too loose, the rings won't slide into the cylinder, and ring breakage is also possible. The key is to keep an eye on the top ring gap. Get the gap close to what it was when you checked ring gap in the cylinder, or just a bit smaller, and things should go well. You might also want to test the fitting of the compressor

The lower end of a later-model Triumph 650 pushrod tube and seals are shown. Note the O-ring inside the tube too. Always renew both seals and do not omit the outer metal ring also pictured. The upper end of the tube also has a seal; both ends have a nasty reputation for leaking. Careful assembly reduces the likelihood of leaking.

tool to see if you can slide it off the rings without excessive force.

If you haven't already fitted the cylinder base gasket, do so now. Also secure the lifters inside of their respective bores. Grease will hold all kinds well, but with Triumphs, it's easy to just stick a piece of hose between the lifters to hold them in place. You do not need to use the original lifter clips installed at the BSA factory, and most likely the bike didn't have them to begin with.

Once the rings are compressed, cut and position two small pieces of wood to span the case opening (see photo) so that the pistons can rest

The BSA head must be tightened completely before installing the exhaust rocker arms. While the Triumph pushrods for each respective motor are all of equal length, the BSA has two long and two shorter pushrods. The long ones go on the center lifters to the exhaust rocker arms as shown.

on them and not move during assembly. The cylinder block can then be lowered gently over the pistons. Look through the bore openings for proper positioning over the pistons. Sometimes, just the weight of the bore will cause the pistons to slide nicely inside, and sometimes a light tap with a plastic hammer is needed to begin the process. Never apply any more force than a light tap as this is how broken rings begin their worthless lives. If the cylinders won't slide over the pistons, loosen your compressors a bit. Sometimes, a ring will pop out before it gets into the bore. If it does, just remove the cylinder

block, reposition the compressor, and try again. The more you do this, the easier it gets, but it can be frustrating for beginners. Just be careful not to force things and you'll get the job done.

With the pistons inside the bore, you can remove the ring compressors and push the cylinder block into the case. On some cylinders you may need to start a nut before fully pushing the block inside the case, and many cylinder base nuts are easier to get on before the cylinder is all the way inside the case. Once all the nuts are on and tightened, it's on to the head. With all engines, cylinder nuts must be checked right after the first run and then after 100 miles. Retighten as needed.

HEAD GASKET

The copper head gasket may be reused if it isn't damaged but it must be annealed. Heat it with a propane torch until it's cherry red and cool it off in a bucket of water before use. Apply a light coating of grease to the gasket prior to installation.

BSA HEAD

Installing the BSA head is very simple. Just install the head hardware and torque the bolts to 25 foot-pounds, beginning with the center bolt and working in a cross pattern from the inside out. The head nuts call for 26 foot-pounds, but since you can't fit a socket on these, most builders tighten them by feel. Accurate measurement is possible with a special torque wrench or by using the torque measurement method described in the wheel section for spoke tightening.

With both Triumph and BSA, it's good practice to torque the head gradually until the final torque specs are reached. I like to go five, ten, and then fifteen foot-pounds in a cross pattern from the inside of the head outwards before final tightening. After final tightening on the BSA, you install the exhaust rocker shafts and then the pushrods. Make sure to loosen the rocker arm adjusting bolts before doing so.

TRIUMPH HEAD

Triumph head installation is a bit more involved and care must be taken or extremely bad leaks will result. Slight weeping may still eventually occur with even the most careful rebuilds, especially with used pushrod tubes. Beginning almost with the Speed Twin, Triumph made running changes to the drain tubes in attempts to keep them oil-tight. Two tubes can look identical to the untrained eye, as the changes were minor, but using a combination of the wrong tube and/or the wrong seal has resulted in serious oil leaks, something I have personal experience with. The tube must be mated to the correct cylinder head and respective guide block in the cylinder and the correct combination of seals must be used with them. Lots of parts swapping by owners has taken place over the years too, such as an earlier or later guide block in the cylinder head, aftermarket parts, and so on.

To reduce the likelihood of leakage, use the best seals you can get, generally English, and use a bit of gasket cement with them. Second, omit no parts, such as the ring band around the lower tube that may seem redundant, but isn't. With the tubes and seals in place, lower the head over them, guiding the tubes into the head with your fingers (see photo). Don't worry if the head does not make contact with the gasket at first. It won't until you tighten the head hardware a bit.

Early unit 650s hold the rocker boxes with four long bolts that also torque the head. The manual shows a pattern of tightening the first center bolt and then each rocker box, and then each side of the head. Later 650 model years and all 500 model years call for a cross pattern. Torque figures for the early 650s are 35 foot-pounds for the 3/8 bolts and 15 foot-pounds for the 5/16 ones.

Late 650s and all 750s with the revised rocker boxes utilize special Allen head bolts positioned inside the rocker boxes. This allows for the head to be completely tightened before installation of the rocker boxes. The 750s also employ two center bolts. The hardware is tightened in a cross pattern from the inside out to 18 foot-pounds. The single inner bolt on the late 650 is tightened to 15 foot-pounds and the two inner center bolts are listed for 16 foot-pounds on the 750.

The 500 does not have a center bolt and the three-eighths bolts are tightened to 25 foot-pounds in a cross pattern from inner to outer.

TRIUMPH ROCKER BOXES

It is a good idea to wait until after the engine is in the frame to install the rocker boxes because it's easier to insert the motor into the frame cradle without them, but we'll cover the procedure now, as it's the next logical assembly step. To install the rocker boxes, first cement the gaskets to the head. Later heads have locating pins. A super-tough metal-reinforced gasket is available for all models and is recommended. All Triumph rocker box gaskets have two holes to hold

A Triumph head is lowered onto the push rod tubes. Note how the fingers are used to guide the tubes into their respective holes.

Always use a torque wrench when doing final tightening. This engine is using an earlier set of rocker boxes with the two long bolts going into the cylinder block. Later models have an internal bolt that allows the head to be completely tightened before installing the rocker boxes.

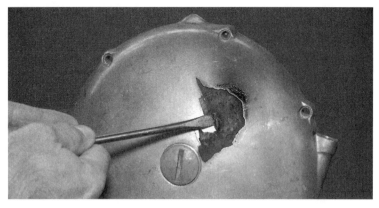

Good primary covers are becoming scarcer and much more expensive every year, so repairing them may be preferable to replacement. This cover was crudely patched with epoxy, which can easily be removed by heating with a propane torch until it softens, allowing us to scrape it off as shown.

Welding aluminum is tricky, but kits that are more like brazing or soldering make this possible for most builders. All you need beyond the kit, which costs about 15 bucks in lots of places, is a propane torch. Cracks can be filled as shown and then the repair ground flush and polished. A good repair is virtually invisible.

A small cutting pliers with this shape is perfect for removing the rivets holding the Triumph patent plate. Just get a good grip and rock the tool to remove the rivet. Be careful with whatever you use because if you cut the rivet off flush, you'll have to drill it out, not an easy job. The old plate was removed by simply prying it off, and sometimes the rivets come with the plate if you're lucky.

and guide the pushrods. Slide the push rods through these holes, being careful not to tear the gasket. Before going for the rocker boxes, check for correct positioning on the lifters by rotating the engine while you lightly push down on the pushrods. The pushrods should move up and down. If one does not, it isn't sitting on the lifter properly. Reset it and retest. Finally rotate the engine until the pushrods are at their lowest point.

Once the push rods are at their lowest point, you can lower the rocker boxes carefully over the head and pushrods. Make sure you have previously loosened the rocker arm adjusting screws. Use the three small rocker box studs as guides to lower the box as straight as you can. Be sure the pushrods contact the rocker arms correctly and then install the larger rocker box nuts/bolts and tighten them to about 10 foot-pounds. Now adjust the rocker arm screws so that they barely make contact with the valve. Next, rotate the engine and check that the rockers move up and down as they should. If you encounter any resistance, stop and check the pushrods; you probably have one off its seat or incorrectly making contact with the rocker arm. Repeat the same process just described with the second rocker box.

Leave the small rocker box nuts and bolts for last. You can strip these bolts (screws on the 500) just by looking at them the wrong way, so be very careful on installation, as they only need five foot-pounds of torque.

SIDE COVERS

You can install the outer covers before or after the top end, but they will at least need polishing first. Simple polishing kits are inexpensive and available from many places and will come with several polishing wheels and usually three sticks of compound: black, red, and white. Unless the cover is in outstanding shape, you'll need to start with the black compound and a sisal wheel to remove scratches.

Really bad covers may need to be sanded first. A circular sanding pad attached to an electric drill works well on many bad scratches and there are lots of other sanding options. At one time, many covers this rough simply weren't worth the effort it took to fix them. Today, however, good covers are becoming very scarce and progressively more expensive, when they can be sourced at all. For this reason, it pays to salvage all but the worst ones.

With the worst flaws smoothed out, switch from the sisal wheel to the spiral sewn cloth wheel and use the red compound. Covers can get pretty hot during this process so gloves are needed. Pretty soon the cover will begin to polish up even better than it was originally if you put enough time into the job. Finish off final polishing with the white compound.

Triumph timing covers have a seal inside that must be replaced. A failure to do so can seriously impact oil pressure. Usually, the seal is the same one used for the points, but there are undersized seals to accommodate a crank tip that needed machining, so check the fit before installing the seal and cover.

You will also need to install Triumph points seals. Allen screws are far better than the stock Phillips screws and full kits are relatively inexpensive.

VALVE ADJUSTMENT

All we need to do now is adjust the valve clearance and then install the valve cover(s). Triumph 500 and 650s require .002 for the intake and .004 for the exhaust. The 750s are set much looser at .008 intake and .006 exhaust. All BSAs are set at .008 intake and .010 exhaust.

Adjustment is simple. Rotate the engine and watch the intake valve action. When the intake valve dips in and then comes back up, turn the engine just a tiny bit more and then adjust both the intake and exhaust valves on the cylinder; repeat the process for the other cylinder. Always recheck settings just to be sure.

Smile, friend. You're looking at a freshly rebuilt Brit twin engine.

This seal in the Triumph timing gear cover must be removed as shown and replaced or oil pressure will suffer, because oil would leak past the worn seal.

The final step for head assembly is adjusting the valves. An A65 is shown. All Brit twin engines will require careful monitoring of valve adjustment during break in. It's a lot easier to use a single feeler blade than the entire set, as it makes it much less likely for the blade to slip out during adjustment, a common problem. This method is especially useful with older Triumphs that require bending the blade quite a bit to get it to fit through the small opening and between the valve and rocker arm adjusting screw.

23 *Putting It All Together*

OVERVIEW

We're almost there. All that's left is installing the engine, frame parts, shocks, wheels, wiring, gas tank…

Okay, maybe we're not as close as we thought. Seriously, once the subassemblies have been rebuilt, we are over the hill. Try to fight the tendency to rush to the finish line, a very common urge after devoting hundreds of hours to restoration work, but one that can result in big problems.

Final details can be completed in different sequences and different approaches, but I'll offer one you can use as a guide. We'll also cover common problems that often arise during the final assembly process and we'll discuss modern parts like the Boyer electronic ignition unit that are not covered in other manuals.

A GOOD FOUNDATION

A standard motorcycle/ATV jack is an ideal assembly stand. Center the frame on it and then get a helper to assist with installing the engine. Install the engine from the left side of the frame (primary engine side) by tilting the top end slightly toward you as it's placed into the frame cradle. Stick it in with the front down a bit too. Triumph claims that you can install the earlier model unit-construction engines in pre-OIF frames by removing only the right two long rocker box bolts, but I've always had fits getting even the box itself to clear the plate that holds the coil mounts. Actually, it's far easier on all Triumphs to install and remove the engine with the rocker boxes off, and I highly recommend it. BSAs do not have this problem, but as a side note, while it's not mentioned in most workshop

A newly rebuilt engine has been placed in its frame, resting on a cycle jack. While everything from milk crates to concrete blocks have been used as assembly stands, the cycle jack allows us to easily raise and lower the bike, making it much easier to install wheels and move the project. Note the absence of rocker boxes, which makes Triumph engine installation much easier.

manuals, you can't remove or install the head on an A65 in an OIF frame unless you remove the top cylinder studs first.

MOTOR MOUNTS

After the motor is inside the frame, loosely install the front mounting bolt. Some front mounts feature multiple bolts. Regardless of which mount or bolts you install first, keep them loose until all are in place, as you will invariably need to shift the engine a bit to line everything up. Don't forget spacers when they're needed (you took notes, didn't you?) and use all the required washers.

Resist the urge to hammer a motor mount bolt (such as the center/bottom one), through the case and frame as this can remove metal. This might not seem like such a big deal but it can have a significant impact on vibration. The BSA manual also shows a lever being used to position the engine in the frame, but this can easily damage fresh paint. It's far better to have an assistant straddle the bike and pull or rock the motor while you line up and insert the motor mount hardware.

Attachment hardware can be replated or replaced. Stainless steel fasteners shown are very popular for good reason. They won't corrode in your lifetime and they add a nice finishing touch. If you want to get even nicer, grind off the forge marks on the bolt heads and polish them. They will look almost as good as chrome and will last much longer.

An old racer's trick is to drill out mounting holes to squeeze in even tighter oversize bolts to further reduce vibration. If during break-in, or even later, you begin to experience excessive vibration, check for loose motor mount hardware, as this is frequently the culprit. Do not omit the head steadies to the frame as these also significantly lessen vibration.

With the engine in the frame, it's a good idea to wrap a few rags around the bottom frame tubes at different points to protect the paint or coating and then wire the frame over the rags to the jack base or stand. This way the frame can't slip off or tip over as you add wheels, forks, and other components.

I like to get my projects rolling as quickly as possible to allow for more convenient movement, so it's on to the forks, shocks, fenders, and wheels. See the fork section for installation and adjustment of the forks.

SHOCKS AND VIBRATION DAMPING

Shocks are very simple to install, but don't forget to attach the fender braces as you do. You might need to use a rubber hammer to knock the shock ends into the frame brackets. If you're installing freshly painted or plated fenders, be gentle with them to avoid scratches. It's best to test fit the rear fender before painting or plating, especially if it's an aftermarket part that will invariably involve some tugging and pulling. Even the stock fender can require some fitting and aligning. You can improve on stock mounting by adding rubber washers and nylon lock nuts wherever you can, as this helps to lessen stress cracks, a universal problem with all Brit twins.

Rubber washers can be employed on many frame and fender mounts to good effect. Sandwich the rubber washer between a steel one and the fender, then tighten the mount until the part is held firmly, but not so tight to completely collapse the rubber and defeat your purpose. The use of nylon-insert lock nuts allows tightening only enough to prevent movement without fear of the fastener loosening up. Rubber mounting the taillight is also highly advisable, as it will increase the longevity of the bulb that tends to fail because the filaments are easily broken by vibration.

On any part that was originally rubber mounted, like Triumph and BSA oil tanks, make sure that you replace the old rubber bushings with new if there's any indication they are age-hardened and/or cracking. A failure to do so will result in one of the few absolute guarantees in life: sooner or later, your oil tank will crack somewhere. Same goes for gas tank mounting.

While my friends often say I tend toward paranoia, it's important to appreciate the real problems created by vibration on brand-new Brit twins and the problems it can create on your newly rebuilt machine.

"Work on twins for vibration faults carried on right up to the close of Meriden in 1973 but the problems were never really overcome," Hughie Hancox said in "Tales of Triumph and the Meriden Factory." Triumph incurred huge warranty costs for replacement of parts cracked by vibration. BSA faced the same problems.

MAKE IT A ROLLER

Install both front and rear wheels but leave everything just hand tight for now as we have aligning to do with both. On the rear wheel, make sure you don't forget the spacer under the speedometer drive. Also see that the drive itself has been cleaned, greased, and checked for operation by rotating the inner ring while observing that the cable drive rotates as it should. Don't forget necessary axle spacers, washers, and wheel adjusters, and be sure to grease the rear axle before installation.

Once the forks are filled to the proper level with oil and the cap nuts tightened, you can install the handlebars. At this point we have a rolling motorcycle. If you have the luxury of a table lift, the bike can be rolled onto it for further assembly. If not, you can leave it on the floor jack or work on the bike as it rests on the sidestand or centerstand.

OIL LINES

With the frame parts attached, we can start running oil lines. It's a good idea to install the oil system first for a simple reason: this way we can't forget and accidentally fire up a dry engine. Yes, it has been done more times than you might think. Very sad scene. It's generally easier to at-tach the oil lines while the engine is a little loose and the Triumph rear motor mounts are off. Be sure you route intake and return lines correctly. The intake line is the one inside, the return on the outside. Some BSAs have a third line; this is much smaller and routes to the head.

Earlier BSAs require a T-fitting to route the line lubricating the head assembly. All BSAs will have a fitting going into the head right above the intake manifold. Triumphs have a variety of different return-line arrangements, but all of them also involve a smaller rubber hose running to the rockers that connects to a steel line attached to the rocker boxes. On 500s this steel line is at the top; on 650/750s the line slips over the rocker shafts on the timing side. All these steel lines require a copper washer on each side. The old ones can be reused if you anneal them. Always use new rubber hose and a clamp where any rubber hose attaches to a metal line. Double check the routing to be sure you haven't accidentally switched the intake and return lines, a catastrophic mistake that is all too common.

Oil coolers are very useful on high-performance applications and in areas where high temperatures severely tax air-cooled engines. The Trident oil cooler shown works very well on any Brit twin and pops up inexpensively at swap meets and on eBay. SRM recommends mounting a thermostat, as oil that's too cold also hurts engines. SRM also recommended a good budget cooler option, a unit from junked Moto Guzzis. Lots of other junkyard options exist. Other oil-cooler temperature control options include a simple bypass tap for use in cold weather. An even simpler, albeit cruder, solution is simply covering the cooler in cold weather.

While oil coolers aren't necessary for many locations, it's hard to deny the benefit of better filtration beyond simple stock screens. The MAP unit shown on this OIF Triumph mounts easily and is very unobtrusive. Many other options exist and all would be very worthwhile improvements.

OIL FILTERS AND COOLERS

While you are routing oil lines, it's very easy to splice in an oil filter and/or oil cooler. Insert these only into the return lines. If you run a cooler, it needs to catch moving air, but don't mount one that blocks the airflow around the head and cylinder cooling fins. One good place to mount an oil cooler is slightly off the left- or right-hand side of the engine. Many owners make a simple bracket attached to the front motor mount bolt. For many regions and applications, an oil cooler is unnecessary. An oil filter, however, is extremely wise on every old Brit, and one can be mounted almost anywhere. MAP markets an inexpensive filter kit that's both easy to mount and for which it is easy to get filters. A lot of small automotive filter brackets can be modified for cycle use too and sourced cheaply from many junkyards.

Now we can tighten up the motor mounts. Next, we add our break-in oil, 30-weight monograde non-detergent. More about this soon. If you haven't already filled the primary case, do so now, and do so even with later Triumphs that fill the primary as they run. Also add 90-weight gear oil to the transmission.

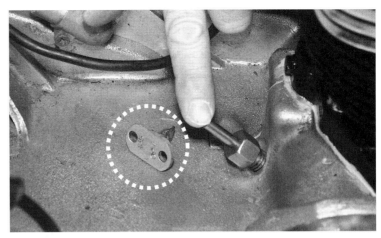

The first step to installing any ignition system is to time the engine statically. The Triumph stock tool is shown in use; the early BSA tool is also shown (it goes in the front timing side of the case). Each tool works the same way: by engaging a notch in the crankshaft.

Once you have all the vital fluids taken care of, it's a good time to see if they're going to the right places. Remove the oil pressure sensor and kick the motor over without the spark plugs (unless you really want a lot of exercise) until oil begins to dribble out of the hole. On early A65s you'll have to pull the return line or the one running to the head and check for oil flow from there or check the return to the tank.

GET THE JUICE LOOSE

There are many ways to wire your Brit Twin ranging from a new factory loom to a simple wiring harness you make yourself, the latter being the cheapest and often also the easiest. In the Budget Brit spirit, this is what we'll do. Since we covered the simple wiring of a Brit twin with a points system in the electrical section, we'll continue from that point and cover installing a Boyer unit and other electrical considerations.

STATIC TIMING

The first step to installing an ignition system is to set the static timing. After the engine is running you should recheck the timing using a strobe light and the timing marks on the alternator rotor. One neat thing about the Boyer unit is that you don't have to time each cylinder separately. Set it up for one cylinder and it's set for both because the Boyer fires both plugs simultaneously.

The Boyer ignition rotor has two reference dots on the magnets. Either one may be used for timing. Both mounting screws are also shown at the bottom of the photo; be sure to use the correct one that fits the thread pitch for your bike. Screws will usually need to be ground down shorter to fit correctly into the cam hole.

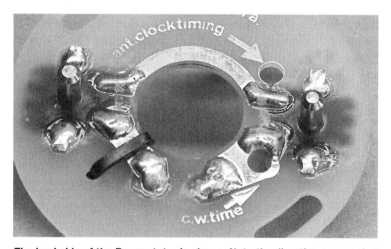

The backside of the Boyer stator is shown. Note the direction arrows that must be matched to the rotation of the rotor. Mark the opposite side of the plastic plate with a marker so that you know which hole to use.

The Boyer plate is installed by aligning the rotor white spots with the correct timing hole as previously established and marked to avoid confusion.

Both the Triumph and BSA have a notch cut into the crank for static timing and an access point for the timing tool (see the photo on page 161). All later Triumphs and BSAs use the same locating tool, but the early BSAs have a different one. All work exactly the same way, however. Simply insert the tool into the access hole at the base of the cylinders and put light pressure on it as you slowly rotate the engine. Soon the tool will click as it slips into the timing notch and also stops the crank from turning. While I don't recommend this because it isn't as accurate, you can get by using a screwdriver to engage the crank slot if you're unable to locate the right tool. Leave the factory tool in place for now, but don't forget it later; you wouldn't be the first person to break one trying to kick the motor over with the tool still in the crank.

BOYER INSTALLATION

The Boyer unit has a small rotor with two magnets that take the place of the mechanical advance mechanism you removed. Put it on the timing shaft lightly and rotate the engine. Note whether the rotor turns clockwise or counterclockwise. (I won't tell you which way because I want you to look for yourself to avoid a mistake.) After noting the direction of rotation, immediately take the next step, and that's marking the Boyer pickup with a marker so you know which hole to use for timing (see photo). The back of the plastic plate is labeled for rotor direction, but you need to mark the front to avoid accidentally using the wrong hole on installation and thereby mistiming the engine.

Install the Boyer rotor so that you have room to advance and retard the ignition plate and also line up the attaching screws with their respective case holes. To check this, just loosely install the rotor and then the stator. You will now sight through the hole you marked on the stator plate and turn the stator so that it lines up with one of the white dots on the rotor magnet. It does not matter which dot you use. Position the stator so that the screws holding it are approximately in the middle position of the slot in the stator. This will allow advancing and retarding the ignition. Tighten down the rotor using the Allen screw supplied with the kit. If it does not, reposition the rotor. Often, you have to grind part of the rotor screw off because it's too long. The kit also ships with two screws; make sure to use the one with the correct thread pitch. It should go in easily by hand.

After the rotor is tightened, you permanently install the stator. Again, be sure the white dot on the magnet is visible through the hole you marked. When it is, tighten the holding screws. The ignition is now properly timed and you can remove the timing tool.

Run two new wires to the pickup plate connections through the case hole and back to the Boyer control box. To seal the case hole from moisture, fill the case hole cavity with silicone sealant or use a rubber grommet.

The Boyer box can be mounted just about anywhere as long as it isn't exposed to excessive heat. Under the seat is the most common place. Boyer provides nylon ties for mounting, but if you don't like these, another good way is to use epoxy to glue the box to a piece of bar stock that can be drilled to bolt up in many locations.

WIRING

Refer to the diagram provided in this chapter to connect the coils and other wires to the Boyer box. Note that the coils are wired in series. Boyer recommends 6-volt coils, but stock 12-volt coils will work for stock applications if they're in good condition. Connect the Boyer hotwire to the ignition switch and the ground wire to a convenient place on the frame.

Install a new battery after placing a rubber or anti-acid pad on the battery box's base. Route the vent tube so that it exits under the bike and not onto a frame part; otherwise, quick corrosion will set in. Even better is a plastic recovery tank (see photo). Most likely the original battery holding straps are long gone; nylon ties work well. Run a 10-gauge wire from the positive side of the battery to ground, unless you have a very late Triumph that uses a negative ground. On the hot (negative) side, run a fused link to the ignition switch. You will also connect the hot wire coming out of either the modern regulator or the stock rectifier at the central terminal to the same terminal on the ignition switch or the wire going to it. If you have a stock regulating system, you also need to run a wire from this terminal or wire to the Zener diode.

Wiring from here can vary according to preference. If you use a switch as shown in the electrical chapter, you can take power from two different switch terminals. The ignition is switched so that one terminal is hot in one key position and both terminals are hot in another. As explained in the electrical chapter, if you wire the ignition to the connection that's hot on both key settings, and run the lights on the single position terminal, the engine will run with the lights off. This also allows isolation of the two systems for diagnostic purposes. Some builders like to wire the lights in a completely different circuit with its own switch and fuse; if so, you can install an inline fuse and switch easily to any circuit. No matter which arrangement you choose, crimp all connectors carefully (if you are using this kind of connector) and use dielectric grease on the connections to keep out moisture and assure reliable performance.

If you're going to use the stock rectifier/diode system, run the two alternator wires to the outside connections of the rectifier. Most electronic regulators will have two wires the same color for attachment to the alternator wires. If your regu-

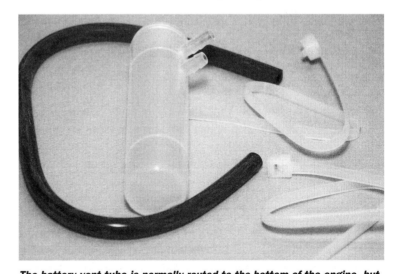

The battery vent tube is normally routed to the bottom of the engine, but a better idea is a small plastic overflow tank. Lots of parts houses sell these. Route the battery vent tube to the lower hole, and then use the upper one for a line to the bottom of the frame. Check the tank routinely, but it seldom fills if the system isn't overcharging. If you do find a lot of fluid in the overflow tank, it's time to check out your charging system as detailed in the electrical chapter.

A later-model Triumph headlight is shown with dried, weather-cracked mounting rubber. These brackets, and those on the front fender too, are very prone to vibration cracking and must be mounted carefully with new rubber.

An aftermarket headlight kit, a common budget alternative, can replace a badly damaged or missing stock headlight. The unit works well if it is properly mounted on insulating rubber washers.

lator has three wires, it is designed for a three-phase alternator, but you can use it for a single-phase system (which is what most alternators are) by using just two of the regulator's wires and taping off the unused one. It does not matter which alternator wire connects to which regulator wire as long as they're the ones for input to the regulator. See the electrical chapter for more details and photos.

Take care when routing wire. It if goes through a fender hole, use a rubber grommet to prevent the wire from chafing through. Be careful routing wire around the frame neck to allow adequate movement of the forks and to prevent pinching wire at the fork stops. Many custom builders like to run wire through the frame, handlebars, and fender brackets to hide the wire, and this does look trick. It can also create a colossal electrical headache, since the wire is hidden. So factor in beauty vs. functionality if you are considering unusual wire routing.

ALIGNMENT

After the front axle is tightened and the forks adjusted (see fork chapter), install the drive chain on the still-loose rear wheel. Sight along the chain as you adjust it to be sure in runs in line with the drive sprocket. Small alignment adjustments can be made with the rear-wheel chain adjusters, but if it's way off, suspect a missing axle spacer or engine mount spacer. You could also have a bent frame or swingarm. Some very poorly made hardtail sections can do this too, as the hardtail incorrectly positions the axle.

We also need to verify that both wheels are in alignment. Take two long, straight boards—angle iron is even better as it's usually straighter—and place them so they contact each side of the rear wheel as a partner holds the bike upright. The front wheel must be in the center of the two alignment pieces. If it isn't, you may have a spacer problem. If these are old rims that are bent, that could account for the misalignment, as could incorrect offset of the wheel when it was laced. Bent fork tubes, or a bent frame are also possibilities. Whatever it is, correct the problem if you want the bike to handle well.

ADJUSTMENTS

With everything straight, tighten the rear axle, the bolts holding the brake plate bar to the frame, and chain adjuster lock nuts. The chain should have about three-quarters of an inch of free play in the upper run with the bike off the jack and on its wheels. Now we can install the foot pegs, brake lever and its rod and adjust it and the brake switch. To wire the brake switch, you need one hot wire to it and a second from the switch to the brake light. You also need a second hot wire to the taillight. Many builders wire the taillight to come on when the ignition is switched on, to serve as an ignition indicator light.

Place the bike on the centerstand or lift as you tighten the brake-adjusting nut to allow spinning the back wheel as you work. Set the adjuster so that there's no drag at all when the brake lever's in contact with the foot peg, but begins to drag when the lever is moved only a tiny bit, and this is when you want the brake switch to come on too. This may take some fiddling, and with cheap aftermarket switches, you may have to compromise with a later actuation for the brake light as these have a tendency to stay on if they are set for very early actuation. Of course, hydraulic brakes are self-adjusting, and only need to be bled after the master cylinder and fresh fluid are added.

FUEL CHECKS

Check the carburetor(s) for leaks before installing. Add a little gas to the fuel tank before either carburetor is mounted, and if the tank has been freshly painted, be very careful if the paint hasn't cured fully. Now connect a line from the carb to the tank petcock and then open the petcock. Hold the carb in the orientation it would have been when mounted on the bike. Depress the tickler until you see gas and then release it and inspect. If the carb continues to dribble gas after you release the tickler, the float or needle is hung up or incorrectly adjusted. Remedy and retest. Check for weeping around the bowl and the drain gaskets too. Also check the seal around the petcocks; you don't want a leak to damage new paint, and a leak at the petcock is extremely common. It can usually be corrected by coating the tap threads with gas-proof sealant and installing a new rubber-lined petcock gasket. The petcock may just be loose, too.

Mount the carb(s) now and route the clutch and throttle cables. It's easiest to install the joining fuel line between dual carbs as they are being installed. Throttle and choke cables can be positioned out of the way with nylon ties to the frame. Grease the handlebar, slide on the throttle, and tighten it. Test for smooth operation now and after installing the gas tank. Turn the forks from lock to lock during the tests to see that there is adequate room for movement.

Because of the vibration problems I mentioned earlier, be extremely diligent as you install the fuel tank. Use all factory mounting rubber and frame attachment braces, or construct suitable substitutes. For example, many shock absorber replacement bushings work well as substitutes for the stock rubber mounts under pre-OIF tanks. With OIF BSAs and Triumphs, make sure that the two side rubber isolators in

Here's a brace to the frame that runs along the bottom of an A65 tank. It's more time consuming to remove and install the brace when removing and installing the tank, so nine out of ten guys don't install it, and that's a mistake. These braces are actually tough to find because so many guys trashed them. Keep yours installed to reduce stresses—and cracks—on the tank.

the frame neck are installed and in good shape, as these prevent the tank from rocking side to side and isolate it from vibration. You can also use pieces of old tire tube held together with nylon ties on the frame spine as replacements for the original rubber bumpers. Whatever you do, do not allow direct metal-to-metal contact between the tank and the frame if you want long tank life. Finish up by running hose from the petcock(s) to the carb(s). Many builders like to install a filter in the main fuel line.

FINISHING TOUCHES

Now we install our seat and side covers. With most Triumphs, you install just one hinge on the seat, and then attach the second one after the first hinge is positioned on the frame posts. BSAs have either a bolt or stud going through two frame tabs and this makes getting to the electrics more difficult. To facilitate access, it is a good idea to pack a socket in your riding tool kit to fit these.

Feel the adrenaline? We're almost there. Attach the exhaust pipes and mufflers. Keep everything loose at first as you may have to tug and pull a bit to align everything. Make sure the kickstart lever does not hit the right pipe or muffler, a common problem with some pipe sets. If you have a set of old pipes, it's best to use them for tuning and break-in to avoid discoloring new pipes. Once the pipes, mufflers and brackets are all together and aligned properly, tighten the assembly.

Before installing the spark plugs, check to see that each one fires when the engine is kicked over with the ignition switched on. Remember, the Boyer unit won't fire under 200 rpm, so a slow turn won't cause a spark as it does with a points system. It needs a fast kick to spark.

Got spark? Congratulations, you're about to experience one of the greatest pleasures a mechanic can have. Tickle the carb(s) after installing the plugs, turn on the ignition, and give it a good kick. Lots of times, the engine will fire on the first shot, others will make you work, but before long your Brit twin will pop and emit it's reborn growl. It doesn't get much better than this.

Be gentle with the throttle and just keep the engine running at a fast idle while you tune in all your sensory apparatus. Use your eyes first and look into the oil tank for a stream of return oil. Listen for hard sounds beyond what you've heard in Brit twins previously. Keep your nose alert for the smell of a hot engine, but it will run hot for a bit even if it is perfect, and will smoke in places too from assembly oil, grease, polishing wax, etc. Don't run the engine too long at a standstill because all Brit twins need moving air to keep them cooled. Direct a big fan onto the engine if you want to run it for any extended time.

After about five minutes or so, shut the engine off, but you can keep that wide grin in place. As you do, check all around the bike for leaks. Let the engine cool a bit before running it again. Now is as good a time as any to celebrate.

IF IT DOESN'T RUN

It happens, but as long as you didn't hear hard clanks or some other evil sound, don't be unduly concerned. It's most likely a simple problem. The three most common are a bad or misadjusted carburetor, mistiming, or valve settings.

First check again to be sure you have a spark at both plugs. Something may have gotten loose or a short could have blown the fuse. If you have spark to just one plug and not the other, it's most likely a bad plug or plug wire if you have a Boyer system. A bad coil or connection between the coils generally produces no spark because you wire the coils in series for the Boyer. Seriously suspect the coils if you have no spark, you checked the wires and plugs, and you have a new Boyer box. Make sure there's power running to the Boyer box too.

Bad or misadjusted points might be possible with stock systems, and with new points it's common for one to close up because it wasn't tightened properly. Also make sure your coil wires are going to the right places, as it may be firing one cylinder when the other one should. On a Boyer, it does not matter which coil goes to which cylinder, as both coils fire simultaneously.

Got spark? Recheck the timing. Are you sure you used the right hole in the Boyer plate? You might want to pull it and confirm that you marked the correct timing hole for the rotation of the rotor.

Timing's okay? Check the carburetor. Does it dribble gas when you depress the tickler? It does? Good. Before we pull the carb, let's do a quick compression test.

Got over 120 pounds in each cylinder? If not, recheck the valve adjustment.

Still low compression? A very common reason for low compression on rebuild is that the valves aren't properly timed. You'll have to expose the cam gear(s), pull the intermediate gear, and reset the gears. If these measures don't work, you'll have to pull the jugs, but these checks/corrections work in the vast majority of low compression cases.

If you have correctly timed spark and good compression, only the fuel system can prevent the engine from running. Pull the air cleaner(s) and make sure the needle moves when the slide does and that the slide opens and closes properly. If it does, give the slide adjustment screw(s) one full turn in and try starting again. You may just have the slide too far closed.

If this does not work, pull the carb(s) and check the primary fuel system as detailed in the carburetor chapter. If this system isn't working, the bike can be extremely difficult to start. If the primary fuel system works properly, check the slide(s) to be sure that the back of the slide is open just a bit when it rests on the adjustment screw. Also check the main jet needle to be sure the snap ring is on the correct groove, and that the main jet passage is free. Be sure the gas is fresh and uncontaminated.

After checking the carburetor, reinstall and try starting again.

No dice? It's time for a second opinion. Sometimes the obvious eludes us and a fresh view sees what we've overlooked. Don't lose your temper; seek advice. One time I worked for days trying to get a rear disk brake to work. I replaced the pads, master cylinder, lines, and then rebuilt the caliper. Nothing worked. A friend stopped by and I moaned about my unsolvable problem. He bent down, looked at the caliper for two seconds and announced, "It looks like the caliper isn't sitting straight on the rotor." It wasn't, the bracket was bent slightly. Problem solved. I'll bet your problem is just as simple, so tap your good allies. A fresh perspective frequently does the trick.

BOYER CHECKS

Boyer boxes do go bad, but I've yet to see a bad one out of the box, and if yours is new, it's not likely to be defective. However, if you're working on a unit you bought at a swap meet, the following should help and may also reveal an installation error. Note that these procedures do not apply to Boyer's new digital micro models but only to the Mark III, the model most commonly used on Brit twins.

The first thing to check on a new installation if you have spark and the bike won't run is that the yellow/black and white/black wires from the stator haven't been reversed to the control box. They should go to the same color wires on the box. If reversed, the unit will fire, but 50 degrees out of time. This is a common error.

To check the box initially for firing, disconnect the two leads going to the stator and then turn on the ignition. Touching the wires together should cause a spark at both plugs. If it doesn't, check to see that you have at least 10 volts going to the box and that the box is also properly grounded. If you have good power and ground connections, the box may be bad, but one or more coils might be causing the problem. Also check the plugs and plug wires to be sure thay are not damaged and connections are solid.

If you suspect the coils, especially if you have a new box, check the coils as explained in the electrical chapter. Better yet, substitute known good coils and carefully wire in the new set. Got spark? Good, one or more coils were bad. No spark? Now you can seriously suspect the Boyer box.

The Boyer can also emit a shower of sparks at the plug. This can be caused by high resistance in the circuit, a bad ground, or the use of coils with very low resistance, under 2 or 3 ohms. Another common ignition problem is a bad cell in the battery. As explained in the electrical chapter, you really can't check electrical systems without a good battery. If you're having electrical problems, replace any old battery with a new one before performing diagnostic testing.

While you can't check what's going on inside the Boyer box, the ignition rotor and stator can be tested. Make sure the magnets aren't loose on the rotor and then check for magnetic power. If the magnets can hold their mounting plate onto your toolbox, they're okay. Use an ohmmeter to check the resistance of the stator pickup coils by placing the meter leads inside of the connectors at the plate. You should get 65-130 ohms across the two stator coils. Move your fingers over the stator coils with the meter attached. If the resistance changes, you most likely have a short or a break in one of the coils.

BREAK-IN

There are almost as many opinions about breaking in an engine as there are engines. Some notions are pretty darn stupid, others make quite a bit of sense. I learned the following routines from a number of veteran bike mechanics and I advocate using them. You may have an alternative process that works just as well.

Unlike modern engines, our old Brits need to be broken in carefully. Again, what's careful to one may not be to others. I was surprised to read that one of my Triumph heroes, Hughie Hancox, ran brand new Triumphs straight off the assembly line to top speed and reported that doing so doesn't hurt them. Mr. Hancox explained that as long as the engine isn't loaded up, which means a lot of throttle at low rpm, it's okay.

Still, I was brought up on the concept of using gentle throttle and speeds of no more than 55 mph during the first 500 miles; I strictly keep to this practice today. I was also taught to use 30-weight non-detergent oil for break-in to promote a good ring seal and I find that this works very well. If you decide to use this thinner oil, you must keep to shorter runs and moderate speeds until you switch to thicker oil.

Another idea I now employ is using leaded racing gas for the first tank, again because this is supposed to improve ring sealing. After the first tank, I revert to super unleaded, which I run in all my old Brits.

Dual carburetors must be in sync. An easy way to see that both slides open at the same time is to use two identical drill bits, one inserted under each slide as shown. A 3/8-inch bit works well for many carburetors. With the drill bits trapped by the carburetor slides, you will be able to detect the action of both slides when the throttle is opened because the bits will tip down.

Change the break-in oil at 100 miles, and the filter too if you have one, then refill with 30-weight again for the next 150 miles. At 250 miles, change the oil again, but this time use what you plan to run regularly. SRM recommends monograde oil in BSAs, and I run either 40- or 50-weight depending on ambient temperatures. I generally do the same with Triumphs, as both personal testing and published reports indicate that monograde oil produces higher oil pressure.

Whatever you do, do not run synthetic oil during break-in; it's way too slippery for the rings to seal. However, 20/50 synthetic oil may be the way of the future for normal operation, as it does clean, cool, lubricate, and withstand high temperatures much better than petroleum-based oil. I have not tested synthetic oils personally, however. Some of these oils contain friction modifiers that can cause clutch slipping, although many owners report no problems at all with use of synthetic oils in wet-clutch engines. For now, I'm sticking to a good brand of monograde oil.

At 500 miles, change the oil again and then begin your normal change schedule. With conventional oil, change the oil and filter every 1,000 miles, especially on BSAs because of the timing-side bush needs very clean oil. It won't hurt your Triumph one bit either to have frequent oil changes.

FINE TUNING

Across the pond our English cousins frequently call this process "sorting" and the finished product "well sorted." They are apt descriptions. No two bikes will need the same attention. Some are pretty well sorted the day they are fired; others will have a variety of kinks that need correction, varying from carburetor jetting to brake adjustment. During this process it is imperative the rider/tuner be both attentive and cautious, as the bad problems are most likely to crop up early. My favorite example is the daredevil who decided to wheelie his Bonneville the first time he went down the street. Unfortunately, when his front forks went up his front wheel didn't. Nasty landing, and a true story.

CARBURETOR TUNING

Nearly every bike will need fine carburetor adjustment. If I failed earlier to persuade you to run a single carburetor, you will now have to synchronize your two carburetors. It won't be the last time either, but you'll get better with practice.

Start by adjusting the cables so that both slides open at exactly the same time, but first you must be able to easily see the effect of turning the throttle. A neat way to do this for most Amal slides is with two 3/8-inch drill bits. You may need to vary the diameter slightly with different carburetors/slide cutaways, but the idea is to have the slide rest on the drill bits so that it just barely touches it and holds the bit straight out of the mouth of the carb.

Unlike the slides themselves, both drill bits can be seen easily when the throttle is twisted; you can tell precisely when the throttle opens for each carburetor because the bit will tip down when the slide lifts. Adjust the cables so the slides lift at exactly the same time and the cables have only a tiny bit of free play.

Once this is accomplished, you can set the pilot air adjustment. Begin by turning each one out one and one-half turns from the fully seated position.

At this point you need to get the bike up to its regular operating temperature; just warming it up a little in the shop will not do. I know it's a shame, but you have to go for a ride. Once the bike's fully warmed up, find a safe place to pull over or loop back to your shop and break out your carburetor adjusting screwdriver.

Each carburetor will need to be adjusted separately. Turn the pilot airscrew in and out in quarter-turns as you listen to the bike. Leave the pilot airscrew where it runs best, and then repeat with the other carburetor.

At this point the engine will be running way above a good idle, so you need to back off the slide screw for both carburetors identically. Do this in very tiny increments until proper idle is achieved. You may need to loosen your cables a bit to reduce idle speed, and this process may

also send you back one more time to sync the slides. Always check to see that the slides are in the same place at idle and also open completely on full throttle.

If you have a single carburetor, use the same procedure to adjust the pilot airscrew and idle speed, but you've no sync problems and half the work.

With the carburetors properly adjusted, the bike should pull smoothly off the line and idle well. There should be no surging or hesitation at cruising speeds. After break-in you can check operation at wide-open throttle. The bike should pull like an angry freight train.

Check the plugs periodically. Rich running may call for a bit more air in the primary circuit, a larger slide cutaway, smaller main jet, or a lower main-jet needle position. Try changing the main-jet needle position before swapping jets. Lean running calls for the reverse of these measures. Be very attentive for signs of pre-ignition caused by a lean mixture as it can quickly and seriously damage the engine.

Carburetor tuning is an art and there are myriad issues with specialized applications, such as racing. Fortunately, stock settings and the previously mentioned procedures will serve the majority of situations. If, however, you'd like to become an Amal super tuner, I highly recommend a booklet published by Victory Library, *Amal Concentric Tuning for British Motorcycles*. It's outstanding and covers everything you'll ever need to know about tuning these carburetors.

CHECK, CHECK, AND RECHECK

Throughout the break-in process, it's imperative to monitor all fasteners for tightness. Valve adjustment must all be checked right after the first run or two and then at the break-in oil change intervals. Carefully monitor cylinder base nuts and head nuts/bolts. Also check both the primary and secondary chains for correct adjustment. With a points system, check the gap on each set.

Hey, guess what? We're there! I hope the sun's shining right now in your part of the world. It's time to ride.

Index

Resources

The following list, while hardly a complete summary of all the good people doing business with Brit twin restorers, contains businesses I most definitely recommend for products and advice. Conspicuously absent, however, is the local shop near you that often proves to be invaluable, and I highly recommend that you find one.

Britech New England
www.triumphday.com/britech
PO Box 371
Southbridge, Mass. 01551
508-764-8624
Good source for high performance, wheel, and suspension parts

British Cycle Supply Inc.
www.britcycle.com
604 Davison St. RR 3
Wolfville, NS Canada B4P2R3
902-542-7478
*Good source for Brit parts;
also has US facility for shipment*

Buchanan Spoke and Rim Inc.
www.buchananspokes.net
805 W. Eighth St.
Azusa, CA 91702
626-969-4655
*Good source for wheel parts,
lacing and truing*

Dave Quinn Motorcycles
www.davequinnmotorcycles.com
335 Litchfield Turnpike
Bethany, CT 06524
203-393-2651
*Specialist in vintage British bikes;
U.S. distributor for Hagon shocks*

Don Hutchinson Cycle
www.triumphman.com
116 Foundry St.
Wakefield, MA 01880
781-245-9663
*Widely acknowledged paint expert and
source for correct Brit paint colors*

E&V Engineering
www.evengineering.com
1924 West M46
Howard City, MI 49329
231-937-6515
*BSA specialist, high performance oil pumps
and roller bearing conversions*

Kim the CD Man
www.classicstyle.com.au/cdmanuals
1 Simon Court
Rosanna VIC 3084
Australia

Klempfs British Parts
www.klempfsbritishparts.com
61589 210 Ave.
Dodge City, MN 55927
507-374-2222
Good source for Brit parts

MAP Cycle
www.mapcycle.com
p7165 30th Ave
North St. Petersburg, FL 33710
727-381-1151
*Manufactures and sells many
high-quality Brit parts*

SRM Engineering
www.srm-engineering.com
Aberyswyth SY23
Dyfed, Wales,UK
(44) 1970-627771
*BSA specialists, roller bearing
conversions in UK*

Walt Lund Machine
21502 99th Ave.
SE Snohomish, WA 98296
800-295-2915
Amal sleeving and repair

Other Whitehorse Books, for your shop . . .

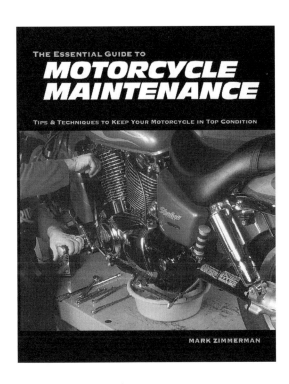

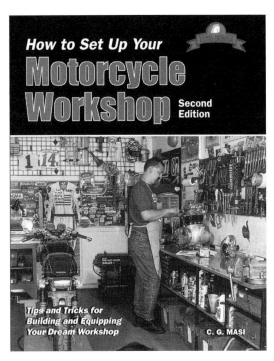

The Essential Guide to Motorcycle Maintenance

by Mark Zimmerman

Veteran motorcycle mechanic and popular author Mark Zimmerman makes difficult subjects easy with his comfortable conversational style and humor. He includes detailed background on how each system of your bike works and what maintenance tasks are required, what tools you'll need, and how to get started. This practical, common-sense guide, with over 500 easy-to-follow color photos and illustrations, covers all brands and styles of bikes, making it a perfect companion to the owner's service manual. Includes hundreds of helpful tips for changing oil, changing brake pads and brake fluid, changing tires, maintaining your chain and sprockets, adjusting your suspension, troubleshooting, and lots more.

Sftbd., 8-1/4 x 10-1/2 in., 256 pp., color illus.

EGMM $29.95   978-1-884313-41-7

How to Set Up Your Motorcycle Workshop (2nd Ed.)

by C. G. Masi

This informative book, now in its second edition, will help you set up your dream motorcycle workshop to make the most of available space, and equip it with the tools necessary to get the job done. Shop profiles are provided to give you ideas of what is possible. Each profile has a layout diagram of the shop with photos as well as ideas and tips from the owner or designer.

Author Charlie Masi also lays out the basic principles of planning and designing workshops, with practical advice on what equipment you'll need. He offers many tips such as: which tools to keep with your bike, which tools you'll need in an emergency, which tools to purchase, which tools you can make, and best of all, how to use them.

Sftbd., 8-1/4 x 10-1/2 in., 176 pp., b/w illus.

MASI2 $19.95   978-1-884313-43-1

... for the fun of it ...

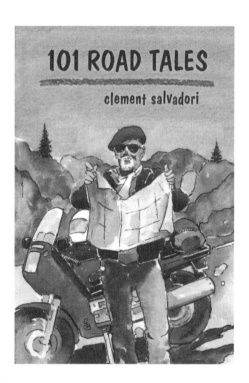

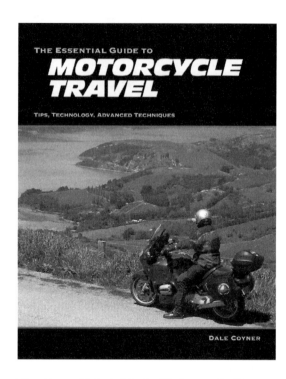

101 Road Tales
by Clement Salvadori

Popular motojournalist Clement Salvadori has been sharing his stories from the road with the readers of *Rider* magazine since 1988. Now, 101 of those engaging Road Tales have been brought together in one book, cleverly illustrated by his long-time friend Gary Brown.

Salvadori loves to travel by motorcycle and loves to write. Combining the two has given him a thoroughly satisfactory life. His contentment and joy of living shine through this collection of columns from the past two decades.

Don't expect a detailed travel guide to places near and far, but rather a guide to the enjoyment of traveling, especially by motorcycle. These tales are spun by an observant and experienced traveler who can make a quick ride on the back roads near his home just as entertaining as a trip across the country. Meet some of the characters he has encountered, laugh with him at some of his blunders, and join him for bread, cheese, wine, and a stupendous vista somewhere away from the hustle and bustle of humanity.

Hdbd., 6 x 9 in., 384 pp., b/w illus.

RT $24.95   978-1-884313-73-8

The Essential Guide to Motorcycle Travel
by Dale Coyner

This book is written to help motorcyclists prepare themselves and their motorcycle for traveling long distances over extended periods. Whether you are getting ready for a weekend trip to the next state, or for a transcontinental odyssey lasting several years, Coyner's book details the fundamentals for riding in comfort, safety, and convenience.

In four major sections, the book covers trip planning, rider preparation, outfitting the motorcycle, and lays out the steps for planning a worry-free trip.

As motorcycle technology has evolved, so have aftermarket accessories, which are made to address virtually every special need. Coyner shows you step-by-step how electrical modifications can be made, and provides specific sections on high-performance lighting and conspicuity, GPS and other cockpit instruments, entertainment and communication devices, cameras and camcorders, ergonomic enhancements, suspension improvements, luggage and storage additions, and trailers.

Sftbd., 8-1/4 x 10-1/2 in., 192 pp., color illus.

EGMT $24.95   978-1-884313-59-2

. . . and the sport of it . . .

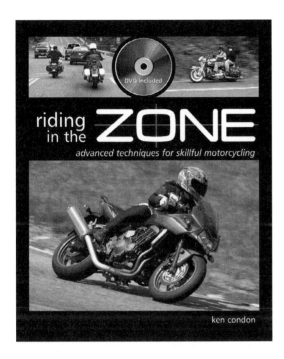

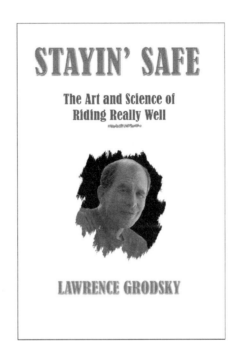

Riding in the Zone: Advanced Techniques for Skillful Motorcycling

by Ken Condon

The Zone is a state of being. It's the experience of being physically and mentally present in the moment, where every sense is sharply attuned to the ride.

Riding in the Zone will help you develop the physical and mental skills that are necessary for you to ride with more confidence and joy.

The book delivers this information clearly and concisely, and is written for those who would rather ride than read. The included DVD helps explain many of the concepts and techniques discussed in the book and provides demonstrations and practice drills to help you implement the lessons quickly and easily.

Ken Condon is a 30-year motorcyclist with experience as a street rider, safety instructor, track-day instructor, and author of the monthly "Proficient Motorcycling" and "Street Strategies" columns for *Motorcycle Consumer News.*

Sftbd., 8 x 10 in., 144 pp., 230 color illus.

ZONE $29.95   978-1-884313-76-9

Stayin' Safe: The Art and Science of Riding Really Well

by Lawrence Grodsky, Edited by Pete Tamblyn

Through the riding courses he taught and his "Stayin' Safe" columns in *Rider* magazine (from 1988 until his untimely death in 2006), Larry Grodsky helped thousands of motorcyclists improve their skills and their ability to ride really well. This collection of Grodsky's columns reveals his ability to illuminate complex and sometimes highly technical subjects with an entertaining and personal style, spiced with his trademark wry wit and keen observations of human behavior.

Readers will be rewarded by the beautifully written observations of a great motorcycle riding instructor who has left his mark on a generation of grateful riders.

Hdbd., 6-1/4 x 9-1/2 in., 352 pp., color illus.

GROD $24.95   978-1-884313-72-1

Call or write for your complete catalog of motorcycling books, videos, tools, accessories, and gear:

800-531-1133
www.WhitehorsePress.com

175